eLearning and Digital Publishing

T0205604

Computer Supported Cooperative Work

Volume 33

eLearning and Digital Publishing

Edited by

Hsianghoo Steve Ching
City University of Hong Kong, China

Paul W. T. Poon
University of Macau,
Macau, China

and

Carmel McNaught
The Chinese University of Hong Kong, China

 Springer

A C.I.P. Catalogue record for this book is available from the Library of Congress.

ISBN-13 978-90-481-6916-0
ISBN-10 1-4020-3651-5 (e-book)
ISBN-13 978-1-4020-3651-4 (e-book)

Published by Springer,
P.O. Box 17, 3300 AA Dordrecht, The Netherlands.

www.springer.com

Printed on acid-free paper

To our colleagues in many countries who share the vision of using technology to open access to learning for the students of the world

To valued colleagues in the Ministry of Education in Taiwan and Feng Chia University in Taiwan who supported this vision

Contents

List of Contributors

CHENNUPATI K. Ramaiah is an Assistant Professor in the School of Communication & Information, Nanyang Technological University, 31 Nanyang Link, Singapore 637718. *ASRamaiah@ntu.edu.sg*

Hsianghoo Steve CHING is a Professor and University Librarian at the City University of Hong Kong, Tat Chee Ave., Yau Yat Chuen, Kowloon, Hong Kong. *hsching@cityu.edu.hk*

Schubert FOO is Professor and Vice Dean in the School of Communication & Information, Nanyang Technological University, 31 Nanyang Link, Singapore 637718. *vd-sci@ntu.edu.sg*

HENG Poh Choo is a graduate student from the Division of Information Studies, School of Communication & Information, Nanyang Technological University, 31 Nanyang Link, Singapore 637718. *hengpc@singnet.com.sg*

Arnold HIRSHON is Executive Director of NELINET (New England Library and Information Network), 153 Cordaville Road, Suite 200, Southborough MA 01772, USA. *ahirshon@nelinet.net*

Lai Chu LAU is an Assistant Librarian in the Law Section of the City University of Hong Kong Library, Tat Chee Ave. Yau Yat Chuen, Kowloon, Hong Kong. *lblclau@cityu.edu.hk*

Philippa LEVY is a Senior Lecturer in the Department of Information Studies at the University of Sheffield, Western Bank, Sheffield, S10 2TN, UK. *p.levy@sheffield.ac.uk*

Y. H. LUI is Professor and Director of the Li Ka Shing Institute of Professional and Continuing Education at the Open University of Hong

Kong, 4/F Shun Tak Centre, 168–200 Connaught Road Central, Hong Kong. *yhlui@ouhk.edu.hk*

Zheng LIU is a doctoral student at the Library of the Chinese Academy of Science, Haidian, Bejing 100080, China. *liuz@mail.las.ac.cn*

Susan McKNIGHT, formerly Executive Director of Learning Services and University Librarian at Deakin University, is now the Director of Libraries and Knowledge Resources at Nottingham Trent University, The Boots Library, Goldsmith Street, Nottingham NG1 5LS, UK. *sue.mcknight@ntu.ac.uk*

Carmel McNAUGHT is Professor of Learning Enhancement in the Centre for Learning Enhancement And Research (CLEAR) at The Chinese University of Hong Kong, Shatin, New Territories, Hong Kong. *carmel.mcnaught@cuhk.edu.hk*

Paul W. T. POON is the University Librarian, University of Macau, Av. Padre Tomás Pereira S.J., Taipa, Macau. *paul_poon_wt@yahoo.com*

Colin STEELE is an Emeritus Fellow, former University Librarian (1980–2002) and Director Scholarly Information Strategies (2002–2003) at the Australian National University, W.K. Hancock Building (043), The Australian National University, Canberra ACT 0200, Australia. *colin. steele@anu.edu.au*

Suzanne THORIN is the Ruth Lilly University Dean of University Libraries, Indiana University, 107 S. Indiana Ave. Bloomington, IN 47405-7000, USA. *thorin@indiana.edu*

Karen WETZEL is the Program Officer for Distance Learning, Association of Research Libraries, 21 Dupont Circle, Suite 800, Washington, DC 20036, USA. *karen@arl.org*

YAN Jinwei is a Professor and Director of the Wuhan University Library, Luojia Hill, Wuhan 430072, China. *yjw@lib.whu.edu.cn*

List of Figures and Tables

Acknowledgements

A work like this—a compilation of intellectual endeavors of a diverse group of authors—is the crystallization of the collective wisdom of these writers. They (their names and affiliations appear on another page) hail from different countries with different areas of expertise. Seeing the usefulness of producing a work like this, they all made time in their hectic schedules to write chapters for this book. For their contribution of time and well-crafted pieces, we as editors would like to extend our profound thanks. In particular, it should be acknowledged with gratitude the contributors' obliging patience and willingness to cooperate when faced sometimes with seemingly never-ending requests from us for textual improvements and small details.

The writers were originally invited to come to Taiwan as speakers in an academic conference with the theme 'Strategic Planning for eLearning and Digital Content' organized by Feng Chia University in Taichung, Taiwan, and scheduled at the beginning of 2003. However, because of the SARS outbreak, the conference was turned into a virtue one with an online mode. The overwhelming majority of speakers graciously agreed to go along with this idea. They produced narrated PowerPoint presentations, and designed online forums and assignment tasks. The result was a very successful eWorkshop, which convincingly demonstrated the power of the emerging technology in teaching and learning. Our gratitude goes to Rebecca Leung and her team at Feng Chia University Library, who organized and coordinated this complex, interactive, international event. For this well-attended and well-acclaimed eWorkshop, we would also like to thank the Ministry of Education in Taiwan, and Feng Chia University for their commitment, and varied and highly competent logistic support. This work has culminated in the development of the International Research Centre for eLearning and Digital Publishing, which is based in Taiwan.

Finally, the editors would like to thank Springer-Verlag for agreeing to publish this book, and Ms Catherine Drury, the very capable Editorial Assistant for Computer Science at Springer in London, for her guidance and advice right from the conception of this book to the final editing and production stage. However, needless to say, the final responsibility for whatever oversights, limitations and blemishes that exist in the book is ours alone.

Hsianghoo Steve Ching, Paul W. T. Poon and Carmel McNaught
February 2005

Chapter 1

ISSUES IN ORGANIZING AND DISSEMINATING KNOWLEDGE IN THE 21ST CENTURY

Carmel McNaught, Paul W. T. Poon and Hsianghoo Steve Ching

1.   The eRevolution, Globalization and Higher Education

That education is of paramount importance to a nation and to humanity is surely beyond any doubt. In the pre-knowledge-based economy, the main purpose of education was to reduce illiteracy so that citizens could become contributing members of the society. However, in the present knowledge-based economy, education has taken on a new dimension because of the pervasive presence and influence of information technology. This remarkable rise in the use of computer technology, and the concomitant changes in all areas of society that have resulted, is coined the 'eRevolution'. The speed of the development of information technology is such that knowledge becomes superseded quite rapidly, and education has to be continuing and lifelong if one wishes to continue to be a productive member of the workforce. Education is thus inextricably linked with the level of economic development of a nation. On a personal level, education enables access to a diversity of ideas and cultures, hopefully facilitating personal growth and understanding across nations and cultures.

It is therefore not surprising that many nations have made heavy investments in building up their educational system and infrastructure. This has included large investments in a range of educational technologies. However, notwithstanding the huge investment and high priority given, educational systems in almost every country these days are criticized as inadequate (both in terms of quantity and quality), and failing to match the expectation of almost all stakeholders. Calls for wholesale educational reform, at both root and branch level, are frequently heard.

Why has education not been able to meet society's needs? This book will focus on only a tiny aspect of that huge question. We will examine the way in

H. S. Ching, P. W. T. Poon and C. McNaught (Eds.), eLearning and Digital Publishing, 1–10.

which technology has impacted on the processes of scholarly communication in higher education. We will show technology as being part contributor to the challenges higher education faces, and also part contributor to the solutions we need to explore. While the contributors to this book are often critical of current university practices and cognizant of the complex challenges that face us, this book is not a 'doom and gloom' scenario. We have compiled this book with a belief that we need to understand issues and challenges in order to be innovative, think 'outside the box', and move forwards.

The world is said to be 'shrinking' as travel becomes easier, and communications technology becomes nearly ubiquitous. At the same time, the need to understand different points of view is becoming increasingly important on this complex and politically divided globe. The world is also 'expanding' in what is often termed the 'information explosion'. To a great extent, this phenomenon has changed previous patterns of teaching, research work, and publishing activities. According to a study 'How much information? 2003' by Lyman and Varian (2003) at the University of California, Berkeley, "print, film, magnetic, and optical storage media produced 5 exabytes [a billion gigabytes] of new information in 2002", and this is the equivalent of almost 800 megabytes of new information per person in the world in a year. Lyman and Varian also "estimate that the amount of new information stored on paper, film, magnetic, and optical media has about doubled in the last 3 years [1999–2002]".

There are several reasons—political, social and economic—for the way this phenomenon of the information explosion has played itself out in higher education, but there are two principal ones. Firstly, the existing reward (appointment, tenure and promotion) system in universities and colleges has spawned a massive quantity of publications, which up to the very recent past mainly appeared in the print formats of monographs, journal articles and conference papers. Secondly, information and communication technology has made web-publishing easier and affordable, so much so that individuals can now publish on the web without a great deal of technical support. In addition, as a reaction to the ever-increasing subscription cost of academic journals that have been, more or less, monopolized by a few multinational mega-publishers, there has been a tendency in recent years for academics to turn to web-publishing so as to make their publications known to their peers more cheaply and more quickly. As a result, the roles of scholars and publishers in this cyber age has become somewhat blurred. This new scholarly communication process has indeed influenced the process of teaching, research and publishing.

The 'shrinking world' is a globally connected one. According to Wagner (2004), there are three dimensions of globalization. First, economically, a world market is created. This means that almost all economic activities are related to those in another country and on a global scale. This is particularly evident in financial markets. Next, culturally, we can see a homogeneous world culture emerging due to the force of mass media (movies, television, news magazines, etc.). However, on the other hand, Wagner also points out that the increasing migration that has taken place during recent decades has led to multiculturalism in most nations. Lastly, from the political viewpoint, globalization brings about the blurring, and even diminishing, of the sovereign nation-state. International blocs, called 'internations', such as the European Union, or World Trade Organization are instruments in this regard. Behind all these dimensions, the driving force is modern information and telecommunication technology. It is technology that has made it possible for different nations in the world to trade with each other with ease and speed. The power of technology brings the mass media programmes to every corner of the globe and turns the world into a global village. Again, it is the 'magic' of technology that facilitates the working and operation of groupings of internations.

'The only constant is change itself' may sound like a cliché, but it is surely one of the predominant hallmarks of this day and age. Some see globalization as a good thing, and some view it as an oppressive and retrograde step for humanity. Judgment very much depends on one's perspectives and what aspects of globalization one is looking at. But, one thing is certain—globalization is inevitable and there is no way to escape from its many impacts. Education is, unavoidably, under the influence of this global change, particularly so in the sector of higher education.

This then is the backdrop to this book. Our universities are facing immense pressures from within because of the increase in the 'publish or perish' syndrome. There are severe budgetary demands on university libraries attempting to enable access to this increasing avalanche of information. University teaching also needs to prepare graduates for a rapidly changing and connected world. We will explore the role of technology in this challenging scenario.

2. Information Literacy, eLearning and Digital Publishing

In this book there are three threads that are constantly intertwined—information literacy, eLearning and digital publishing. Of the three, 'information literacy' is the hardest to define clearly, but is also a foundation principle for the other two. In Chapter 3 we define information literacy as involving 'accessing, evaluating, managing and communicating information', and as a pre-requisite for constructivist learning. Figure 1-1 shows two ways to illustrate the relationship between these three threads.

The depiction on the left emphasizes the differences between the three concepts, foregrounding particular combinations in order to achieve effective curriculum development, effective design of educational materials and open access to education. Several of the chapters in this book are located in the overlap spaces and are concerned with effective curriculum development,

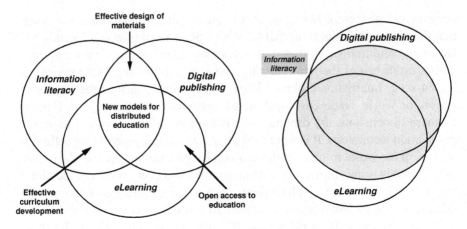

Figure 1-1. Two depictions of the relationships between information literacy, eLearning and digital publishing

effective design of materials and opening access to education. Some are case studies and some are overviews of the literature in these important areas.

On the right, information literacy is merged more closely into eLearning and digital publishing, emphasizing its significance for both areas—as the glue that connects eLearning and digital publishing. The title for this book emerged from this second depiction of the relationships. However, we will use the 'dispersed' diagram on the left for ease of illustration in the later figures in this chapter.

3.   Overview of the Terrain of this Book

This book was designed to occupy a unique niche in the literature accessed by library and publishing specialists, and by university teachers and planners. It examines the interfaces between the work done by four groups of university staff who have been in the past quite separate from, or only marginally related to, each other—library staff, university teachers, university policy makers, and staff who work in university publishing presses. Information literacy has been in the province of librarians, but rarely do librarians influence the nature of the curriculum by working together with teachers. In our information-rich society this is a real waste. Over the past few years university policy makers have invested a great deal of money and energy into providing an infrastructure for university teachers to use in developing eLearning courses for students who are both on-campus and off-campus. However, the feedback from teachers' experiences with eLearning into policy making is often somewhat ad hoc and thus valuable lessons are not heard. Finally, staff in university press offices are often seen as marginal to the real scholarship of the university and many academics consider them as purely a convenient printing and digitizing service.

Yet all four groups are directly and intimately connected with the main functions of universities—the creation, management and dissemination of knowledge in a scholarly and reflective manner.

In figure 1-1, the confluence of all three areas of information literacy, eLearning and digital publishing is labelled 'new models for distributed learning'. The convergence of distance and campus-based learning that has occurred through eLearning brings new meaning to terms such as 'schools without walls'. The model used in this book does not focus on the differences between face-to-face and off-campus learning. Rather, it points out if we have the systems and processes to enable knowledge to be collected, managed and disseminated, then we have much greater potential to provide education locally, globally, on- and off-campus.

Figure 1-2 extends this model by adding both a layer of institutional policy and the broader cultural milieu that our increasing interest in, and concern with, global education demands we acknowledge. Of course, this

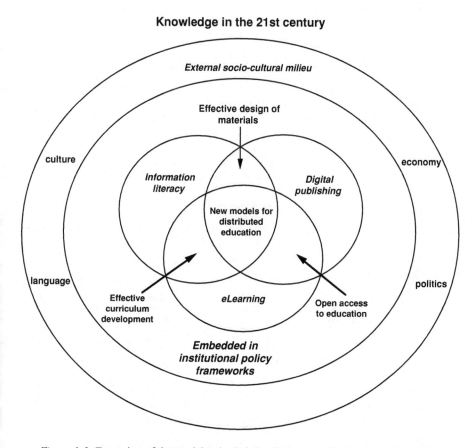

Figure 1-2. Extension of the model to include institutional policy frameworks and the external socio-cultural milieu

two-dimensional representation is far from the reality of the multi-dimensional connections that exist, but it suffices as an illustration of that complexity.

4.   Structure of this Book

The structure of the book has three main sections: the first has primarily an educational focus, the second a focus on digital publishing, and the third builds on the first two sections to examine overall implications for the growth of knowledge and scholarly communication.

This collection brings perspectives (in alphabetical order) from Australia, Hong Kong, People's Republic of China, Singapore, Taiwan, United Kingdom and United States of America. Various chapters, therefore, examine the central concerns of information literacy, eLearning and digital publishing with different lenses. Figure 1-3 shows the chapters in this book mapped

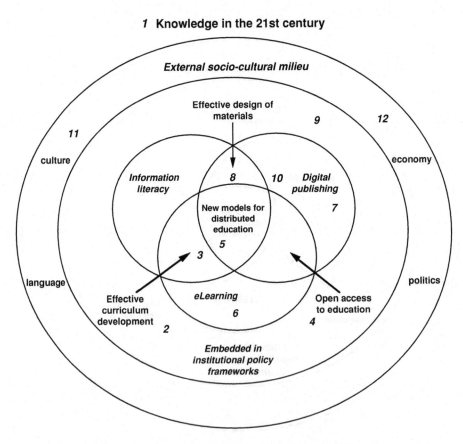

Figure 1-3. Approximate locations of the chapters in this book

into the spaces of figure 1-2. While one point has been indicated, in reality each chapter touches on several areas with 'tentacles' reaching across the whole domain. 'The whole is more than the sum of the parts.' Our ability to understand the extent of the shifts that are occurring in modern universities, and still need to occur in the next few years, relies on our ability to synthesize ideas and experiences from a wide range of university staff. This is just what we hope this book offers.

The contributors to this book are all experienced in their own professional areas. Most of the authors are information specialists and/or university teachers. Many have responsibility for policies concerning eLearning in their institutions. Also several of the library staff already work actively in digital publishing. These authors already bridge across domains. Their combined experiences offer an opportunity to understand the complex nature of emerging models for the provision of education through electronic means to all students in all places. Against the backdrop of the challenges outlined briefly in section 1.1, the chapters in this book were written as a coherent whole to respond to and meet these challenges.

4.1.   *Focus on eLearning and Distributed Education*

The first group of chapters focuses on eLearning and distributed education. We begin with a case study that shows clearly changing responses to global educational markets. In Chapter 2, Y. H. Lui, after looking at the opportunity afforded by the new information technology for distance education, examines how Hong Kong (as a free market for distance education) imports and regulates offshore programmes and courses, and how the Open University of Hong Kong, with which Lui is affiliated, plans and operates the provision of non-local programmes in Hong Kong.

Carmel McNaught, in Chapter 3, delves into the meaning of information literacy. Her article also develops a model of eLearning around the types of learning activities afforded by the web, and discusses the role of technology in assisting graduates to achieve important capabilities such as critical thinking and problem solving. These elements combined explain the synergy between information literacy and eLearning—two important themes of this book. She suggests that current challenges in eLearning may be overcome with reference to models for online communities, of which community digital libraries is one.

The next two chapters address various aspects of implementation of eLearning and distance education. They offer a detailed and useful reference to education providers and regulators in other countries to use in their own strategic planning. An effective and user-friendly eLearning programme is predicated on a robust support system, of which the library services is a key part. In Chapter 4, Susan McKnight, formerly of Deakin University in Australia, points out that to be successful in delivering online education, a university must have a significantly different infrastructure and culture than that normally provided for on-campus students. By using Deakin University as a case study, McKnight outlines the elements that constitute the new infrastructure. From Deakin's experience, it is clear that not just a few more new service components are required, but also a totally new organizational structure to deliver the library and information service to the online students needs to be in place. In addition, to drive this all, a new mindset is necessary to create a new service culture.

Chapter 5 by Karen Wetzel of the Association of Research Libraries (ARL) in the US is written from the perspective of an eLearning provider under the aegis of a professional membership association. Online Lyceum, the subject of her chapter, is the distance education component of ARL. Wetzel chronicles the issues and challenges of putting a course online—from design and development of the digital course environment and course content to administration and course delivery—as experienced by Online Lyceum. She also describes its conceptual underpinnings and the business model, and ends her chapter with some very useful success factors and lessons learned.

Having looked broadly at the eLearning from an organizational and institutional perspective, we turn, in the last chapter in this section, to the experience of eLearning from the perspectives of eLearners themselves. This is a deliberate plan, so that the focus of the learner is not lost in the labyrinth of systems and policies. Chapter 6 is penned by Philippa Levy of the University of Sheffield in the UK. She focuses closely on how learners 'orient' themselves in an online environment, using some of the findings of a practice-based case study evaluation project that examined participants' experiences of a networked learning approach to professional development. In this chapter, the voice of the participants is clearly heard.

4.2.   *Focus on Digital Publishing and Electronic Content*

Part two of the book has its focus on digital publishing and electronic content, and it consists of three chapters. Chapter 7, jointly written by Chennupati K. Ramaiah, Schubert Foo and Heng Poh Choo of the Nanyang Technological University in Singapore, is an overview of electronic publishing (EP). It reviews the current status of EP and its business models, and then highlights a number of the trends of EP. Of particular interest to understanding digital publishing in a globalized world, is the section that examines EP in both developed and developing countries. This chapter is useful in providing a background for the subsequent chapters in the book.

In Chapter 8, Hsianghoo Steve Ching and Lai Chu Lau of the City University of Hong Kong take on one of the most pressing problems of eLearning—that of plagiarism. They suggest that digital publishing offers a solution to this enormous problem; they offer a detailed plan for this process that has benefits for enhancing student learning and for making high-quality work available to the scholarly community. University libraries have an active role to play in this process.

The last chapter in this section, Chapter 9, is authored by Arnold Hirshon of NELINET (New England Library and Information Network) in the US. It is written from a library consortium's perspective on how to implement collaborative consortial purchase for libraries in the face of the ever-increasing prices of electronic resources. Both Chapters 8 and 9 offer solutions to major problems which are innovative and go beyond existing practices in many universities.

4.3. *Implications for the Growth of Knowledge and Scholarly Communication*

The final section of the book examines the implications for the growth of knowledge and scholarly communication. Chapter 10, by Colin Steele of the Australian National University, begins by explaining the reasons for the current scholarly publishing crisis. Steele then highlights the future pattern of the creation, distribution and access of knowledge, information and data. He presents a strong case for the 'liberation' of publishing through open access ePrint repositories and ePresses.

The final two chapters are specifically on scholarly communication itself. Chapter 11, written by Jinwei Yan and Zheng Liu of Wuhan University in China, presents a Chinese perspective of scholarly communication. Basing on a sampling survey that the authors carried out, this chapter describes the current status of scholarly communication in China and highlights some future trends that are likely to emerge. Understanding the nature of scholarly communication in China is essential if a truly global flow of information is to occur which can lead to knowledge based on perspectives from both East and West.

The final chapter of this book, Chapter 12, takes an overview of the global changes in scholarly communication. The author, Suzanne Thorin of Indiana University in the US, traces the history of scholarly communication, and in doing so, outlines the inadequacies of the traditional scholarly communication. This chapter also looks at the emerging trends of how scholars are conducting and disseminating the results of their research. The book thus ends with a sense of scholars exploring emerging spaces and new strategies for conducting and disseminating research.

5.   Higher Education in Transition

Today's higher education is, no doubt, in transition, and at a critical crossroads. In order to survive and thrive, universities and colleges have a significant amount of restructuring and reforming to do. Universities and colleges should realize that the eRevolution does not sound the death knell for them, if they adjust their ways of operation. Instead, technology can rejuvenate them and enable new and more sustainable directions. With these two points in mind—a mindset for constant change and reform, and the realization that technology is a powerful enabling instrument rather than a hindrance—higher education can find new directions to the satisfaction of all of its stakeholders. The words of John F. Kennedy, spoken in 1960 still have resonance today: "We stand today on the edge of a new frontier...a frontier of unknown opportunities and perils, a frontier of unfulfilled hopes and threats. The new frontier of which I speak is not a set of promises—it is a set of challenges." It is hoped that the chapters in this book offer some strategies for meeting the challenges universities worldwide face in the 21st century.

References

Lyman, P., & Varian H. R. (2003). How much information? 2003. Retrieved February 14, 2005, from http://www.sims.berkeley.edu/research/projects/how-much-info-2003/

Wagner, P. (2004). Higher education in an era of globalization: What is at stake? In K. Jaishree, K. Odin & P. T. Manicas (Eds.), *Globalization and higher education* (pp. 7–23). Honolulu: University of Hawaii Press.

PART ONE

FOCUS ON eLEARNING AND DISTRIBUTED EDUCATION

Chapter 2

THE PROVISION OF NON-LOCAL PROGRAMMES IN HONG KONG: THE EXPERIENCE OF THE OPEN UNIVERSITY OF HONG KONG

Y. H. Lui

1.   Chapter Overview

Using advanced technology, it is now easier for education institutions to deliver courses and programmes at a distance, reach students in other places, and foster international collaboration. There is a growing trend for education services to be exported from one country to another. While exporting countries/institutions may find this trend acceptable at least from a financial point of view, opinion is divided over whether such development is beneficial to the importing countries.

This chapter examines how Hong Kong (as a free market) imports and regulates offshore programmes, and how the Open University of Hong Kong (OUHK, a distance university) considers and operates the provision of non-local programmes, with their component courses, in Hong Kong. It provides a useful reference for regulators and education providers in designing a proper framework to facilitate the import of good quality offshore programmes and to make the import 'win–win' to all parties concerned (including the local operators, the local students and the local community).

2.   Introduction

Rapid advances in communication and information technology not only accelerate the trend of globalization but also change people's way of learning. Technology, especially the Internet, offers new opportunities to create, store, manipulate, access and distribute information, and provides new learning

H. S. Ching, P. W. T. Poon and C. McNaught (Eds.), eLearning and Digital Publishing, 13–28.
© 2006 *H. S. Ching, P. W. T. Poon and C. McNaught.*

environments and channels. By taking advantage of these new communication and information technologies, education institutions are now better placed to deliver courses at a distance, reach students in many places and foster international collaboration.

There is a growing trend for education as a service to be exported and imported among different countries. While exporting countries/institutions may find this trend acceptable at least from a financial point of view, opinion is divided over whether this development is beneficial to the countries importing programmes. On the one hand, advocates believe that importing offshore programmes should bring in several benefits, for example:

- making use of other countries' expertise and infra-structural investments in education;
- reducing local government's funding commitment to education as non-local programmes are often imported and provided on a self-financing basis;
- enabling programmes and courses offered to be more responsive to local development needs because offshore courses are already available elsewhere and can be introduced very quickly into the domestic market;
- increasing the opportunity for local people to get an overseas tertiary education qualification, as they are not required to study abroad which may be more expensive and time-consuming;
- enabling local students to obtain an international perspective on knowledge, ideas, values and practices; and
- providing a chance for local students to learn in an international language (for example, English) so that they can develop better language skills to communicate and interact with the international community.

Chan and Mills (2000) reported one successful Australian/Hong Kong partnership.

On the other hand, critics express their concerns about the potential problems and risks associated with importing programmes. Among other things, these include the following issues:

- *Quality*: How can the quality of imported programmes be controlled? Can the standard of programmes be maintained when they are operated in the local culture? Are the domestic and imported programmes of comparable quality?
- *Local relevance*: Are the curriculum and content of the offshore programmes relevant to the local market and can they can meet local conditions and needs?
- *Support for student learning*: To what extent can offshore course providers provide learning support (for example, library facilities,

computer laboratories) to students? Is such support sufficient to facilitate student learning to meet course objectives?

- *Political considerations*: For instance, would offering offshore programmes reduce the domestic government's investment in and commitment to education, thus slowing down the development of the local education infrastructure? Will importing programmes result in a significant outflow of money and cause a problem to domestic balance of payments?

Obviously, all these issues have to be carefully considered and analysed before a decision about whether, and if so how, to import offshore programmes is made. To better understand the issues, it is useful to refer to other nations' experiences in importing programmes and courses. Global Distance EducationNet (DistEdNet) is a network supported by the World Bank and administered by the Commonwealth of Learning that strives to achieve this aim. The East Asia Global Distance Education Network is one of the regional sites of the DistEdNet hosted and managed by the Centre for Research in Distance and Adult Learning at The Open University of Hong Kong.

Hong Kong is known to be a free economy. Basically, there are very few restrictions on the import and export of goods and services. The education market is no exception. Local education institutions are permitted to operate offshore where appropriate. Similarly, overseas institutions are also allowed to conduct their programmes in the territory, provided that they can meet certain requirements.

Among the nine degree-awarding tertiary institutions in Hong Kong (see http://www.ugc.edu.hk/english/fund_inst.html for the eight government-funded institutions), the Open University of Hong Kong (OUHK, formerly known as the Open Learning Institute of Hong Kong; see http://www.ouhk.edu.hk/) is the first university offering programmes by distance education. The OUHK began offering distance programmes in 1989. Besides operating in Hong Kong, it also provides certain programmes in several major cities of mainland China. While the University exports programmes to mainland China, it also conducts programmes developed by overseas education institutions in the local market.

This chapter examines how Hong Kong (as a free market) imports and regulates offshore programmes, and how the OUHK considers and operates the provision of non-local programmes in Hong Kong. It is hoped that the chapter can serve as a useful reference for regulators and education providers in designing a proper framework to facilitate the import of good quality offshore programmes for the benefit of local communities and students.

The remainder of the chapter consists of two main sections. The next section introduces the regulatory framework for offshore programmes in Hong Kong, with particular attention being paid to the requirements in registration, operations and advertisement. The following section examines the OUHK's strategies, policies and experience in the provision of non-local programmes. In particular, the reasons why a distance university imports offshore programmes will be explored and the operational processes needed to offer these programmes will be outlined.

3.   Regulatory Framework for Offshore Programmes in Hong Kong

Hong Kong is a market with very little restriction on export and import of education programmes. To ensure effective control over the conduct of imported programmes, the Hong Kong Government enacted the *Non-Local Higher and Professional Education (Regulation) Ordinance* in July 1996, which became effective from June 1997. Specifically, the Ordinance has two objectives:

1. to protect Hong Kong consumers by guarding against the launching of non-local programmes which do not meet some pre-determined registration criteria; and
2. to enhance Hong Kong's reputation as a community which values internationally recognized higher academic and professional education.

The responsibility for implementing the legislation rests with the Education and Manpower Bureau which set up the Non-local Courses Registry to carry out the regulatory tasks. In essence, the legislation establishes a system of registration to regulate the conduct of offshore programmes offered in Hong Kong. The programmes subject to regulation include all offshore programmes leading to the award of non-local higher academic qualifications (sub-degree, degree, postgraduate and other post-secondary qualifications) or professional qualifications. These regulated programmes need to fulfil certain requirements with regard to registration, operations and advertisement.

3.1.   Registration Requirements

The legislation stipulates that it is an offence to conduct regulated programmes without registration or exemption. To offer offshore programmes in Hong Kong, operators must secure their registration or exemption status before conducting them. Applications must be made to the Registry at least 4 months before programme commencement.

To register, an offshore programme must meet the following three broad criteria:

1. *Comparable standards.* If the programme concerned is leading to a non-local higher academic qualification awarded by a non-local institution,

   - the awarding institution must be recognized by the relevant accreditation authority and the academic community in its home country;
   - there must be effective control measures in place to ensure that the programme is of comparable standard to that of a programme leading to the same qualification operated in its home country; and
   - the comparability in standard must be recognized by the institution itself, the home academic community and the home accreditation authority.

2. *Professional recognition.* If the programme to be registered leads to an award of a non-local professional qualification issued by a non-local professional body,

   - it must be recognized by the professional body for the purpose of either awarding the qualification or preparing students for the sitting of the relevant professional examinations; and
   - the professional body must be generally recognized as an authoritative and representative professional body in the relevant profession in its home country.

3. *Financial matters.* The operator has to make proper arrangements for payment and refund of the programme fee to the satisfaction of the Registry.

Once an application is accepted and approved, the Registry issues a certificate of registration to the operator. A registration number is assigned to each registered programme and the operator is required to show the number in all relevant promotional materials.

It is worth noting that not all offshore programmes require registration. The following three exceptions are allowed in the legislation:

1. *Programmes conducted in collaboration with eleven specified local tertiary* institutions (the nine degree-awarding institutions; the Hong Kong Academy for Performing Arts; and the Hong Kong Shue Yan College, an independent liberal arts college). These programmes will be exempt from registration on the condition that the institutions' executive heads can certify that the programmes concerned fulfil the criteria required for registration, both in terms of the awarding institution's professional body's standing and the programme's quality assurance and recognition status.

2. *Programmes conducted purely by distance learning.* These refer to programmes conducted solely by means of mail or telecommunication (using television, radio or computer networks) and without the relevant institutions, professional bodies or their agents being physically present in Hong Kong to deliver any lectures, tutorials or examinations, etc.
3. *Programmes conducted solely by local registered schools or local institutions of higher education* (as these programmes are already covered in regulations of other legislation).

To decide if an offshore programme meets the criteria for registration or exemption from registration, the Registry will normally consult with the Hong Kong Council for Academic Accreditation (HKCAA) for expert advice. As an independent self-financing statutory body responsible for accrediting programmes' academic quality and standards, the HKCAA charges fees on a cost-recovery basis and these fees are borne by relevant applicants. The Registry records all registered and exempted programmes in a register which is available for public inspection free of charge.

3.2.   Operation Requirements

Besides registration requirements, all regulated programmes are also required to fulfil certain operation requirements. These cover arrangements for payment and refund of tuition fees, premises to be used for teaching, and reporting of certain information required by the Registry:

- The tuition fee *payment* arrangement of regulated programmes needs to be approved by the Registry and stated clearly in relevant documents provided to students. The operators are obliged to issue a written receipt showing the purpose of a payment within 30 days of its receipt.
- To protect students against sudden or unexpected financial loss, the legislation requires a non-local programme operator to *refund* the relevant part of the tuition fee if the programme ceases to be conducted due to cancellation of its registration/exemption status or its premature cessation. The refund must be made to the affected students within 1 month; otherwise the operator commits an offence and is liable to fine and imprisonment.
- For safety purposes, all regulated courses must be conducted in *premises* approved by the Registry or exempted premises (registered schools, specified local tertiary institutions, education purpose-built/designated premises and hotel function rooms). Operators need to

furnish particulars of the premises to be used for conducting the courses and get prior approval from the Registry for using them.

- To ensure that the registration criteria are met continuously, operators of registered and exempted programmes are also required to submit *annual returns* to the Registrar for scrutiny. If there are any changes in particulars that may affect the registration criteria (such as the operator, the course content, the arrangements for payment and refund), the operators must notify the Registrar and the students in writing within 1 month of such changes.

3.3. Advertisement Requirements

The advertisements made for offshore programmes also fall within the ambit of regulation. The legislation sets out clearly that an offence is committed in the following two circumstances: (1) publishing advertisements to induce enrolment in regulated programmes not registered or exempted, and (2) publishing false or misleading materials in any advertisements on any regulated programme or purely distance-learning programme.

To facilitate consumers in identifying the registration and exemption of non-local programmes, both registered and exempted programmes need to show their registration numbers and exemption status respectively in their advertisements. Furthermore, the advertisements must also contain a standard statement saying that "it is the discretion of individual employers to recognize any qualification to which the programme may lead".

It must be stressed that Hong Kong's regulatory framework of offshore programmes is merely a system of registration rather than a system of quality recognition. Throughout the regulation process, there is no assessment or guarantee of any individual programme's quality, nor its comparability to local degree programmes. An offshore programme's registration or exemption from registration is just an assurance of the awarding institution being a recognized body, and the programme being of comparable standard to that of any identical

Table 2-1. Number of registered and exempted programmes

	Number	Proportion (%)
Registered programmes	411	42
Exempted programmes	572	58
Total	983	100

Source: The Non-local Courses Registry, Hong Kong. (Retrieved February 2, 2005, from http://www.emb.gov.hk/index.aspx?langno= 1&nodeid=1250)

Table 2-2. Geographical distribution of non-local programmes

	Registered programmes	%	Exempted programmes	%	Total	%
Australia	152	37	137	24	**289**	**29**
Canada	8	2	6	1	**14**	**2**
Mainland China	17	4	52	9	**69**	**7**
UK	181	44	332	58	**513**	**52**
US	41	10	34	6	**75**	**8**
Others	12	3	11	2	**23**	**2**
Total	**411**	**100**	**572**	**100**	**983**	**100%**

Source: The Non-local Courses Registry, Hong Kong. (Retrieved February 2, 2005, from http://www.emb.gov.hk/index.aspx?langno=1&nodeid=1250)

home programme and recognized as such in the home country. It is entirely up to individual students to decide whether a programme is acceptable for the purposes of admission, employment, etc. This illustrates why the standard statement is needed to alert stakeholders of the potential recognition issue.

Table 2-1 shows the number of non-local programmes offered in Hong Kong and table 2-2 gives their geographical distribution. As at 26 January 2005, there were a total of 983 offshore programmes conducted in the territory, out of which 42% (411) and 58% (572) are registered and exempted programmes respectively. The programmes mainly come from Western countries such as Australia, Canada, the UK and the US. The UK is the largest exporter accounting for more than half of the programmes, followed by Australia. It is estimated that annually Hong Kong students spend hundreds of millions of dollars in taking these non-local programmes.

Having understood the macro regulatory framework in Hong Kong, in what follows we turn to examine how the OUHK collaborates with overseas institutions to conduct non-local programmes in the local market.

4.   The Open University of Hong Kong's Experience

The OUHK was founded by the Hong Kong Government in 1989, with a mission to provide higher education to adult learners, principally through a system of open and distance education. As compared with other conventional universities in Hong Kong which generally offer government-funded higher education in largely face-to-face mode to full-time students, OUHK has the following four salient features:

1. *Open access.* Except for full-time associate degree, professional and postgraduate programmes, there are no admission requirements for

OUHK's sub-degree and degree programmes. Programmes are open to anyone aged 17 or above. Students with lower qualifications can start with pre-foundation programmes to bridge them up to the university level. Although open access is allowed, the University adopts the principle of *"lenient entry, stringent exit"* (寬進嚴出) and has rigorous quality assurance mechanisms in place to control the quality and standard of its programmes and courses. To complete a course successfully, students must pass both the coursework and the final examination.

2. *Distance learning.* The OUHK is the first university offering distance education in Hong Kong. Except for the programmes taken by full-time students, all other programmes are delivered in distance mode. For each course, students are given a comprehensive self-study pack which is specially developed to cater for the needs of working adult students. To support students' learning, courses are generally supplemented with online learning, audio-visual materials and optional face-to-face tutorials as appropriate. In addition, every student on a course is also allocated a part-time tutor who provides academic comments and advice via telephone or Internet. This type of flexible learning mode allows students to circumvent the time and place constraints and to plan their own pace of study.

3. *Credit system and transfer.* The University adopts a credit system to deliver its courses. Each distance course is given a credit value that contributes towards an academic qualification. According to their own needs and interests, students may choose courses and accumulate credits at their own pace until reaching the required total credits for a qualification (90 credits required for the award of Higher Diploma, 120 credits for an ordinary degree and 160 credits for an honours degree). No fixed time limit is set for the completion of most programmes. Students who have obtained relevant qualifications from other local or overseas tertiary institutions can also apply for credit exemption and advanced standing.

4. *Self-financing.* OUHK is a self-financing university. Only in the first few years of its establishment did the University receive funding from the Government for its recurrent expenditure. Since that time the University has basically operated on a self-financing model and has relied on tuition fee income to cover its running costs. Occasionally, the Government provides dollar-to-dollar matching grants to finance the University's capital projects on a merit basis. While the tuition fee for a degree at the OUHK and other conventional universities is roughly the same, about 82% of the latter's running costs is financed by the Government. To some extent, this reflects the cost-effectiveness of OUHK's distance education model as compared with the conventional education system.

The OUHK offers programmes and courses through its four Schools and one Institute, namely the School of Arts and Social Science (A&SS), School of Business and Administration (B&A), School of Education and Languages (E&L), School of Science and Technology (S&T), and Li Ka Shing Institute of Professional and Continuing Education (LiPACE). The four Schools offer hundreds of distance courses contributing to programme awards of certificate, diploma, higher diploma, associate degree, degree, master and doctoral degree by the University. Each semester there are around 25,000 students enrolled in courses and annually there are about 4,000 graduates from these sub-degree, degree and postgraduate programmes. So far over 120,000 students have studied in OUHK's distance courses at different levels and in various disciplines.

4.1.   *Li Ka Shing Institute of Professional and Continuing Education*

The OUHK conducts non-local programmes through its extension arm, LiPACE, which has the role to provide education opportunities not covered by other Schools. Specifically, LiPACE offers a variety of flexible and high quality professional and vocational learning opportunities (with an emphasis on face-to-face teaching) to the public. At present, major programmes and courses offered by LiPACE include: taught programmes and courses offered in collaboration with professional bodies and/or developing professional competence, some of which may lead to the award of certificates and diplomas by the Institute alone or jointly with relevant professional bodies; tailor-made training courses organized for private and public organizations; full-time programmes; and non-local undergraduate and postgraduate programmes offered in collaboration with overseas universities. Students enrolled on these programmes will receive their awards from the overseas partners upon completion of their studies. This rich smorgasbord of offerings needs to be carefully planned and organized.

4.2.   *Strategic Considerations*

Although not spelt out clearly, the University has several considerations when formulating its strategies for conducting offshore programmes and courses. These considerations include:

1. *Partnership.* In comparison with conventional education, distance learn-ing is still new in most people's minds and its recognition is yet to be improved. Being a young distance university with a short history, the University considers collaboration in provision of non-local programmes

as a good way to partner with prestigious offshore universities and to raise its profile in the international academic community.

2. *Programme choices to students.* To a self-financing university, limited resources are certainly a constraint on its programme development. In particular, developing distance programmes are quite costly and time-consuming. To respond to market demand in those areas that have no or low capacity of internal provisions, importing offshore programmes is taken as a quick and cost-effective alternative by OUHK to enhance its course offerings and afford more choices to students.

3. *Drawing on others' expertise.* It is also hoped that through collaboration with overseas institutions in provision of their programmes in Hong Kong, the University may draw on partners' expertise and experience of programme development in those areas where OUHK is not strong enough or under-developed.

4. *Financial contribution.* Financial contribution is another major consideration. Being self-financing, the University hopes that offering offshore programmes may bring in additional income to fulfil its self-financing mission.

4.3. Policies on Non-Local Programmes

Based on the strategic considerations, some internal policies have been developed to guide the launching and provision of non-local programmes.

For administrative convenience and efficiency, the University mandates its extension arm, LiPACE, as the only unit to conduct non-local programmes. However, to avoid conflict with other Schools' interests, in most cases LiPACE cannot offer any non-local programmes similar to those currently offered or under planning to be offered by the Schools. Generally, when there are any ideas for offshore programmes collaboration, LiPACE consults with other Schools first. Only if they have no objections will it proceed to explore the proposal further.

As explained below, the University has established a rigorous quality assurance mechanism to monitor the development and conduct of non-local programmes. A cautious approach is taken to assess carefully both the quality of offshore programmes and the reputation of potential partners. Though these programmes are awarded by the overseas partners who are responsible for the control of academic standard and quality, it is understood that as a local operator providing student learning support, any wrongdoing in the programmes would also endanger the OUHK's image and reputation. Therefore, as a general policy, the University only considers collaborating on quality programmes offered by prestigious overseas partners.

To avoid public confusion, promotion and enrolment of non-local programmes are done separately from the OUHK's own programmes. In all promotion materials, it is clearly indicated that the programmes will lead to the awards of overseas partners rather than the University's.

The offshore programmes conducted or to be conducted must expect to be financially viable. In the past years, LiPACE has phased out some offshore programmes which could not attract sufficient market demand for whatever reasons. These include Certificate in Professional Photography (New York Institute of Photography, US), Writing Business English Course (via the Internet, School of Continuing and Professional Studies, New York University, US), Master of International Trade and Investment Law (Deakin University, Australia), Master of Arts (Public Policy) and Graduate Certificate in Public Policy (University of New England, Australia).

4.4.   Quality Assurance Mechanism

Quality is one of the major concerns in OUHK's policy on offering non-local programmes. To ensure all programmes' quality, the University internally has a rigorous quality assurance mechanism covering programme development, management and monitoring.

There is an approval process for the development of offshore programmes at both the Institute and the University levels. Any idea or plan to offer offshore programmes must first be approved by the LiPACE Director who will make a general judgement about the programme quality, the relevant partner's reputation and the potential market demand. If the idea sounds acceptable, the Director will consult with other Schools to get their endorsement before proceeding further.

Once a green light is given, a Programme Planning Team (PPT) will be formed within LiPACE to take responsibility for reviewing the standing and reputation of the overseas institutions, assessing the quality of the courses, ascertaining the market demand and handling other issues related to planning and development. The team consists of both academic and administrative staff. If no relevant subject expertise is available internally, outside experts would be invited to provide academic advice. The PPT will prepare a programme proposal with a budget which will first be examined by the Institute's Executive Board (IEB) and then by the University's Committee on Professional and Continuing Education (COPACE) for approval. COPACE is a sub-committee set up by the University Senate to oversee the operation of LiPACE's non-credit bearing courses (including non-local programmes). The Committee is chaired by the Vice President (Academic) and its membership consists of Deans of other Schools and representatives of the University's Human Resources Unit and the Finance Unit.

The proposal of an approved programme will become an internal definitive programme document. Any modifications must follow set procedures to get approval. In addition, the approved programme will also be subject to close monitoring from time to time.

In the management and monitoring of the non-local programmes, two basic principles are worth noting. First, since the programme's awarding institution is the overseas partner rather than the OUHK, it is the former party that has the primary responsibility to maintain the academic quality and standard of all non-local programmes. As a local operator, the OUHK plays a supporting role to maintain and enhance each programme's academic quality. It can provide advice and suggestions but it cannot enforce any academic changes unilaterally. Second, if either party would like to initiate changes, a prior consultation with the counterpart will usually be made to see whether the proposed changes are reasonable and acceptable, and if so how they can be implemented in a proper way.

On both sides, a programme coordinator will be appointed to manage the day-to-day operation of the programme. Where necessary, the programme coordinators may refer matters to a jointly set up Programme Management Committee (PMC), which is responsible for overseeing the approved courses. The Committee is usually chaired by the LiPACE Director or the counterpart's Faculty Dean. Membership consists of the programme coordinators and other relevant academic and administrative staff. Each year the PMC will have at least one meeting to review the programme's operation and quality, including programme curriculum and materials, appointment and performance of instructors, assessment methods and standards, relevance of the programme to the needs of the local community, feedback from students and instructors, and any other matters of concern.

If local teaching is required for an approved non-local programme, both parties would agree on the minimum requirements of local instructors to be recruited. There will also be a series of measures (including class visits, a student consultative committee and student evaluation surveys) to monitor the appointed local instructors' performance in class.

4.5.   *Existing Non-Local Programmes on Offer*

Table 2-3 provides the distribution of OUHK's non-local programmes by level and by country of partners. It can be seen that a majority of these programmes are at postgraduate level. This follows because as a young university the OUHK itself has naturally focused more on undergraduate programmes in its early development, and so there has been some space for importing offshore postgraduate programmes.

Table 2-3. Non-local programmes offered by OUHK

	Sub-degree	Degree	Postgraduate	Total
Australia	—	1	12	**13**
UK	2	1	1	**4**
Mainland China	3	1	—	**4**
Total	**5**	**3**	**13**	**21**

Among the imported programmes, most fall into the areas uncovered or under-covered by other Schools. These areas include accounting, finance, nursing, gerontology, occupational health and safety, traditional Chinese medicine, journalism, public relations, interior design and law. These courses are delivered in different learning modes, including taught (teaching by overseas academics or local staff), distance mode or their combinations.

4.6.   Contributory Factors to a Programme's Success

The OUHK launched the first non-local programme (Master of Accounting in collaboration with Curtin University of Technology in Australia) in February 1996. So far there have been 26 courses developed, out of which more than 80% are being successfully conducted in terms of satisfactory student enrolment and feedback, and financial contribution. From this limited but fruitful experience, several striking points about the success of a non-local programme can be identified.

Partners' prestige is essential to the success of non-local programmes as good names are often perceived to be associated with good quality. Prestige may benefit a programme's launching and subsequent promotion. Equally important is a partner's experience and commitment in operating programmes offshore because student support in non-local programmes hinges very much on an effective administrative and coordination system. Regardless of how prestigious an institution is, lack of experience and commitment certainly affects the quality of services provided to students.

The programmes to be conducted should be of good *quality and reputation.* Quality and reputation may be reflected by recognition of relevant professional bodies, high ranking or rating given by independent associations, high enrolment number at home, etc. Another indication is the identity of a local operator. If the operator is a local university rather than a private profit-making organization, people generally have greater confidence in the programme because they believe that a university has a more rigorous and effective quality assurance mechanism in selecting and monitoring offshore programmes.

A successful programme should have a curriculum and/or award *relevant to local development needs*. For example, as an international business and financial centre, there has been a great demand for business and finance programmes in Hong Kong. In recent years, people have become more concerned about an aging population and health problems. Imported health-related programmes are becoming more popular.

To most people, distance and online programmes are still quite a new approach to learning and have yet to become popular. This is the same situation in Hong Kong, where the demand for pure distance or online offerings is still not very high. Students generally prefer to have a *taught element* built into their courses to supplement their studies. Face-to-face sessions are valuable in that they not only provide an opportunity for students to have interaction and discussion with their instructors and fellow students (thus obtaining the actual and psychological support from their peer group), but also serve as an effective mechanism to enhance local supplementation to the imported course materials and to set checkpoints to monitor their study plan and progress (Fung & Carr, 2000).

Student support is also a crucial factor in determining a programme's attractiveness and competitiveness. It is often heard that students choose offshore programmes conducted by local universities (instead of private organizations), partly because of their confidence in a university's quality assurance mechanism, partly because local universities generally have better support in terms of library resources and computer laboratories provided to facilitate student learning.

In a rapidly changing world, people are more aware of the importance of lifelong learning. Besides studying for a single qualification, they are also concerned about whether, and if so how, a potential *progression path* is available for their studies. A programme that has a clear and direct progression path will almost certainly have a greater chance of attracting higher enrolments, retaining those students for longer and, overall, having a higher programme completion rate.

As the Hong Kong continuing education market is highly competitive, there are a number of local and offshore programmes offered in different subject areas. Students are known to 'shop around' to compare different aspects of similar programmes. To attract prospective students to a particular programme and engage their interest in enrolment, active *promotion* is required and *pricing* also needs to be very competitive.

5.   Conclusion

Following the trend of globalization and rapid technological development, it is increasingly popular for universities to extend their programmes and campuses beyond national boundaries. Queries have been raised whether such movement is beneficial to the country and the students at the receiving end.

This chapter has reported Hong Kong's experience in regulating imported programmes and the Open University of Hong Kong's experience in operating imported courses and programmes. It provides a model of how a free economy can set up its regulatory framework to ensure the orderly conduct of non-local programmes and to protect local consumers. Further, the enactment of this model by a distance university is shown in the example of the Open University of Hong Kong through the explanation of OUHK's strategies, policies and mechanism in the provision of non-local programmes in its domestic market. It is hoped that these experiences are of value to other universities engaging in international partnerships. Ultimately, it is hoped that local students and the local community will increasingly benefit from these global partnerships.

Acknowledgement

The author wishes to thank Dr. Bob Butcher for comment on this chapter.

References

Chan, F. T., & Mills, J. J. (2000). Collaboration for success in open and distance education: A case study of Australia and Hong Kong. International Distance Education and Open Learning Conference. Retrieved November 15, 2004, from http://www.ouhk.edu.hk/cridal/gdenet/ Policy/Global/EAP3B.html

East Asia Global Distance Education Net. Retrieved February 2, 2005, from http://www. ouhk.edu.hk/cridal/gdenet/

Fung, Y., & Carr, R. (2000). Face-to-face tutorials in a distance learning system: Meeting student needs. *Open Learning, 15*(1), 35–46.

Hong Kong Government (1996). Non-Local Higher and Professional Education (Regulation) Ordinance. Retrieved February 2, 2005, from http://www.justice.gov.hk/home.htm

Chapter 3

THE SYNERGY BETWEEN INFORMATION LITERACY AND eLEARNING

Carmel McNaught

1.   Chapter Overview

The chapter opens with a discussion of what is involved in designing university programmes in the 21st century. The need to produce graduates with key capabilities who can work effectively in a complex, changing world is highlighted. Information literacy is one of these key graduate capabilities.

The distinction between information and knowledge is central to understanding the meaning of information literacy, and the relationship between information literacy and eLearning. The chapter is predicated on a broad approach to the meaning of information literacy. The model that is described is based on that developed by the American Association for School Librarians (AASL) and moves information literacy into a place beyond that of information retrieval and evaluation. The model emphasizes that an information-literate person actively uses information to further personal learning and growth with respect to all facets of her or his life, and also is an active and participatory member of human society.

A pragmatic approach is taken to the description of skills needed in being an efficient and effective seeker and user of information. The importance of planning information searches and prioritizing potential sources of information is stressed, as is the need for active engagement with information to seek understanding. It is at this point that the bridge between information literacy and learning occurs—the transformation of information into knowledge that is demonstrated in the production of a unique product (be it an essay, report, media object, etc.). The skills involved in evaluating the appropriateness of any product are also essential.

The themes of personal construction of knowledge and social learning are maintained in the discussion of learning and eLearning. A constructivist

H. S. Ching, P. W. T. Poon and C. McNaught (Eds.), eLearning and Digital Publishing, 29–43.

approach to describing learning as a personal construction of knowledge is taken. A model of eLearning is developed around the types of learning activities afforded by the web. Four areas are explored: communication between teacher and students; assessment and feedback to students; study management and skills support; and resources/content for learning. Learning is enhanced when all four aspects are utilized in some way or another. However, the power of the web is underutilized if communication technologies are not included as a strong feature of eLearning designs.

Finally, the emergence of models for online communities is explored. The example of DLESE (Digital Library for Earth System Education) does illustrate a possible model for how digital libraries can support the development of a community of information-literate people working in a particular (albeit broadly conceived) discipline area. The chapter ends with some reflections on the possibilities for information literacy on a global scale and the role of community digital libraries in the realization of that aim.

2.   Designing University Programmes for the 21st Century

There is almost a mantra these days about the increasing rate of change in all institutions. What is remaining the same? What is changing? Higher education rests on the premise that student learning can be facilitated by operating in a planned environment. If we don't believe that we should return to the days of unstructured discovery learning that many of us tried in the 1960s and 1970s (either as learners or teachers) and found very unsatisfying. Basically, not only does the curriculum need to be planned, but also the nature of the total student experience over, usually, a period of years needs to be considered if curriculum alignment (Biggs, 1999) is to occur and result in demonstrable benefits for students. Many university programmes are designed by choosing an appropriate set of content topics, and insufficient attention is paid to other details of educational design. However, there are several aspects to good curriculum planning. The aims need to be clearly spelt out; this is often best done by specifying reasonably precise learning outcomes or objectives. Choosing content topics for programmes (and their component courses), planning teaching and learning activities, and setting assessment tasks for the students need to be done together, and all these three aspects of planning need to be done with the learning outcomes in mind. This is shown in a simple form in figure 3-1.

Thus, a general description of educational design might be 'a planned process of making curriculum decisions about how best to support student learning in some defined area'. It is worthwhile spending a little time looking at the meaning of learning. Learning is a complex process. How do students learn the important ideas they need to know? Do they assimilate

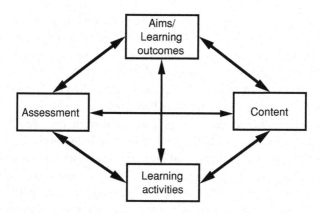

Figure 3-1. Simple representation of an aligned curriculum

information which they then reproduce? This might be possible for certain facts, but even then, if the facts are all unrelated, it is hard to remember them. Learning is much easier if connections can be made between ideas and facts. How can these connections be made? Is it by rules, as in a system of information processing, much like the way a computer can be programmed? This might be possible for learning fixed processes which are always the same, for example, a laboratory procedure such as setting up an electrical circuit from a diagram, or routine clinical procedures such as taking a patient's blood pressure. But sets of rules are not enough when learners need to solve a problem they have not seen before, or when they want to design something quite new (a bridge, a poem, or a plan for doing new research). Something else is needed then. In these cases, learning appears to be a complex process where knowledge is constructed from a variety of sources. What students learn depends on what they already know, how they engage with new ideas, and the processes of discussion and interaction with those they talk to about these ideas.

Another way to look at the complexity of learning is to examine the diversity of beliefs about what constitutes learning. In the literature, one contrast to emerge with some consistency is between academic teachers who think of learning as reproducing knowledge (and of teaching as organizing and presenting the knowledge to be reproduced), and others who think of learning as a process in which understanding is constructed by the student with the assistance of the teacher (e.g. Trigwell, Prosser, & Taylor, 1994). This is often called the instructivist/constructivist paradigmatic divide. Roblyer's (2002) approach of looking at the relevant emphases of 'directed instruction' and 'constructivism' is perhaps more helpful. She does not adopt an either/or approach but instead discusses the relative emphases of design aspects in each paradigm. A constructivist approach involves a focus on learning through posing problems, exploring possible answers, and developing products and presentations, in contrast to a focus on transmitting hierarchically constructed content and skills. This then implies that the constructivist approach emphasizes pursuing global goals that specify general abilities such as problem solving and research skills; anchoring learning tasks in meaningful, authentic situations; group work rather than individualized work; and alternative learning and open-ended assessment methods.

The paradigms that people adopt for the design and development of educational environments reflect their prior knowledge and experience, the manner in which they were taught, and implicit (or explicit) models of teaching and learning they have experienced in their own educational undertakings. The adage that 'people teach as they were taught' may be extended to 'people design educational environments based upon their experiences (and perceptions) of teaching and learning'. 'Directed instruction' may well be useful in many specific situations, but our ultimate goals in education are 'constructivist'. The outcomes of education, especially if we take a lifelong view of learning, are more likely to be described by broad capabilities, such as the list of clusters of abilities noted by Nightingale *et al.* (1996): thinking critically and making judgments; solving problems and developing plans; performing procedures and demonstrating techniques; managing and developing oneself; accessing and managing information; demonstrating knowledge and understanding; designing, creating, performing; and communicating. In a globally connected world where challenges are inter-disciplinary, these capabilities become more essential.

So, designing appropriate university programmes involves working out how the ultimate broad educational goals we have can best be met by specific choices of activities and assessment within individual small modules, units or courses. There needs to be alignment between stated learning outcomes, student activities and assessment. This needs to occur across various levels of skill and understanding. There are implications for the level of achievement in that these need to be specified clearly; for example, it may be that full mastery is expected for some foundational aspects of the discipline but that variation in the attainment of graduate capabilities is expected (and that is certainly what occurs!). The art of educational design lies on being able to work across both programmes and courses, and being able to map student learning across an entire degree or diploma programme.

3.   Exploring the Meaning of Information Literacy

Information literacy is integral to the development of many of the capabilities above. If we combine several of these capabilities, we come up with something close to a useful working definition of information literacy:

Information literacy involves accessing, evaluating, managing and communicating information.

The difference between information and knowledge is often not clearly defined, and indeed there often a strong overlap in normal conversation. The analogy of the difference between the bricks and mortar, and the house can be useful. Information is the bricks, and learning skills and processes constitute the mortar. Combining 'bricks' of information together using appropriate strategies (mortar) can result in a new house of knowledge. Knowledge is constructed from information. Thus, an information-literate person is someone who can find and select the right information for any given task. In this sense, information literacy is a pre-requisite for learning in a constructivist framework.

With this basic definition in mind, let us take a more detailed look at information literacy standards and skills. The American Library Association and Association for Educational Communications and Technology (ALA & AECT, 1998) produced a list of nine information literacy standards. By standards is meant goals or benchmarks. There are three areas with three standards in each area. The three areas are information literacy, independent learning, and social responsibility. The fact that information literacy itself is a subset of the information literacy areas is an illustration of the challenges that occur when one tries to define the boundaries of information literacy. What is helpful about this framework is the sense of moving from a more neutral skills orientation to a value-laden position of social connectedness. The nine standards are shown in figure 3-2 with the centrality of the information literacy area highlighted.

One other useful term is 'critical literacy'. This essentially encapsulates all nine of the standards described above. Van Duzer and Florez (1999) describe critical literacy as encompassing "a range of critical and analytical attitudes and skills used in the process of understanding and interpreting texts, both spoken and written". The term is often used with adult language learners but its applicability is much wider. It is useful to be reminded that aural (and oral) skills are also needed in developing high levels of information literacy. In our multilingual societies this reminder is especially important.

3.1. Skills of an Information-Literate Person

Just what does a learner need to do in order to carry out a successful information search? What skills does s/he need? Eisenberg's (2001) Big6™Skills (table 3-1) are a useful set. They indicate clearly the complexity of information searching but also highlight that information searching is best approached in a

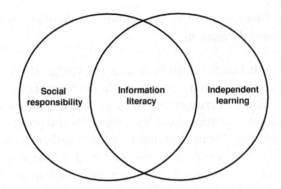

Information Literacy
Standard 1: The person accesses information efficiently and effectively.
Standard 2: The person evaluates information critically and competently.
Standard 3: The person uses information accurately and creatively.

Independent Learning
Standard 4: The person pursues information related to personal interests.
Standard 5: The person appreciates literature and other creative expressions of information.
Standard 6: The person strives for excellence in information seeking and knowledge generation.

Social Responsibility: contributing positively to the learning community and to society
Standard 7: The person recognizes the importance of information to a just society.
Standard 8: The person practices ethical behavior in regard to information and information
            technology.
Standard 9: The person participates effectively in groups to pursue and generate information.

Figure 3-2. Nine information literacy standards (after ALA & AECT, 1998, pp. 8–9)

methodical and meticulous manner. A lot more than random Google searches
is involved!

4.   eLearning in University Curricula

What about the 'online' or 'e' aspect? The key thing here is not to
think of online learning as being totally different to learning which occurs
in traditional face-to-face education. The learning process is not different
(after all, students are still people with the same neural pathways), but now
we have new tools and options to use in designing learning environments.
Siemens (2004) produced a comprehensive map of the range of tools that can
be used in the plethora of post-secondary educational offerings; these include
synchronous, asynchronous, collaborative and mobile tools. In his mapping,
the communicative nature of the tools is fore-grounded.

Let's focus a bit more closely on how student learning is linked to the design
of online learning environments. Initial discussions between educational

Table 3-1. Big6™ Skills (Eisenberg, 2001) (The 'Big6™' is copyright © (1987) Michael B. Eisenberg and Robert E. Berkowitz. www.big6.com)

Stage	Details of the process
1.Task definition	1.1 Define the information problem. 1.2 Identify information needed.
2.Information seeking strategies	2.1 Determine all possible sources. 2.2 Select the best sources.
3.Location and access	3.1 Locate sources (intellectually and physically). 3.2 Find information within sources.
4.Use of information	4.1 Engage (e.g. read, hear, view, touch). 4.2 Extract relevant information.
5.Synthesis	5.1 Organize from multiple sources. 5.2 Present the information.
6.Evaluation	6.1 Judge the product (effectiveness). 6.2 Judge the information process (efficiency).

designers and teachers often focus on the potential of online technology. What does 'going online' offer that can enhance or replace face-to-face modes of operation? In the last 15 years, I have been working as an educational designer in environments involving technology. While the technology has changed dramatically, a basic discussion about the overall functions of technology in education is helpful; the educational needs of learners remain largely the same. I usually describe the functions that technology can enable as: communicative interactions between the learner and the teacher, and between learners; opportunities for learners to get feedback on their learning; detailed study support; and provision of content resources that student can engage with. In table 3-2 some examples of how this can be done are listed.

Content resources are the most commonly used feature of the web (though, in my opinion, the communicative function of the web is much more powerful and much more interesting), and hence worth specifically commenting on. Most of the content one sees in online courses is not interactive and engaging; it is textual and static. How can we develop content materials where we put photos, videos, animations, simulations and quizzes to good educational purpose? I often use the following checklist to assist staff in deciding where time, effort and money is best spent in the development of online content. In the examples below, content is not static but is explored, interrogated and acted upon by learners. Smolin and Lawless (2003) distinguished between technology literacy, visual literacy and information literacy. The examples below all require technology literacy and visual literacy; the degree of information literacy required by the learner depends on the complexity of

Table 3-2. Relationship between functions of technology and particular strategies (after McNaught, 2002)

		Function of technology	**Some strategies to consider**
Access to information and tasks	Enabling Communication	1. Learner–learner/ learner–teacher interaction	• Online tutorial sessions • Online role plays • Feedback to class on practical or field work reports • Continuous evaluation form • Workspace for team assignments • Moderated discussion forums
		2. Learner self-assessment/feedback on learning progress	• Self-help quizzes (for formative assessment purposes) • Publishing work for peer review • A current collection of assessment materials and supporting documentation • Samples of previous assignments/project work (with documented student permission) • A collection of past/recent exams and sample tests (where appropriate) • Provision for electronic submission of assignment work
		3. Study programme management/study skills support	• Direct access to a clear course guide or description • A current timetable/timeline related to outlining face-to-face tutorials, lectures, lab/field work and online activities (with times, dates and location details) • Online learning activities clearly described/linked to curriculum outcomes • Current contact details of lecturers, teachers and tutors • A structured collection of Frequently Asked Questions and/or glossary • Links to information on the Library and student support services • Lecture outlines • Laboratory notes • News announcements
		4. Content resources for students to engage with	• A structured collection of learning resources • Clear links to related Library resources and databases • A structured and validated collection of annotated web links • Multimedia simulations, tutorials, etc.

the task associated with the content. Examples of the educational purposes expensive online content should have are to:

- show features not commonly seen, e.g. photos of specific building faults, geographical or geological features, anatomy dissections. The possibility exists of adding 'hotspots', line overlays, etc. These can be linked to quiz questions.
- represent things that are not visible, e.g. molecular structures, chemical equations, distributions of numbers.
- illustrate processes, e.g. chemical reactions, material flow in factories, expansions of gases. Here animation and/or simulation provides an aid for students in conceptualizing the process.
- demonstrate procedures, e.g. videos of laboratory procedures, interviewing skills; and
- show professional practice, e.g. Excel spreadsheets in accounting.

The interdependence of the functions of technology is shown clearly in the depiction Feitz (1997) has of the learner in the 21st century. The learner has access to, and selects from, learning resources (information and tasks), some of which are enacted in the learning space. This learning space could contain communication areas for working with other learners and/or a range of self-assessment tasks. Guidelines are constantly available in the learning objectives area. Note that the role of the teacher is one of a learning facilitator, a guide to assist knowledge construction rather than a source of information. It is clear that this view of the 21st century learner, nested in a well-structured and well-resourced learning environment, is one that puts more onus on the learner to be active in seeking information and using it to construct knowledge. All the information literacy skills outlined above are essential in a constructivist online environment. One final point to note is that the power of the web is underutilized if communication technologies are not included as a strong feature of eLearning designs (see figure 3-3).

5.   The Future of Information-Rich Learning Environments

The argument thus far highlights the synergy between information literacy and eLearning. Online environments facilitate access to and retrieval of information. They can also facilitate learners' communication with teachers and other learners that can be useful in evaluating the usefulness of any resource. The two aspects of the wealth of information and the possibility of an online community which can explore and work with that information to construct knowledge have lead to the rosy promises for the future of eLearning that have been predicted for some time (e.g. Siemens, 2003).

38

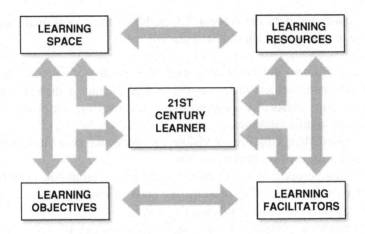

Figure 3-3. Interactions in a 21ˢᵗ century learning environment (Feitz, 1997) © State of
Victoria (Department of Education & Training) 2002

One example of the 'hype' around eLearning has been the growing interest
in 'learning objects' and the building of object repositories. Reuse of expensive
resources has driven this movement (Littlejohn, 2003). Well-known examples
are MERLOT in the US (http://www.merlot.org/), eduSourceCanada in
Canada (http://www.edusource.ca/), and the Ariadne Foundation in Europe
(http://www.ariadne-eu.org/). The well-publicized move of the Massachusetts
Institute of Technology to make its online courses available as learning objects
for others to use (MITOpenCourseWare; http://ocw.mit.edu/) has made the
link between discrete learning objects and whole course units much more real.

However, the packaged modular approach to the provision of learning
resources is not plain sailing. The crux of the matter is the tension between
producing something which is generic enough to fit many educational contexts
(including subject matter, and teacher and student preferences), and yet
adaptable/customizable to fit each context in an educationally satisfying way.
Parrish (2004) is a recent authoritative review of this tension. Also, as Boyle
(2003) pointed out, eLearning does not have a good track record in designing
learning materials; why should the somewhat more complex job of designing
reusable learning objects be done better?

ELearning is often said to be 'not working' or 'not living up its expectations'. In a challenging report entitled 'Thwarted innovation. What happened
to eLearning and why', Zemsky and Massy (2004) concluded that "eLearning
took off before people really knew how to use it" (p. iii). That is undoubtedly
true but, at this point, where do we go? Zemsky and Massy suggest that wide-
reaching changes are needed—to the current university process for quality
curriculum development, to funding models, and to relationships between
corporate and collegial education. They even suggest that all the technical and

Table 3-3. Implications of the challenges of using technology

Enabling communication

Positive contribution	*Challenges*	***Implications: need for***
Multiple perspectives on the value of a resource	'Dead' forums where queries or ideas are not answered	Skilled online facilitators
Potential access to others working in the same field	Finding others with similar learning needs	Online communities that have defined goals
Building links between 'experts' and novice learners	Without support, few novice learners will make this type of outreach	Organizations which have an active educational outreach

Access to information and tasks

Positive contribution	*Challenges*	***Implications: need for***
More information available to more people	Chaotic and fragmented nature of the web	Guidelines to facilitate searching
Cross-referencing through hyperlinking	Poor navigation; being 'lost in the web'	Good navigation models
Large number of perspectives because there are multiple publishers	Difficult to find evidence of the authority of much material	Models of how to display information with adequate authentication
Finding appropriate information in a given area	Often only low-level information is found, or information is out-of-date	Dedicated subject repositories with staff who keep them up-to-date
Being able to self-assess	Often only low-level multiple choice questions are available	Tasks that are demanding and can have customized, possibly real-time, feedback from others

market issues surrounding learning objects need to be fixed before eLearning can be successful. This is not pragmatic and we need to find a middle ground.

The most educationally interesting and potentially most rewarding aspects of using technology in education are summarized in table 3-3 under the two broad themes of 'enabling communication' and 'access to information and tasks'. Challenges or problems that occur frequently are listed in the second column. These 'challenges' are often due to poor educational design and explain to a certain extent the contexts that have led to reports such as Zemsky and Massy's (2004) doom and gloom scenario.

In the final column under 'implications', there are references to material in subject domains, to actions involving that material and to groups of people working together to maintain and support the collections of material. Material, activities and people—these three elements are all needed. Wegner (1998) coined the phrase 'community of practice'. He proposed that there are three fundamental elements in a community of practice: a knowledge domain, practices based on the knowledge, and a community of learning practitioners. This implies that future effective information-rich learning environments might be, to some extent, communities of practice. What might one of these communities of practice look like?

Several of the functions listed under 'implications' are currently performed by university (and other) libraries, digital repositories and professional subject organizations. The potential of a combination of all three together could be a way forward. Examples of organizations that have these characteristics can be found in a relatively recent move towards the creation of 'community digital libraries'. Digital libraries have existed for some time, with the focus being on how to best gather relevant and accessible digital collections. Cole (2002) described the three primary constructs of digitization projects as digital collections, digital objects and metadata. His checklists of principles for these constructs are recommended for those embarking or refining a digital library.

However, the 'people' aspect also needs attention. As Wright, Marlino and Sumner (2002) commented, "a community digital library is distinct through having a community of potential users define and guide the development of the library". They are writing about a community digital library dealing with the broad subject domain of earth system education. The Digital Library for Earth System Education (DLESE) website (http://www.dlese.org/) has this description which clear shows the three elements of material, activities and people:

> The Digital Library for Earth System Education (DLESE) is a distributed community effort involving educators, students, and scientists working together to improve the quality, quantity, and efficiency of teaching and learning about the Earth system at all levels.
>
> DLESE supports Earth system science education by providing:
>
> - access to high-quality collections of educational resources;
> - access to Earth data sets and imagery, including the tools and interfaces that enable their effective use in educational settings;
> - support services to help educators and learners effectively create, use, and share educational resources; and
> - communication networks to facilitate interactions and collaborations across all dimensions of Earth system education.
>
> Retrieved February 8, 2005, from http://www.dlese.org/about/index.html

DLESE is a partnership between the National Science Foundation (NSF); the DLESE community that is open to all interested in earth system education; the Steering Committee; and the DLESE Program Center, a group of core staff. The concept of the library took shape in 1998, and is now governed by an elected Steering Committee that is broadly representative of the diverse interests in Earth system science education. Its future growth and development is guided by the DLESE Strategic Plan, which outlines the broad functionalities of the library to be developed over the next 5 years (2002–2006). Its goals cover six core functions: (1) collection-building; (2) community-building; (3) library services to support creation, discovery, assessment, and use of resources, as well as community networks; (4) accessibility and use; (5) catering for a diversity of user needs; and (6) research and evaluation on many aspects of community digital libraries (see http:// www.dlese.org/documents/plans/stratplanver12.html).

It is this final core function that was the reason this example has been chosen for this chapter—there has been extensive evaluation research on the model. A search of the Association for Computing Machinery (ACM) digital library (http://portal.acm.org/dl.cfm) on 'dlese' yields 200 papers. Some of those of particular relevance to the educational potential of DLESE are Khoo (2001); Marlino and Sumner (2001); Wright, Marlino and Sumner (2002); Sumner, Khoo, Recker and Marlino (2003); and Sumner and Marlino (2004). These series of papers show a clear endeavour towards ensuring that the needs of the earth system education community are a strong driving force towards the development of policy for the library—an online community that has a true synergy between learning and information literacy.

As Lynch (2002), so aptly commented: "... digital libraries are somehow the key construct in building community, making community happen and exploiting community. Indeed, much of what we have learned about designing successful digital libraries emphasizes the discipline of user-centered design. Effective digital libraries are designed both for purpose and audience, very much in contrast to digital collections".

5.1.   Concluding Comments

In conclusion, let us return briefly to the concept of graduate capabilities that I postulated as being central to the planning of effective universities programmes in the 21st century. The achievement of a population of graduates who have the capacity to evaluate complex, often ill-defined, issues and options with an analytical and open-minded approach is becomingly increasingly urgent. In this chapter, I have suggested that embedding information literacy is one key to good educational design for university programmes. Further, the functions and tools that technology affords us should be used more intelligently in the design of our educational programmes. Community digital libraries seem to offer a model that universities should examine carefully, not as something 'out there' but as an option for close integration with university education.

If community digital libraries become more pervasive, while still retaining their fresh responsiveness to their user communities; *if* more discipline domains are served by such community digital libraries; and *if* university libraries take on the role of being liaison between these community digital libraries and university teachers, then the synergy between eLearning and information literacy could become a foundation for the design and development of effective university programmes. It may well be that the future of the global community depends on new models such as this.

References

American Association of School Librarians and Association for Educational Communications and Technology (1998). In 'Information literacy standards for student learning'. *Information power: Building partnerships for learning*, chapter 2. Chicago: ALA Editions/ American Library Association. Retrieved February 8, 2005, from http://www.ala.org/ala/ aasl/aaslproftools/informationpower/informationpower.htm

Biggs, J. (1999). What the student does: Teaching for enhanced learning. *Higher Education Research & Development, 18*(1), 57–75.

Boyle, T. (2003). Design principles for authoring dynamic, reusable learning objects. *Australian Journal of Educational Technology, 19*(1), 46–58. Retrieved February 8, 2005, from http:// www.ascilite.org.au/ajet/ajet19/boyle.html.

Cole, T. W. (2002). Creating a framework of guidance for building good digital collections. *First Monday, 7*(5). Retrieved February 8, 2005, from http://firstmonday.org/issues/ issue7_5/cole/index.html

Eisenberg, M. (2001). A Big6™ Skills Overview. Retrieved February 8, 2005, from http://www.big6.com/showarticle.php?id=16

Feitz (1997). Presentation at the Successful Schools Conference. Summarized on SOFweb, Department of Education and Training, Victoria, Australia. Retrieved February 8, 2005, from http://www.sofweb.vic.edu.au/lt/pguide/vision/viscurric.htm

Khoo, M. (2001). Community design of DLESE's collections review policy: A technological frames analysis. In *Proceedings of the 1st ACM/IEEE-CS joint conference on digital libraries*, (pp. 157–164). Roanoke, Virginia, US. New York: ACM Press. Retrieved February 8, 2005, via http://portal.acm.org/dl.cfm

Littlejohn, A. (Ed.) (2003). *Reusing online resources: A sustainable approach to eLearning.* London: Kogan Page.

Lynch, C. (2002). Digital collections, digital libraries and the digitization of cultural heritage information. *First Monday, 7*(5). Retrieved February 8, 2005, from http://firstmonday.org/ issues/issue7_5/lynch/index.html

Marlino, M., & Sumner, T. (2001). The digital library for earth system education: Building community, building the library. In *Proceedings of the 3rd ACM/IEEE-CS joint conference on digital libraries* (pp. 80–81). Houston, Texas. New York: ACM Press. Retrieved February 8, 2005, via http://portal.acm.org/dl.cfm

McNaught, C. (2002). Adopting technology should mean adapting it to meet learning needs. *On The Horizon, 10*(4), 14–18.

Nightingale, P., Te Wiata, I., Toohey, S., Ryan, G., Hughes, C., & Magin, D. (1996). *Assessing learning in universities.* Sydney: Professional Development Centre, University of New South Wales.

Parrish, P. E. (2004). The trouble with learning objects. *Educational Technology, Research and Development, 52*(1), 49–67.

Roblyer, M. D. (2002). *Integrating educational technology into teaching* (3rd ed.). Columbus, Ohio: Merrill Prentice-Hall.

Siemens, G. (2003) The whole picture of eLearning. Retrieved February 8, 2005, from http://www.elearnspace.org/Articles/wholepicture.htm

Siemens, G. (2004). Categories of eLearning. Retrieved February 8, 2005, from http://www.elearnspace.org/Articles/eLearningcategories.htm

Smolin, L., & K. Lawless, K. (2003). Becoming literate in the technological age: New responsibilities and tools for teachers. *The Reading Teacher, 56*(6), 570–577.

Sumner, T., & Marlino, M. (2004). Digital libraries and educational practice: A case for new models. In *Proceedings of the 4th ACM/IEEE-CS joint conference on Digital libraries* (pp. 170–178). Tuscon, AZ, US. New York: ACM Press. Retrieved February 8, 2005, via http://portal.acm.org/dl.cfm

Sumner, T., Khoo, M., Recker, M., & Marlino, M. (2003). Understanding educator perceptions of 'quality' in digital libraries. In *Proceedings of the 3rd ACM/IEEE-CS joint conference on digital libraries* (pp. 269–279). Houston, Texas, US. Washington, DC: IEEE Computer Society. Retrieved February 8, 2005, via http://portal.acm.org/dl.cfm

Trigwell, K., Prosser, M., & Taylor, P. (1994). Qualitative differences in approaches to teaching first year university science. *Higher Education, 27*, 75–84.

Van Duzer, C., & Florez, M. C. (1999). Critical literacy for adult literacy in language learners. ERIC Digest. Retrieved February 8, 2005, from http://www.ericdigests.org/2001-1/critical.html

Wegner, E. (1998). *Communities of practice: Learning, meaning and identity.* Cambridge: Cambridge University Press.

Wright, M., Marlino, M., & Sumner, T. (2002). Meta-design of a community digital library. *D-Lib Magazine, 8*(5). Retrieved February 8, 2005, from http://www.dlib.org/dlib/may02/wright/05wright.html

Zemsky, R., & Massy, W. F. (2004). Thwarted innovation. What happened to eLearning and why. University of Pennsylvania: The Learning Alliance. Retrieved February 8, 2005, from http://www.irhe.upenn.edu/WeatherStation.html

Chapter 4

CHANGING THE MINDSET: FROM TRADITIONAL ON-CAMPUS AND DISTANCE EDUCATION TO ONLINE TEACHING AND LEARNING

Susan McKnight

1.   Chapter Overview

This chapter outlines a case study of one institution's journey towards using eLearning in its distributed education outreach. Deakin University's distinctiveness and competitive advantage is enhanced by its online teaching and learning initiatives, which are a major plank of its strategic plan. By taking a 'whole of enterprise' approach to online teaching and learning, Deakin is able to leverage off its considerable investment in distance education support services and technological infrastructure, enhancing experiences for all students, regardless of whether they are on-campus or remote to the University. This chapter outlines how Deakin University established the policy and infrastructure framework, and changed the mindset of academic staff, to progressively introduce online resources and learning experiences to enhance, and where appropriate, transform teaching and learning.

2.   Introduction

There is increased competitiveness in the globalized higher education market, made possible by the increased use of information technology to deliver online education. Many universities have been using information technology to complement face-to-face teaching for some time and are now trying to capture a segment of what is considered a vast market for online higher education courses. However, to be successful in delivering online education, or eLearning, to students who will never set foot on a university

H. S. Ching, P. W. T. Poon and C. McNaught (Eds.), eLearning and Digital Publishing, 45–67.
© 2006 *H. S. Ching, P. W. T. Poon and C. McNaught.*

campus requires a significantly different infrastructure and culture than normally provided for on-campus students.

Traditional distance education providers have a long history, culture and infrastructure for supporting students who may never venture on campus. This chapter outlines the success factors required for an effective eLearning environment using Deakin University, Australia, as a case study. To successfully maintain its profile in the global education environment, Deakin University has strengthened its commitment to modern distance education, and is consolidating its competitive advantage in distance and flexible learning afforded through network technologies and eLearning.

The main driver for eLearning should be the desire to improve learning outcomes and experiences for students. As an established distance education provider, Deakin University has long strived to mainstream services established for off-campus students, recognizing that if issues of isolation, time and place could be resolved for the traditional distance education student, then all users of the services would benefit, as everyone could be provided with more flexible options for learning and access to support services.

As a result, Deakin University's *Deakin Online* and *Deakin Online Campus* initiatives build on the existing strengths within the University, not only in teaching, research and student support, but also in its knowledge of on-campus, distance and online education. These initiatives are also underpinned by a culture within the University for student-centred learning, and a commitment to providing higher education opportunities to students who, for whatever reason, do not want to attend a physical campus. Deakin's history of using technology to enhance access to and participation in learning, rather than making decisions driven more by technology than pedagogy, supports the *Deakin Online* and *Deakin Online Campus* initiatives in enhancing learning outcomes for all students, regardless of their mode of study.

ELearning at Deakin University is built upon clear planning and policy frameworks that articulate what is to be achieved and why. The University's strategic plan and operational plan establish the vision and targets for the online learning initiatives and these are supported by policies, guidelines and processes, including characteristics of best practice in teaching and learning, responsibilities of management, academic and support staff and students, and the guidelines for assuring quality and legislative compliance. A key purpose of this chapter is to explain this framework.

In addition to Deakin University's planning and policy framework, organizational structures have been modified to ensure that eLearning is appropriately resourced and services aligned to achieve success. Further, a number of initiatives have been put in place to change the mindset, that is to achieve cultural change, so that all within Deakin University are assisting in the transition from a traditional on-campus and off-campus paradigm to a very flexible system for delivering teaching and support services and resources.

Students have a choice as to how they study, and quality assurance measures support the students graduating with discipline-specific and generic skills that are required in a modern world.

3.   Background of Deakin University

Deakin University has an established reputation as a provider of excellent distance and on-campus education. Deakin's vision is to be Australia's most progressive university, internationally recognized for the relevance, innovation and responsiveness of its teaching and learning, research, partnerships and international activities.

Deakin University was established in 1974 and began teaching in 1977. The University has over 30,000 students enrolled each year, and specializes in student-centred education and lifelong learning. It has five campuses across the State of Victoria: two in Melbourne, the capital; two in the second largest city, Geelong, which is 70 km from the capital; and one in Warrnambool, a thriving regional centre 270 km from Melbourne. Deakin has five faculties: Arts, Business and Law, Education, Health and Behavioural Sciences, and Science and Technology. It offers awards from undergraduate degrees to research and professional doctorates.

All Deakin students have choices about the way they study. Students can attend lectures on campus and receive face-to-face teaching. Each year, approximately 15,000 distance education, online and multi-mode students access online curriculum and receive comprehensive study packages including state-of-the-art computer-aided learning, simulations and videos to facilitate their learning. Flexible delivery allows students to study on-campus or off-campus, full-time or part-time, or using a mix of study modes. With Deakin, students can take a degree from anywhere in the world—on campus, at home, or where they work. Students studying on-campus, online or off-campus take exactly the same Deakin degree.

In 1995 Deakin was named 'Australian University of the Year' for its innovative use of information technology in undergraduate teaching. In 1997 it won a five-star rating from the Graduate Careers Council of Australia. In 1999, Deakin became the first university in Australia to be awarded the coveted University of the Year for a second time, this 1999 award recognizing the University's productive partnerships with business and industry.

4.   Deakin's Strategic, Operational, and Teaching and Learning Plans

The University's focus on eLearning, and the creation of *Deakin Online* and the *Deakin Online Campus*, are founded on the goals of the University's

Strategic and Operational Plans and the objectives of the Teaching and Learning Management Plan.

'The Competitive Edge', Deakin University's Teaching and Learning Management Plan 2000–2002, provided the initial impetus for online learning initiatives. Its language reflected the realities of the time, which emphasized the need to take a broader-than-national view of the University's marketplace and to focus on strategies that would specifically assist with extending higher education opportunities to students regardless of their country of residence.

There were two relevant objectives relating to eLearning in that plan. These were titled 'Going global' and 'Creating Deakin's virtual campus'. Taken together they set the strategic vision for how Deakin's flexible learning support services could support Deakin as a global university.

With the appointment of a new Vice-Chancellor in 2003, Deakin University undertook a complete review of its strategic planning framework and developed a new 5-year strategic plan, with an annual operational plan to guide actions throughout the period. Online learning remained a key strategy in the new Plans.

The University's current (2004) Strategic Plan states that Deakin's goal for teaching and learning is to "provide excellent undergraduate, postgraduate and professional development programs of contemporary relevance that are available to students wherever they are located and developed in partnership with potential employers, industry, government and professional bodies."[1]

Considerable energy has been expended in articulating steps required to achieve this goal. Two of the strategies articulated to achieve this goal are:

> Ensuring Deakin's distance education courses and services set world standards for excellence, are aligned to student needs and make innovative use of technology including, where appropriate, the delivery of the course online; and
> Progressively introducing online resources and learning experiences to both distance education and campus-based programs to enhance, and where appropriate, transform, teaching and learning by:
>
> - ensuring that staff and students have appropriate information technology and teaching and learning skills that make them competent in the use of online environments and facilities;
> - providing a supportive, comprehensive, coordinated and integrated technological infrastructure to support excellence in teaching and learning and the delivery of online services;
> - ensuring that online courses have exemplary content and learning design through the adoption of best practice methodologies and world-class standards;
> - encouraging and facilitating supportive research and experimentation in online teaching and learning and establishing vehicles for using the

results of research to continuously refine online teaching and learning strategies and practices; and

- assuring the quality standards of online learning programs, content, design and pedagogy using benchmarking with world-class online and distance education teaching and learning providers.[1]

The goal and strategies clearly articulate the forward directions of the University and its commitment to enhancing student learning regardless of their location. There is an explicit acknowledgement of many inter-related elements that are required for a successful eLearning strategy: skills for both teacher and learner to successfully use the online environments; appropriate information technology infrastructure; the integration or coordination of systems that support eLearning; the use of research and scholarship to inform continuous improvement in online learning; and the importance of standards, monitoring and benchmarking to strive for best practice. The goal and strategies also emphasize the importance of using technology "where appropriate". Technology is not the driver.

The University's 2003 and 2004 Operational Plans (no longer public documents) included specific actions and targets that are aimed at ensuring implementation of the University's eLearning goal. The relevant 2004 initiatives are listed below. The accountable officer, in the main, is the Pro Vice-Chancellor (Online Services) assisted by the Executive Director, Learning Services.

Promoting Innovation through Online Teaching and Learning:

- ensure that all units have at least a Level 1 online presence by the beginning of Semester 1, 2004;
- ensure that all students commencing an undergraduate degree in 2004 will study at least one unit online (Level 3 online presence) in their course;
- enable all undergraduate students new to the University in 2004 to complete an IT skills development program as part of their orientation;
- conduct a survey and achieve at least 60% satisfaction in respect of students' evaluation of Deakin Studies Online (DSO);
- develop and obtain Academic Board approval for a policy regarding 'Quality Online Elements in Courses and Units' and conduct an audit of at least 20% of units against the policy;
- ensure that all staff using DSO in 2004 complete, or have completed, a training program on using the technology effectively;
- by July 2004, complete an IT Skills Audit of the remaining 50% of Deakin's staff; and
- by November 2004, 70% of staff who require training to have completed an IT Skills development program.

Thus, the direction towards online learning that was articulated in 2000 has now been firmly embedded in the functional and operational plans of the University.[2] Many exciting eLearning initiatives have been achieved since 2000, including the acquisition of a new, enterprise-level learning management system, WebCT Vista, and the restructuring of the major academic support units of the University to better focus support for the online learning initiatives. Deakin has now mainstreamed its eLearning initiatives.

Rather than maintaining the 'global' and 'virtual' tags, new terminology was introduced in 2003 to describe the University's eLearning initiatives, and *Deakin Online* and the *Deakin Online Campus* were created to consolidate and coordinate the online teaching and learning infrastructure and service delivery.

There is still strong support for traditional distance education; however, more and more distance education is being enhanced by online learning opportunities. To quote from the University's 'Online and off-campus learning' page:

- Deakin prepares its graduates to be confident and competent using online technologies and in online environments.
- Deakin uses online technologies to enrich learning experiences and add flexibility and value for all students.
- Deakin's online campus provides distance education students with additional access to online resources and services and opportunities for interaction.[3]

5.   Deakin Online and the Deakin Online Campus

The aim of *Deakin Online* is to establish an enterprise level system with consistent branding by having the one system interface that will:

- provide access to information about the University to the general and academic communities;
- provide a link for an enterprise wide solution to knowledge management within the University community through a portal;
- provide the structural basis for the *Deakin Online Campus* and *Deakin Studies Online*; and which will achieve reduced training, support and maintenance costs for the University (see figure 4-1).

The *Deakin Online Campus* provides a comprehensive learning environment through integrated networked technologies to:

- enrich learning experiences for off-campus and multi-modal students as well as for on-campus students;

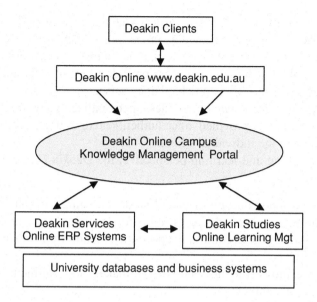

Figure 4-1. Deakin Online infrastructure

- foster improved learning outcomes, accepting current limits on how much time we can expect students to spend using a computer and being online. This will change as the population accepts the electronic environment more and more, and as external network services improve;
- foster improved learning outcomes consistent with the University's policies and guidelines on teaching and learning, for example with respect to graduate attributes, excellent teaching, excellent courses, experiential learning, internationalizing the curriculum, and appropriate assessment;
- expand enrolments, especially in postgraduate coursework where most students are off-campus;
- adopt technologies that are appropriate for the task. Appropriate use of technology matches the needs of sound pedagogy with the capabilities of the technology;
- implement a mix of people, pedagogy, and technologies (for example, Internet, print, communication strategies, synchronous and asynchronous delivery) which services the mixed nature of Deakin's students from a single source; and
- enhance access to academic and administrative support services through *Deakin Online*.

The successful online campus must provide an environment that goes well beyond the actual learning resources and interactions associated with teaching and learning. It will emphasize the social and community aspects of the online experience that provides, for the eLearner, what the physical and social fabric of a face-to-face university provides on-campus students. For example, the online campus can provide chat spaces that facilitate conversations that would normally take place in the cafeteria. It can provide access to services for student welfare, such as counselling and chaplaincy services.

The *Deakin Online Campus* provides a personalized view of services and resources, with access provided, once authenticated, to those services which are appropriate to the individual's logon.

From a teaching and learning perspective, the *Deakin Online Campus* is for:

- all off-campus and multi-modal students, being their home campus for university life, an access point for teaching and learning, and a means to engage in communication and collaboration with other course participants;
- all on-campus students who wish to make use of online teaching and learning resources;
- all higher degree by research students, providing access to research resources, supervisors and collaborative networks; and
- all staff who interact with students and deliver teaching and learning services and other support online.

The *Deakin Online Campus* enriches learning experiences, fosters improved learning outcomes and enhances access to academic and administrative support services through *Deakin Online*.

6.   Policy Framework

To implement an eLearning strategy, a university must provide an appropriate policy framework that supports the vision and directions of the organization. The following outline the major policies that have been enacted to support Deakin's online teaching and learning initiatives.

The major policy that underpins the *Deakin Online* and *Deakin Online Campus* initiatives is the 'Online Technologies in Courses and Units Policy'[4]. The Policy states:

- Deakin University shall progressively introduce basic online elements into all of its award courses and more extensive online elements into selected courses.
- Deakin will use online technologies for the purpose of enriching teaching and learning experiences where value can be added for students and cost effectiveness is demonstrated.
- Deakin will substitute online for other methods under specific conditions where there are demonstrable benefits to the learning experience.

- Deakin will only develop courses in primarily or wholly online mode for strategic purposes.
- From 2004, all students commencing a Deakin Bachelor degree course shall undertake and pass at least one wholly online unit, unless exempted by the Chair of Academic Board.

The Policy is pedagogically driven, not technology-driven, and focuses on learner outcomes. It is consistent with the University's Strategic and Operational Plans and articulates the principles, implementation procedures, training and support, as well as monitoring, evaluation and quality assurance measures in place to assist implementation.

The Deakin Categories of Online Activity, Appendix A to the Policy, defines three levels of online unit being: Basic Online (for all units); Extended Online (which uses more online functionality than the Basic Online units); and Wholly Online.

The Code of Good Online Practice[5] elaborates the principles and values that govern Deakin's Online Campus as stated in the Online Technologies in Courses and Units Policy. The Code is

> intended to provide guidance for organizational units, staff and students to ensure that programs and services reflect good practice, resulting in a high standard of quality for the online teaching and learning environment. ... General principles of good practice in higher education require interpretation and adaptation if these new technologies are to make a positive contribution to the university experience of today's diverse cohorts of students. Learning from experience and modifying practice as a result of experience are cornerstones of success.

The Code includes sections on University Good Practice, Joint University and Faculty/ Division Good Practice, Faculty Good Practice, Staff Good Practice, and Student Good Practice.

Students, of course, need to be able to access the *Deakin Online Campus*, whether from on-campus computer laboratories or from work or home. The Student Access to Computers Policy[6] is concerned with private student access to computers and other information technology, and the expectations of Deakin University in this respect. It states:

- The University expects that all students enrolled in Deakin courses will have access to a personal computer and to the Internet and electronic mail (subject to equity issues).
- Minimum hardware and software requirements will be specified annually by the University taking into account technological developments and teaching requirements.
- It is intended that a computer satisfying the minimum specification when new will, with appropriate upgrades, continue to meet the developing requirements of the University for at least 3 years.

- The University will continue to provide and support on-campus computer facilities and computer laboratories sufficient for general academic needs in computer classes and will continue to make these facilities available to students out of class times, subject to an annual review of needs and demands.
- The University will provide and support Library computer facilities for accessing information resources, online databases and catalogues, selected course materials, past examination papers, electronic reserve and other digital materials required for study purposes.

The background to this policy explains the rationale:

Deakin University has identified computer literacy and competency in Information Technology (IT) as essential generic skills that all Deakin graduates should possess. Certain IT skills are necessary in order to make use of databases and electronic library facilities, and basic word-processing and spread sheet skills are also generally required. More advanced, or specialized, IT skills are required in certain disciplines. The University also makes extensive use of IT and the Internet for course information, enrolment, examination timetable, release of results and other services. In general, students at Deakin University will be required to make use of computers and other information technology at various times during their coursework and in certain aspects of academic administration.

Another supporting policy relates to the University's responsibility to make online learning resources available to students who have disabilities. The Accessibility of Electronic Materials Policy[7] supports the University's compliance with the Australian Disability Discrimination Act (1992) (DDA) and articulates Guidelines for Creating Accessible Electronic Materials and the Techniques for Creating Accessible Electronic Materials as outlined by the World Wide Web Consortium 5 May 1999, 'Web content accessibility guidelines 1.0: W3C recommendation'.[8] There are other policies and guidelines covering copyright compliance and student conditions of use of information technology services.

7.   Organizational Change

Two key organizational changes have occurred as a result of the University's online teaching and learning initiatives, as well as more subtle changes within faculties.

Learning Services was established to play a major part in enabling Deakin University meet its Strategic Plan for teaching, learning and research. It is the primary academic support unit of the University and was formed in 2000 from the merger of what was the Office of Flexible Learning, the Centre for Academic Development, Learning Resource Services and the Library. This organizational restructure had its gestation in the Teaching and Learning Management Plan 2000–2002 Objective 'Creating Deakin's Virtual Campus'.

Many other universities have merged information technology support with library services. However, Deakin's Learning Services focuses on content, whether it is information resources from the library or curriculum resources. It is designed to bring together a blend of professionals aimed at ensuring that the online learning environment is a seamless mix of all services and resources required by students for a successful education. Today, Learning Services comprises four organizational units:

The *Teaching and Learning Support Unit* (TLSU) is responsible for educational design, academic professional development, management of the enterprise-level learning management system, and research and evaluation on teaching scholarship and pedagogy. Staff in TLSU work closely with academic staff and other teaching and learning support staff employed by the faculties to design curriculum resources and learning environments, and provide expert advice on the most appropriate means of achieving the desired learning outcomes. Within TLSU is the Learning Systems Group, which is responsible for the training and support associated with Deakin Studies Online. Universities rarely insist that academic staff have teaching qualifications, so it is the responsibility of TLSU to work with the Faculties to provide an introduction to teaching at Deakin, especially teaching in an online environment, as well as specific training on WebCT Vista, the application supporting Deakin Studies Online. Deakin University, however, from Semester 2, 2004, is requiring all new academic staff to complete a Graduate Certificate in Higher Education as part of their probation, and this will include pedagogical issues for online teaching.

Learning Resources is responsible for translating the education designs for curriculum material into the actual resources used by teachers and learners, whether interactive online environments or static web pages, multimedia CD-ROMs, audio- and video-tapes, printed material, and accessible curriculum resources for students with disabilities. This Unit is also responsible for monitoring the quality of learning resources and for establishing the guidelines for copyright compliance and web accessibility.

Access and Information Resources incorporates the traditional technical services functions of a library (acquisition, cataloguing, collection management) but is also involved, more and more, with managing information resources and systems for digital objects (eReadings, digital information for students with a disability, and digital course materials, with an emphasis on complying with copyright, intellectual property and disability discrimination legislation and policies).

Library Services provides the traditional public services of the library. It is responsible for reference and information services, resource delivery including loans, inter-campus and off-campus loans, inter-library loans and shelving, the information literacy and liaison programs, and collection development. The information services provided for off-campus and online students are crucial in supporting online and distance learning. Access to all library services and resources is available from the Library's home page. However, there is a special page for off-campus students to facilitate their access to resources and services.

As Deakin is a multi-campus institution, there has been a concerted effort to acquire serial resources, in particular, in electronic format so that students, regardless of location or campus, can access these resources. In 2004, the Library provided access to over 60,000 eJournals, 300 eBooks and 160 online databases. However, print resources are still provided to off-campus and online students. They request the items from the catalogue and these are dispatched to the student, either by courier or express post, for next-day delivery to most locations within Australia.

In addition, there are a number of online tutorials provided by Library Services that provide a wealth of training opportunities to students who never come on campus for traditional information literacy training.

As of April 2004, Learning Services employed approximately 280 people in 237 effective full-time positions across five campuses. There is a wide variety of professional categories represented within Learning Services, including: librarians and library technicians; academic staff with specialist skills in education design, research and evaluation, and professional development; instructional designers; graphic designers; programmers and web developers; IT system and database administrators; photographers; editors, desktop publishers and publishing support officers; printers and finishers; video and audio producers; accountants; business managers; copyright experts; and administrative and clerical staff.

The purpose statement of Learning Services is "we help people teach and learn" and this guides the services and interactions of staff with customers within the University, the academic staff and students.

Within the Deakin Online framework, all parts of Learning Services must work together to ensure that the online learning environments used by students are easy to use, and integrate access, as seamlessly as possible, to all learning materials, whether curriculum content or support information resources. When working online, from a student's perspective, there is a very blurred distinction of where the curriculum ends and the information resource support provided by the Library, begins. It is up to Learning Services staff to make sure that the distinction is not important and that resources are either directly available within DSO, or that links to traditional library services, such as the library catalogue, and key information resources, such as past examination papers or recommended reading material, are easy to access on a unit-by-unit basis.

Library Services staff have developed an extensive range of options to assist academic staff to integrate library services and resources into their DSO environments.[9]

The professional skills of staff in Learning Services are also being used in other sections within the organization. For instance, Library cataloguing staff are working with editors, content developers, multimedia experts and IT staff to identify metadata schema and systems to provide the necessary functionality to better manage courseware intellectual property, and to link the course materials planning and production system with the digital object repository of course-related learning objects. This cross-over in working relationships adds further weight to the need to manage significant cultural change, as staff have had to develop new work processes and new skills, and form new teams within the organization, as well as continue to serve their traditional customers within the University. Over time, it is likely that there will be further organization change within Learning Services, most likely integrating faculty liaison functions with training and support services.

Another key organizational change was the appointment of a Pro Vice-Chancellor (Online Services) to coordinate all aspects of the *Deakin Online* and *Deakin Online Campus* initiatives. The position is part of the Senior Executive of the University and so ensures that matters relating to eLearning are kept at the forefront of key decision-makers. The Pro Vice-Chancellor has no line management responsibility but works closely, in particular, with Learning Services, the Information Technology Services Division, Academic Administrative Services Division (student administration) and faculties to make sure that there is alignment with University plans and that services and new online initiatives are coordinated across the University.

The increasing move towards online teaching and learning has also resulted in additional administrative and teaching support positions being established within the faculties. The number of positions varies from faculty to faculty, depending on the degree of reliance on traditional distance education and online modes of delivery. The faculty appointments work closely with Learning Services staff and assist Associate Deans (Teaching and Learning) and Unit Chairs to plan the work schedule of new and revised curriculum resources.

8.   Philosophy and Culture

The University's Strategic and Operational Plans, and the operational plans of faculties, administrative divisions and Learning Services are developed in collaboration with staff and, most importantly, students. This way, there is close alignment with identified needs and the academic programs and services provided to meet these needs. The emphasis on eLearning is embedded in the University's Strategic Plan, as already indicated, and strategies and actions for supporting eLearning appear in all operational plans.

Without students, there is no need for a university. To be successful in the online educational environment, the entire university must work together to create a student- or learner-centred virtual campus. The Pro Vice-Chancellor (Online Services) plays a key role in ensuring that all parts of the University work together. The needs of the student must be paramount and the focus of all actions. Therefore, the emphasis for planning and implementation must be undertaken from the point of view of the student. The question "Will this help the student be successful at university?" should be asked when undertaking annual planning exercises.

It cannot be overstated how important it is to have a service culture amongst staff that recognizes the special circumstances of distance and online students. Even the best plans will not be implemented effectively unless staff understand and are committed to providing the same level of opportunities for access to all university services as those provided for on-campus students.

Deakin University has been very successful in providing excellent resources and services for distance education and online students. One of the keys to this success is the philosophy that ensures mainstreaming of services designed to resolve access and learning problems experienced by off-campus students so that these services benefit all students. In this way, barriers to learning are reduced, and efficiencies are gained by incorporating the required services into the normal workflow within the University, rather than having to establish duplicate sets of services, one serving on-campus students and another serving distance and online students.

9.   Changing the Mindset: Cultural Change

Although Deakin University has been involved in distance education since its inception over 25 years ago, there has been a need for cultural change to maximize the likelihood of success of the *Deakin Online* and *Deakin Online Campus* initiatives. There is no single way to achieve cultural change. Rather it takes a myriad of initiatives, and sustained emphasis, to achieve change. In addition to the high level plans and policies, and organizational restructures that contribute to cultural change by highlighting the organizational emphasis, the following are some of the additional initiatives that have been put in place to commence this ongoing process to change the mindset from traditional on-campus and distance education to that of flexible eLearning options to enhance teaching and learning for all students, regardless of mode of study.

As already indicated, there has been an increased need for integration and coordination of services across the University. The Pro Vice-Chancellor (Online Services), the Executive Director of Learning Services and staff from the Teaching and Learning Support Unit of Learning Services play a major role in communicating with faculty and divisional staff about eLearning and distance education issues. Articles are posted on the University Portal, included in the University newsletter, and reports provided to Academic, Faculty and School Boards.

A major contributor to achieving cultural change was the process employed to select new information technology applications, such as the learning management system that supports Deakin Studies Online. A small steering committee oversaw the process. It was assisted by a number of specialist teams, the composition of which came from across the University and included staff from faculties, representatives from administrative divisions and students. The teams developed selection and success criteria after receiving input from over 1,200 students and 400 academic staff who participated in online surveys and focus groups. The short-listed vendors then conducted presentations at all campuses and made their system available for detailed testing and 'play' by anyone interested. Participants in the presentations and testing activities provided feedback to the Steering Committee who then made the final recommendation to purchase. At the end of a very extensive process, there was 'buy-in' and excitement about the possibilities offered by the online delivery system chosen, WebCT Vista.

The Deakin Online Implementation Group was established to oversee projects established to implement the various software applications required for the eLearning framework, such as WebCT Vista and the software used for the redevelopment of the University's web gateway. This group identifies roadblocks to successful implementation and escalates any issues to the Pro Vice-Chancellor (Online Services). It also identifies changes required in the broader policy and administrative environment for forwarding to relevant committees. This group, with members from across the University, helps to break down silos of isolated activity and thinking, and ensures that everyone is aligning activity and new ideas in line with the overall University objectives for online education.

Although not directly related to the *Deakin Online* initiatives, the University's Academic Board, in 2003, established a standing committee, the Information Services Committee, which replaced the previous Library Committee and Information Technology Committee of the Board. This new Committee is responsible for establishing and monitoring quality assurance standards for information systems and information management as these relate to academic matters (teaching, learning, and research) and academic administration. The University's Planning and Resources Committee established, in 2004, an IT Strategy and Standards Sub-Committee to be responsible for advising on resourcing issues and technical standards. These initiatives highlight the complex nature of managing and leveraging IT in a university environment to ensure the success of eLearning.

In 2003, through the Deputy Vice-Chancellor (Academic), Learning Services introduced the Online Teaching and Learning Fellows Scheme. The aim of this scheme is to enhance the dissemination and implementation of exemplary online practice throughout the University. The objectives of the Online Teaching & Learning Fellowship Scheme are to:

- recognize, support and develop Deakin University's existing expertise in online teaching and learning;
- provide an opportunity for Fellows to actively engage in the development of online teaching and learning environments for Deakin University;
- provide advanced professional development in the design, implementation and maintenance of exemplary online teaching and learning practice;
- encourage peer-based professional development through skill-sharing and mentoring; and
- support the implementation of the Learning Management System within the teaching programs of the University.

The Scheme provides support as well as specific professional development in learning technologies to enable Fellowship recipients to:

- align online teaching and learning with University strategic objectives;
- implement quality online teaching and learning environments using the facilities available through WebCT Vista;
- experience the dynamics of online teaching and online learning;
- integrate online teaching and learning strategies into their teaching portfolio; and
- expand the understanding of online teaching and learning throughout the University.

The Online Teaching and Learning Fellows are champions of online learning within Deakin, and are change agents within the faculties. The 2003 Fellows showcased their work at an internal teaching and learning conference and their work has been used to create 'Teaching Online: Stories of Contemporary Practice at Deakin', a valuable resource for all academic staff.[10]

The 'Attributes of Excellent Courses'[11] and 'Attributes of Excellent Teaching'[12] were developed in consultation with academic staff and students and provide the benchmark by which teaching and courses will be judged. The 'Attributes of Excellent Courses' articulates sound academic quality, demonstrated relevance to students and evidence of external recognition as the means by which to judge courses. An excellent teacher is expected to underpin practice by scholarship, incorporate sound principles of teaching, support students and their learning, and adopt an inclusive and learner-centred approach. These attributes include the appropriate use of technologies to enhance teaching and learning.

Another opportunity to foster excellence in online teaching is to acknowledge excellence and reward best practice. To this end, the Vice-Chancellor's Awards for Outstanding Teaching are used to recognize excellence in online teaching and scholarship.

The University is establishing a Centre for Knowledge Technologies and Online Teaching and Learning within the University. This initiative will focus scholarship and research into areas that will promote excellence in eLearning and online teaching. The Centre will have a Director and another professorial-level position, and will be supplemented by researchers from the faculties, Learning Services and others from outside the University. It will be a means of attracting research grants to further develop insights into what constitutes excellence in online teaching and learning. One research project underway is investigating workload implications of using a learning management system, which will inform the University's academic workload model. Another is a longitudinal evaluation of DSO's implementation processes.

Academic staff, in the main, have embraced DSO as a means of enhancing teaching and learning at Deakin. However, the level of comfort experienced by teaching staff is directly related to their competency in using the online tools. Adequate time for professional development must be factored in to the implementation of learning management systems to enable faculty staff to gain the skills and to experiment with online technologies. This is an ongoing requirement, as new versions of software require re-skilling of academic and administrative staff.

10.   Technology Support

Integration of numerous applications is required to deliver *Deakin Online*. There are a number of complex interfaces between systems so that the learning and teaching environment is as useful, and user-friendly, as possible. The portal developments supporting *Deakin Online* and the *Deakin Online Campus* have gone a long way towards simplifying this integration from a user perspective. Work is progressing on having a 'single sign-on' authentication system; however, realistically there will always be applications or resources,

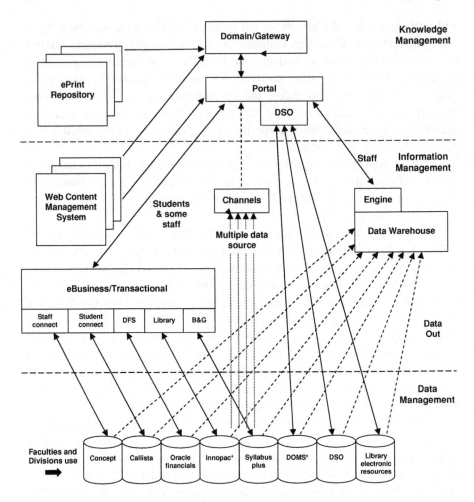

Figure 4-2. Deakin University application architecture

especially some of the library's external online information services, that will require an additional authentication step (see figure 4-2).

The enterprise administrative systems are based on ORACLE databases and, with a new project on data warehousing and data mining, will enable significant sharing of corporate data that is not yet achievable. It is envisaged that these systems will enable a knowledge management/ sharing system that will greatly enhance decision-making and administration across the University.

One of the crucial factors for success in an eLearning environment is the reliability of the technology infrastructure. The network and server systems must be robust, scalable and available 24 hours a day, 7 days a week throughout the year. Students access the University's online services at any time throughout the day and night, and there is an increasing number of international students who live in different time zones. Therefore, a 24-hour IT Help Desk is provided to receive problems and questions. To underpin this service, however, Deakin University has had to review its in-house IT support services so that there is a person (or persons) on site for an extended period who can reboot a server or notify a vendor that a problem has been experienced. The extension of on-site IT support is still under negotiation, as industrial issues relating to shift work and penalty rates have to be resolved. Even the weekly scheduled IT maintenance window, when the Information Technology Services Division undertakes routine maintenance and upgrades, has to be relocated to a time that is less inconvenient to students. (No time is the right time if you want access to the online environment!)

Relationships with key vendors play an important part in ensuring the availability and quality of the online teaching and learning systems. To this end, Deakin has special partnerships with SUN, ORACLE and WebCT.

11.   Student eLearning Support Initiatives

In addition to assisting academic staff to work effectively in the online environment, and to design pedagogically sound online spaces for teaching and learning, the University has an obligation to assist students as well.

The Deakin Learning Toolkit (DLT) is a resource distributed to all Deakin University students (and staff) to assist them in their eLearning both on-campus and off-campus. The University has been producing this award-winning CD-ROM since 1998. It contains a wealth of information on the University's eServices and facilities, as well as providing students with all the Deakin-recommended software for use on their own computer. The Toolkit is supplied on two CDs and allows the user to:

- review most information without being actively connected to the Internet;
- return many times to search and find information as required;
- work at their own pace without using other resources such as a phone line or an Internet service provider; and
- use the Deakin Learning Toolkit as a convenient information resource for all eLearning at Deakin.

The CD-ROM provides a wealth of useful programs to allow users to browse the Internet, read email, access library facilities and participate in online conferences. The DLT CD-ROMs are available for both Windows and Macintosh computers and are sent to all off-campus students as part of their enrolment package. New and returning on-campus students collect the DLT from various locations on each campus including Student Information Centres, Bookshops, Student Association Offices, Information Technology Services Front Desks and the Library.

An online version of the Deakin Learning Toolkit, accessible only to University staff and students, is also available. The online site contains the latest versions of software on the DLT and information that was not available at the time of production.

The DLT is an example of a successful collaborative project that has brought together the resources and services of all faculties, the Division of Student Life (for assistance in study and other personal matters that influence student life), the Information Technology Services Division, Academic Administrative Services Division and Learning Services.

In addition to the DLT, students receive a booklet titled 'Learning in the Online Environment' which is aimed at specific skills and information to facilitate and enhance student-learning outcomes. This booklet is also available online. From 2004, the Deakin Learning Toolkit and 'Learning in the Online Environment' information have been combined so that there is one resource for students. Induction sessions for new and returning students focus on the importance of becoming familiar with the contents of the revamped Deakin Learning Toolkit.

12.   The Changing Physical Campus

The eLearning initiatives have also had an impact on the physical fabric of the campus. At Deakin University, the intention is for on-campus students to access and benefit from the online learning initiatives, not just those students who study at a distance. Therefore, in addition to the obvious expansion of central computer rooms, for additional servers and network services, there has been a major upgrade to on-campus computing laboratories and common spaces to enable easy access to the online teaching and learning systems.

Wireless networking facilities have been included in libraries, Internet cafes and some lecture theatres. Computer laboratories have been upgraded to include more workstations and general lecture spaces have been refurbished to include the latest IT communications equipment.

There is considerable cost in providing the IT infrastructure required to develop and maintain excellent eLearning services. Deakin uses a centralized model to mandate the standard of computing hardware and software for both staff and students. Staff workstations are centrally leased so that there is regular updating and refreshment of the technology. However, the standards for student computers are maintained at a level that is within the financial reach of most students, and services are designed for delivery on the standard hardware platform. The Deakin Learning Toolkit is provided to students at no additional cost so that they have all the required software for their online learning at Deakin.

13.   The Challenges

There are a number of additional challenges to be met if the *Deakin Online* and *Deakin Online Campus* initiatives are to be a solid success. Below is a brief list of some of these.

The University is competing in a competitive employment marketplace that challenges our ability to attract and retain IT professionals that are required to develop and support the eLearning initiatives.

The challenge to maintain a competitive advantage amongst other higher education institutions requires a delicate balance between being at the bleeding edge on new technologies as opposed to being at the leading edge. It is very important to make sure that technology decisions keep in mind the student, so that the technologies do not outpace the capacity of the majority of students to benefit from the technology. The technology has to be robust and easily accessible.

Budgets must take into account the rapidity of change in technology, and the significant cost of updating hardware and software, and for maintaining interfaces between upgraded corporate applications. This rapid change places an enormous demand for ongoing professional development and training of academic and general staff, as well as of students.

The complex legal environment regarding intellectual property, moral rights, and copyright, especially in the digital environment, poses challenges for compliance and management.

Should universities develop their own content, or share/ lease content developed elsewhere? Deakin University has long been sharing and licensing curriculum resources for distance education. The demand for interactive online learning environments, and the high costs associated with developing and maintaining these, will result in the need to develop partnerships with additional institutions, including traditional universities and private publishers and media companies, to enable online delivery of rich content.

14.   The Success Factors

This chapter has provided a brief snapshot of eLearning at Deakin University. There are many challenges to be met when moving from a face-to-face or distance education paradigm to one of flexible, student-centred online learning. There needs to be a whole-of-university approach to eLearning, even if the approach adopted is to encourage devolution rather than the centralized approach favoured at Deakin University.

By including the objectives and goals for online learning into the University's planning and policies, there is a framework to guide resourcing decisions and actions within the University. By establishing targets for deliverables, the whole University community knows what is expected of them and when. It fosters a common understanding of priorities and directions, and, as long as the planning processes include staff and students, generates a great deal of buy-in and goodwill towards the new goals.

I have focussed on the need to achieve cultural change, to change the mindset of academic staff and students away from traditional notions of on-campus and off-campus, where more discrete offerings and services can survive, to a much more integrated approach to teaching, learning and support delivery that is required in the online environment. The need for restructuring of organizational units may be necessary to maximize value and facilitate cooperation and coordination.

The need for robust and scalable technology infrastructure is a given, as is the need for 24×7 help desk support for online teachers and learners. Working with technology and publishing partners may improve the level of service and functionality, or reduce the costs of participating in eLearning.

In addition to these, other key success factors for online teaching and learning should include the following strategies:

- Consult students regularly.
- Involve academic staff in IT decision making.
- Provide peer support for students and staff.
- Focus on teaching and learning, rather than technology.
- Focus on highly adoptable uses of technology and use open standards.
- Nurture innovators and early adopters.
- Monitor learning outcomes and continually improve all aspects of online teaching and learning.
- Reward excellent teaching in the online environment.

The main emphasis must be on the learning outcomes, not the technology.

15.   Endnotes

1. Deakin University Strategic Plan 'Taking Deakin University Forward'. Retrieved January 21, 2005, from http://www.deakin.edu.au/vc/docs/TDUF04.pdf
2. Deakin Online Management Plan 2003–2007. Retrieved January 21, 2005, from http://theguide.deakin.edu.au/TheDeakinGuide.nsf/0/db963375aa298c9fca256ea60083a6c0?OpenDocument

3. Online and off-campus learning. Retrieved January 21, 2005, from http://www.deakin. edu.au/online_offcampus/

4. Online Technologies in Courses and Units Policy. Retrieved January 27, 2005, from http://theguide.deakin.edu.au/TheDeakinGuide.nsf/0/c7f602b0582206bbca256e64000f4c 50?OpenDocument

5. Code of Good Online Practice. Retrieved January 27, 2005, from http://theguide.deakin. edu.au/TheDeakinGuide.nsf/0/093e73da39d40f7fca256e62007b8ee0?OpenDocument

6. Student Access to Computers Policy. Retrieved January 27, 2005, from http:// www.deakin.edu.au/dlt2005/it_deakin/rules/student_access.html

7. Accessibility of Electronic Materials Policy. Retrieved January 27, 2005, from http:// theguide.deakin.edu.au/TheDeakinGuide.nsf/0/1698c56218aa198cca256e5f0011854d? OpenDocument

8. World Wide Web Consortium 5 May 1999, 'Web content accessibility guidelines 1.0: W3C recommendation', W3C. Retrieved January 21, 2005, from http://www.w3.org/TR/ WAI-WEBCONTENT/

9. Online Library Resources to Support DSO. Retrieved January 21, 2005, from http://www.deakin.edu.au/library/services/dso/options.php

10. Teaching Online: Stories of Contemporary Practice at Deakin. Retrieved January 21, 2005, from http://www.deakin.edu.au/teachlearn/cases/

11. Attributes of Excellent Courses. Retrieved January 27, 2005, from http://theguide.deakin. edu.au/TheDeakinGuide.nsf/0/ad62654ffe4471f8ca256e60007e5dda?OpenDocument

12. Attributes of Excellent Teaching. Retrieved January 27, 2005, from http://theguide.deakin. edu.au/TheDeakinGuide.nsf/0/666ce41463e0639fca256e61000197cb?OpenDocument

Chapter 5

DEVELOPING AND MANAGING A PROFESSIONAL DEVELOPMENT DISTANCE-LEARNING PROGRAMME: THE ARL/OLMS ONLINE LYCEUM

Karen A. Wetzel

1. Chapter Overview

The chapter describes the development, administration and future directions of the Online Lyceum, a distance education programme which is under the auspices of the Association of Research Libraries (ARL) and its professional development capability, the Office of Leadership and Management Services (OLMS). There are unique opportunities and challenges involved with being housed within a membership association that differentiates the Online Lyceum from university-based distance education programmes. This case study will outline important issues for others who are interested in creating their own distance-learning programme business model. Both the conceptual underpinnings of the Online Lyceum and the business model are explored. The vision, goals, financial model and administrative structure are all examined so that readers obtain a comprehensive overview. Successes and lessons learnt are used to inform the strategic planning process used by OLMS to ensure that the Online Lyceum will continue to grow and be an integral part of the ARL.

2. Distance Education and Professional Development

Distance learning, once something new and untried, is now largely deemed necessary as a valuable learning tool to reach a broad and diverse audience that may otherwise not be served. No longer the infant it once was, we have learned a great deal about the factors that make this mode of learning valuable. But recognizing the worth that distance learning can provide alone is not enough.

H. S. Ching, P. W. T. Poon and C. McNaught (Eds.), eLearning and Digital Publishing, 69–88.
© 2006 H. S. Ching, P. W. T. Poon and C. McNaught.

Distance learning needs to be developed as a cogent part of an organization's strategic planning in order to support its mission, fulfil a missing need, take advantage of new opportunities, and integrate with overall goals. Beyond these essential parameters, funding, long-term maintenance and planning are key to making online learning a success. In the case of the Online Lyceum, the distance-learning capability of the Association of Research Libraries' Office of Leadership and Management Services (ARL/OLMS), the decision to develop a distance-learning programme was made in recognition of the larger ARL mission and goals while also maintaining the standards of the already established OLMS training programme.

The Online Lyceum provides, via the Internet, professional development courses to the library, higher education and information technology communities. ARL's Office of Leadership and Management Services has been offering professional development workshops and organizational development consulting services for library professionals for over 30 years. Workshop topics range from library management skills to service quality assessment. The adult learning model is the framework for these professional development experiences; this model focuses on teaching concepts that learners find meaningful through skills practice for immediate and long-term application of the freshly received information. As an ARL programme, however, it is helpful to first understand the context from which the Online Lyceum was formed.

3.   The Online Lyceum and ARL/OLMS

The Association of Research Libraries (ARL) is a not-for-profit membership organization that represents 123 of North America's leading academic and research libraries. The Association's mission statement serves as the guiding force for all its programmatic activities and clearly defines how it serves its members:

The mission of the Association of Research Libraries is to shape and influence the forces affecting the future of research libraries in the process of scholarly communication. ARL programmes and services promote equitable access to and effective use of recorded knowledge in support of teaching, research, scholarship and community service. The Association articulates the concerns of research libraries and their institutions, forges coalitions, influences information policy development, and supports innovation and improvements in research library operations. ARL operates as a forum for the exchange of ideas and as an agent for collective action (ARL, 2004).

This mission statement, adopted in 1994, set the tone for how the Online Lyceum was formed and operated. In addition, the decision to create the Online Lyceum was largely influenced by, and would need to consider, the alignment of this new endeavour with the overall ARL strategic priorities. Every year, the ARL Board of Directors reviews the organization's mission and strategic objectives and agrees upon a priority order for engaging those objectives. In essence, they decide which, of all the objectives, we should pursue most vigorously given current environmental conditions, including Association needs, professional issues (for example, recruitment), the economic market and so on. The ARL is comprised of nine main programme areas that each focus on at least one of the strategic objectives and often more. The OLMS focuses on management and staffing objectives, and encompasses five programme areas to meet these objectives: Organizational Development Consulting, Training and Leadership Development, Information Services, Distance Learning, and Diversity. ARL's strategic objective for staffing is, "To identify on an ongoing basis the capabilities and characteristics required for research library personnel to serve best their constituencies and to assist member libraries and educational programmes in the recruitment, development, and effective use of staff," and for management it is, "To assist member libraries in augmenting their management capabilities" (ARL, 2004). As you may infer, the presence of two strategic objectives that deal specifically with staff and staff skills underscores the centrality of what the OLMS does relative to the Association overall and the importance of developing staff skills in our member libraries.

In August 1998 several priorities emerged regarding professional development needs in libraries, and the advent of distance learning as a training option caused us to explore options for distance education delivery of OLMS content by pilot testing a number of technologically enabled learning events. Various issues emphasized the importance of moving in this new direction. An obvious first factor that prompted us to look at distance learning was the opportunity to leverage eLearning capabilities to support the Association's mission and priorities by providing training and leadership development opportunities to meet the expanding needs of library professionals and staff working in ARL member libraries and in the greater library and education communities. An increasing number of participants were attending OLMS's face-to-face events, and online learning could not only fulfil those current needs but offered the possibility of expanding OLMS training to a larger population and in new ways. For example, in-person training events are wonderful for introducing concepts and for initial practice of new skills. Having a distance-learning infrastructure would allow us to not only replicate this training online, but could also be used to expand on participants' learning following in-person events or to offer supplementary modules that are best introduced over time. This approach—a blended curriculum—was an emerging professional development theme when we began the Online Lyceum and the possibilities for enhancing OLMS training and leadership development were exciting. Another priority that was moving us in the direction of online learning was that the costs associated with participating in OLMS in-person institutes were at times a barrier to participation. Though we have always been conscientious with registration prices, airfare and lodging costs for multiple nights could be significant, especially in tight economic times.

In addition to these benefits, the opportunity to enter a formal partnership with an ARL member institution—Southern Illinois University Carbondale (SIUC)—provided a great incentive to create the Online Lyceum. SIUC's Library Affairs department had the necessary infrastructure to support online course development and our relationship with them as an ARL member library made the partnership all the more attractive. As part of the partnership agreement, SIUC would develop, house and maintain the technological backbone of the Online Lyceum. Their contribution of these services pro bono for the initial distance education courses was significant in getting the Online Lyceum programme started. Thereafter, SIUC development services would be paid for on an hourly basis.

It was therefore recognized that the Online Lyceum would need to sustain an organizational structure that: develops new models for the provision of training and leadership development programmes; delivers programmes that are fundamental to the ongoing success of library professionals and, in turn, library users; serves a diverse and geographically dispersed clientele in a variety of new learning environments; and harnesses the potential of innovative distance education technologies in a planned and coordinated way to serve its constituents. However, in order to weigh the potential of the Online Lyceum and to make a best argument for support from ARL and its member libraries, it was essential to also measure the risks of this project proposal. Four primary risks were identified.

4.   Weighing the Risks

The first risk, as indicated above, was that any distance-learning initiative would need to clearly align with the Association's strategic objectives. The success of the Online Lyceum would be largely determined by the same trait that has made ARL a leading organization: careful and constant dedication to our member libraries' wants and needs. Without this tie, no case could be made to support exploration in this new direction. Thus, the way the Online Lyceum was created had to align with Association objectives and speak directly to the current priorities of the Board in order to receive support from Association leadership during its pilot phase. By following the path set by OLMS's long history of providing valuable training to library staff and through careful consideration of expressed member desires, however, we were able to make a case that would meet ARL's strategic objectives. Next, then, Online Lyceum development would need to be carried out to make sure the needs of ARL members were met first and foremost.

Revenue implications were a secondary but vital concern in order to ensure the programme's long-term viability. Though most of the ARL programme areas are largely or wholly supported by membership dues, OLMS is different from other ARL programmes because it is built on a largely cost-recovery budget, with only a small fraction of its overall budget subsidized by dues. The remainder of the funds needed to operate OLMS comes from revenue generated from consulting, training and publication sales. The fact that the OLMS uses a cost-recovery model is highlighted because revenue generation was a second risk to consider and is one of the important factors that plays into our every decision related to the Online Lyceum. In 1998, distance learning was a relatively new market and there was little external data to support a business case for investing in this set of activities. The few fully developed distance-learning programmes in existence did not provide viable comparative data because they were not cost-recovery operations, as is OLMS. Also, we were not able to find financial success stories of distance-learning providers who actually broke even between costs and revenue generated at the end of the year. Further, library professionals, on a whole, were just beginning to experience online learning and could find that this delivery medium might not suit their professional development needs. Even if the courses attracted an initial attendance, there was the question of how to retain and attract new learners.

A third major risk was technologically based—the possibility that the technology would disrupt the learning experience, or that the demands of the online environment may prohibit participant use. As is true for many service-based organizations, the Online Lyceum's success is greatly dependent on word-of-mouth recommendations from people who have had a high-quality experience with it. Thus, it was essential that technological errors be minimized, giving participants seamless interaction with the content and facilitators. To optimize participants' experience and create the most accessible environment possible, it was decided that Online Lyceum courses would be designed for users who had a 22 KB modem or faster and would be built for access by the most commonly used browsers and multimedia plug-ins. In addition, the courses would be housed at SIUC, which has two dedicated servers, including one backup server to minimize possible downtime.

Finally, we were working on an assumption that much of the existing OLMS content could be converted and made available in the web-based environment and that the medium would meet the learning needs of our primary community, librarians. The nature of OLMS workshops is interactive and dynamic, and it was uncertain whether this exchange would play out effectively online. The lack of distance-learning models also meant that there was little information on online learner tendencies and best practices in creating online courses, so there was the further assumption that our knowledge of adult learning would translate well into this new environment. If our assumptions proved untrue, there was the possibility of insufficient participation or available content to support the project.

When measuring the benefits against the risks, however, it was decided that the number of advantages offered by distance-learning offset and outweighed the possible risks, and a pilot course would be created to launch a distance-learning capability within the OLMS. Some of the decisions that we made in order to avert the risks when designing this first course and developing the distance-learning programme—and what worked, what didn't, and why—will be discussed further below. Before we look more closely at that process, however, it is important to first take a look at the goals that would set the tone and lead us in our development. With backing from ARL membership, an Online Lyceum mission statement was created to clarify the following key objectives:

- increase and ensure access to professional development opportunities for ARL member libraries;
- facilitate anytime, anywhere learning opportunities that are interactive and engaging;
- enhance the technology skills of professional librarians and staff and encourage innovation in the use of technology in libraries;
- take a leading role in the creation of professional development opportunities that are accessible from a distance and expand access to Online Lyceum programmes by creating organizational alliances that are mutually beneficial to Online Lyceum participants and partners;
- expand access to non-ARL academic libraries and to geographically and economically disadvantaged libraries; and
- generate strong and diverse support for Online Lyceum programmes through sound financial and human resource management and effective marketing and promotion.

With these aims squarely in mind, OLMS funds were redistributed so that a percentage would act as base funding to create the pilot Online Lyceum course, *Training Skills Online*.

5.   Content and Curriculum Development

In its inception, it was decided that the first Online Lyceum courses would be built from translating in-person events into an online format. This method allowed us to work from proven material that was already in place, thereby limiting the amount of start-up time and costs that would be associated with creating new, untested content. The premier course, *Training Skills Online: Facilitating Effective Learning*, took material from the popular in-person training event and moved it into a distance-learning format with assistance from the education design and technology staff at SIUC.

The first step in this process was to clearly define our audience. Online Lyceum participants are members of a sophisticated and increasingly diverse workforce. Typically, participants have full-time positions in a library, some with MLS degrees, some as information technologists, and many in functionalist roles such as human resources or staff development. They come from all types of libraries, with a variety of educational and employment backgrounds. Their learning needs vary, from seeking desired content to choosing the most effective mode of delivery. Some are technologically proficient and others struggle with the web-based mode of delivery. Overall, though, all our customers ask for and expect high-quality content and the ability to easily and intuitively navigate the courses. They also want access from their workstation or from their home computer, depending on what is most convenient for their schedules. Taking into consideration the diversity of scheduling needs, the Online Lyceum offers 24-hour access to course content; each course has an additional 2-week window of access allowing participants extra time to complete all readings and review assignments, and real-time chat sessions are scheduled throughout the course to fit a range of time zones and scheduling needs.

Another aspect that distinguishes Online Lyceum participants is that the people who enrol in our courses want to develop new and immediately applicable job skills for the library environment, rather than taking courses that lead to a degree. The Online Lyceum is not currently affiliated with an academic unit or certifying agency, although participants who have completed the course assignments and evaluation receive a Certificate of Completion from ARL/OLMS. Often, our participants' secondary interest is enhancing their vitae for their tenure or continuing appointment portfolio, but that is seldom their primary motivating factor. These distinctions lead us to think and refer to these adult learners as *participants* rather than students. This may appear to be just a matter of semantics, but is in fact quite fundamental to the way we approach our relationship with them as adult learners with explicit professional development objectives. To help clarify this distinction, it will be helpful to look at the adult learning framework that OLMS curriculum is based on and that would inform the content development of *Training Skills Online* as well as to discuss some of the challenges associated with translating this core model to fit the online medium.

The adult learning model is based on the belief that "learning that results in increased self awareness, changed behaviour, and the acquisition of new skill sets must actively engage the individual in the learning process" (OLMS, 1996). David Kolb (1984), adult learning specialist, describes this learning process as a cycle. The cycle includes two initial stages, where the adult learner first observes and then reflects on the specific action or experience and his or her own response to that experience. The learning cycle ends with two phases that serve to take these observations and assimilate them into a conceptual framework that lets the learner relate the concepts to past experience, enables the learner to derive implications for future action, and tests and applies that learned knowledge in different situations.

Working with SIUC, *Training Skills Online* was created using the licensed WebCT course software. However, in order to incorporate the best practices of the adult learning model as well as to provide for the interactive nature we wanted to make sure were a part of the online courses, limitations of this software made it necessary to individualize the course environment. The WebCT environment was customized using home-grown scripts to create 'journal' items. These are learning activities and assignments that could be put into a participant journal, to which facilitator feedback is added, and the journal retained by the participant after the course as a learning resource. The journal is a key component of the Online Lyceum, presenting participants with questions that are designed to elicit thoughtful responses to the complex topics covered in the course material, rather than relying on the more standard multiple-choice 'quizzes' that are frequently a part of standard distance-learning courses. Journal activities take participants through the first phases of the cycle and provide participants with an opportunity to reflect on past learning experiences and consider how to incorporate new skills and techniques into your future work. Journal assignments mimic the second half of the learning cycle by having participants practice course concepts to ensure that the content relevance is better understood and then easily applied in the workplace. The assignments are submitted for review and feedback from the facilitators. The journal items are thought provoking and take advantage of the expert facilitation that distinguishes the Online Lyceum.

As a strategic premise, Online Lyceum administrators realized that, in the growing distance-learning arena, the Online Lyceum needed to build on the best practices of the OLMS and create a learning environment that would be sustainable over time and would meet the individual needs of participants and their institutions. As such, Online Lyceum courses are built on an interaction-driven model that: (1) provides one-on-one and group contact with content experts to facilitate interaction and provide feedback to course work; and (2) promotes interaction among fellow participants to provide an environment where knowledge, skills and experiences are learned, shared and applied in a cohort experience. The courses also incorporate creative content development using multimedia, graphics, etc. to keep participants engaged, to support a variety of learning styles, to enrich the learning experience, and to maximize the courses' impact. In addition, the Online Lyceum requires completion of an evaluation form at the end of each course to measure participant satisfaction and enable us to respond to and meet participant expectations.

The Online Lyceum is unique in its approach to web-based professional development because of its emphasis on the close interaction with facilitators. Though this approach is not uncommon in distance education programmes offered for students, it is much less prevalent as a professional development option for working professionals. A more common model for professionals—for example, offered through a corporation as part of its employee-training programme or through an association for its members—is modules that act as written tutorials and link to reference materials, but without any interaction with a facilitator or with other participants. The Online Lyceum, on the other hand, works closely with facilitators to design the course content, including assignments, journal activities, chat sessions, multimedia and bibliographies. Facilitators are typically assigned no more than 15 participants per course; two facilitators are assigned to courses with over 15 and up to 30 registered participants. This ratio allows facilitators to track participants' posted activities and assignments, engage with participants, respond to questions and submissions in a timely manner, and guide weekly chat sessions.

The importance of facilitators cannot be overstated. Participants' experience with the course content is meaningful and successful in large part due to the hands-on interaction with and feedback from experts in the field. Facilitators bring to Online Lyceum courses:

- in-depth knowledge of and experience with the course topic,
- strong communication skills,
- teaching experience,
- a commitment to libraries and professional development, and
- interest in helping others.

During this initial course development it was also decided to create an individualized look-and-feel to brand the Lyceum courses, rather than relying on a packaged design. *Training Skills Online* was first offered in January 1999 to 40 participants.

6.   The Online Lyceum Business Model

After the successful creation of the pilot *Training Skills Online* course, the next major step in establishing the Online Lyceum was to find start-up funding to fully develop the distance-learning programme. A business plan developed in fall 2000, nearly 2 years after a first course was piloted, provided a framework for the true development of the programme. The business plan projected that, with basic operations funded through a small dues allocation and support from OLMS, the Online Lyceum could break even financially—that is, have a revenue stream equal to its annual expenses—in 3 years.

To support the Lyceum during this development phase, beginning in 2001, $US 30,000 in dues was reallocated from the OLMS Information Services program, which manages OLMS publications. A program officer for distance learning was hired and programme supplies (office space, computer, etc.) were purchased out of these existing OLMS funds.

Key to the development and success of the Online Lyceum has been the support of ARL member libraries through this dues-based funding. Because of the cost-recovery nature of OLMS activities, the ARL membership granted the Online Lyceum dues support to offset development costs for new courses with the expectation that it meet its 3-year break-even goal. Therefore, in developing the Online Lyceum's business plan, certain considerations were made to ensure that the programme would be able to meet that expectation:

- Courses are timely and relevant in order to sustain multiple offerings, so that registration fees can remain low and yet provide a consistent revenue stream to eventually cover the course's initial development costs.
- The Online Lyceum learning environment takes advantage of reusable objects in order to minimize development costs.
- The Online Lyceum pursues additional external funding, primarily grants, to allow for enough flexibility to take advantage of unique learning opportunities and to cover costs of new course development.

In planning this new programme, it was important to put into place an infrastructure that would be strong enough to fulfil the ongoing cost recovery demands through tumultuous economic times. As was mentioned above, the Online Lyceum is a partnership effort of two parent organizations, ARL and SIUC. To handle the day-to-day workings and strategic planning of the Online Lyceum, the ARL/OLMS infrastructure consists of one program officer who has direct responsibility for full-time management of the programme, including but not limited to: marketing and promotion; managing course creation and development; and coordination of registration, billing, ongoing courses, facilitators and participants. The Southern Illinois University Library Affairs team provides technological and educational design expertise to the Online Lyceum and consists of the following staff working on a part-time basis: two managers, one programmer (up to about 20% time), one instructional designer (up to about 20% time), and a pool of approximately five students who work on the material as part of their in-house training on web tools.

The SIUC partnership allows the Online Lyceum to support learning and application of new technologies with a department that provides experience in the distance-learning field as well as an established technological infrastructure, including server housing and support, and access to licensed distance-learning software. A memorandum of understanding is revised and signed annually, outlining specific projects and goals for the year and including terms and a rate for services rendered, paid for on an hourly basis.

Working with a partner has obvious benefits. ARL is able to draw upon essential SIUC staff with instructional design expertise and coding skills as well as technology (servers, software, etc.) available from the University, while working toward mutually interesting and beneficial goals. Working in a partnership also naturally includes challenges. Some of the challenges of working in this type of relationship arise from the two organizations' needs to develop new courses, expand capacity, enhance quality and recover operating costs. Although some of these functions can be engaged jointly, most of these areas must be addressed at separate institutional levels. In essence, some of the pressures faced by SIUC and ARL are competing interests. For example, SIUC Library Affairs' parent organization is an academic institution and its primary institutional responsibility is to provide quality-learning tools to SIUC students and academics. SIUC Library Affairs plans its own yearly course creation and management based on an academic calendar that emphasizes student and academic teacher demands. Online Lyceum course creation and management is in addition to their primary workload and is scheduled around University requests. The Online Lyceum, on the other hand, works on a calendar year and its primary goal is to provide professional development courses that can be scheduled at convenient times for working professionals. At times, the number of Online Lyceum courses to be developed and offered in a given year can be tempered by the availability of SIUC time and human resources, with a necessary 4 months development time for each course from the time content is handed off to SIUC. Thus, much attention is paid to making decisions that are in the best interest of both partners, or at least seek to inflict the least amount of harm. Again, the relationship between ARL and SIUC is not a vendor/client one. It is a partnership, and so decisions based strictly on business efficiency are not always pursued; instead, the two organizations work together to explore issues and needs and create mutually agreeable solutions in order to satisfy both our separate and common goals.

7.   Successes and Lessons Learned

Four areas were identified as measures to Online Lyceum effectiveness: financial success, participant satisfaction, course completion and the successful incorporation of new skill sets. We have been successful in each of these measures; however, not surprisingly, we have also learned lessons along the path to meeting those aims.

7.1.   *Financial Success*

Financial success is the primary indicator of programme effectiveness. As has been previously stated, in order for the programme to continue, the Online Lyceum courses needed to generate enough revenue to cover the costs associated with their development and to allow for the creation of new courses, and it was decided that the Online Lyceum's financial plan would be reviewed quarterly to ensure that it achieve its revenue targets. We were able to meet our goal of reaching financial break-even in our third year through careful selection of timely and highly relevant topics facilitated by experts in the field, thereby ensuring continued popularity and applicability of our courses and steady registration streams. Course planning that allowed us to minimize initial costs by working with existing OLMS content has been an effective strategy, but also has made us realize that some topics may work better in an online environment than others and has let us learn more about maximizing instructional design for distance learning. For instance, although our first course, *Training Skills Online*, was well received, feedback has made us realize that some training is better done in person. Most people who have taken *Training Skills Online* tell us that the content is very strong and that the presentation is as useful as they could have expected in a web-based environment. But this topic focuses on face-to-face interaction skills and more than half of the past participants in this course say they would have preferred an in-person session to an online course, so they could practise the skills learned in a live laboratory setting and receive feedback on actual demonstrated work. And though the *Training Skills Online* course example is given here, other courses have received similar feedback. Staying true to OLMS' professional development focus while recognizing the limits and possibilities of distance learning has caused us to be especially careful in our topic selection when deciding what will work well online—more focused, concise, high-quality courses whose topics can be effectively practised online—and what topics are best reserved for face-to-face workshops.

In addition, we were able to meet our financial goals by taking advantage of in-house OLMS training staff expertise to help minimize costs, both in creating content and, more often, in facilitating courses. Although the solution was effective early on, the growth of the programme has pointed out the need to have a cadre of facilitators to work with who have specialized knowledge and who are sufficiently trained in instructional design and online facilitation. Access to such a cadre continually provides new topics as well as reduces the heavy workload on OLMS trainers that has accompanied the growing programme. It further allows for needed flexibility in scheduling; without these additional facilitators, the number of times a course could be offered was limited and therefore restricted registration and revenue. The decision to develop this core group has also enabled us to work more frequently with OLMS adjunct staff as well as to create new connections with content experts outside of OLMS.

Another successful track has been our pursuit of external funds to assist with the Online Lyceum's creation of new courses. In 2000, a National Leadership Grant from the Institute of Museum and Library Services funded the creation of three new courses and forwarded our decision to pursue blended curricula. Using topics identified by member library directors and other leaders in the field, these courses were created and piloted as part of the ARL Leadership and Career Development Program, a year-long programme that is a combination of two intensive leadership institutes and the three online courses. We now have the added benefit of being able to offer these courses as part of our public offerings, so that we have a continued source of revenue. A different external funding model is cost-sharing partnerships. This model was used for the original *Accessible Web Design* course with the University of Wisconsin, Madison, with course content being created by a University library staff member. Although this model provided us with enough flexibility to take advantage of new opportunities by sharing expenses—and then revenue from courses—with a partner institution, it was unfortunately not practical in the long term. The amount of staff time required to administer the course was not considered in the revenue sharing, and became prohibitive to offering the course. We were eventually able to change this original agreement and it became a valuable lesson to consider for future such partnerships.

Finally, our experience in developing the Online Lyceum's first courses showed that the costs of course development—moving the completed contents into the online format—could be prohibitive, running as high as $US 20,000 per course. These costs are based on the hourly payment to SIUC for instructional design, HTML and JavaScript coding and multimedia and graphic creation, as well as payments to content providers. It does not take into consideration ARL staff work or other indirect ARL costs. Since the earliest courses, we have made several structural changes in order to maintain affordable registration fees and recover direct and indirect costs. The most significant structural change was migration to a new online environment. Whereas the first five courses were developed in the WebCT environment, subsequent courses were built in our own home-grown system so that development and edits could be made more easily and in less time, and reusable objects could be taken advantage of more frequently, primarily through standard scripts for course functions and through server-side includes. This decision has also allowed us to work in and continue to develop a distinctive learning environment.

7.2.   Participant Satisfaction

The second crucial measurement of Online Lyceum effectiveness is participant satisfaction. At the end of each course, Online Lyceum participants are required to complete an online evaluation form that provides detailed feedback on course content, the online learning environment and the applicability of learning. These evaluations gather qualitative and quantitative data to provide information about participant satisfaction with Online Lyceum courses as well as are integral in identifying areas for improvement. It was recognized that the courses and approaches would be tested and refined over time in order to provide the most effective and high-quality distance-learning environment possible, and to keep content current. Since 1998, over 900 participants having taken our courses, many of who have returned for multiple courses and indicated in their feedback that they have recommended our courses to others. Those past participants in management positions, for instance, have frequently sent staff to courses they themselves have found useful. The course evaluation forms have also shown that participants rank the courses highly on many levels: the course topic and its delivery, the facilitation, and the learning environment. As the Online Lyceum has grown, so too has the credibility and availability of distance learning generally and the capability of the Online Lyceum in particular to deliver high-quality, highly facilitated and highly effective courses. Despite these positive signs, however, wide-ranging budget cuts have severely restricted professional development funding at a large number of libraries, and so we now find ourselves faced with the dilemma of lower registrations despite high satisfaction levels. Nonetheless, a critical mass of professionals who are comfortable using web-based learning as a professional development option has gradually grown and, with this growth, the Lyceum evolves.

The evaluation forms have not only shown satisfaction, but have provided us with valuable feedback that has led us to make a number of significant changes. We have refined the course journal to allow participants to edit their work, created email prompts to alert participants when they have received comments in their journals, installed a new chat software client, and have completely revised one course to refine and expand the content as well as to increase opportunities for interaction, a move that has generated a large amount of positive responses. Based on feedback, we have also identified areas where more information needed to be shared with participants, particularly as many are first-time users of online learning. This additional information ensures that they are comfortable in the online arena without the technology or course layout impeding their learning process. In effect, the evaluations support our need to understand customer satisfaction and foster continuous innovation.

7.3.   *Course Completion*

Course completion is another indication of success in that a high completion rate also shows a level of interest in the course and indicates that the participant found it was of value enough to finish. At the end of each course, participants who work through all assignments and complete the evaluation form receive a Certificate of Completion from ARL/OLMS. Participants then use the certificates as indication of their commitment to and completion of continuing professional education. Considering the demographics of our customers—adults with full-time, often management- or administrative-level positions—our course completion rate is quite high. Over 75% of participants who have taken an Online Lyceum course are able to successfully complete it. For participants who get too far behind in their coursework due to demanding work schedules and/or personal events, we allow them to opt out of the current offering and re-enrol in a later session—something we offer without charging a second registration fee. And though the Online Lyceum has been successful despite a lack of academic credits, we have received enough requests for this type of recognition (continuing education units) that we have pursued a relationship with a like-minded association that will allow us to provide this added incentive mid-2004.

7.4.   *Acquisition of New Skills Sets*

The successful incorporation of new skill sets by participants is the final indicator that Online Lyceum course goals have been met; however, it is by far the most difficult to measure. Post-course feedback is used to gather information about training effectiveness and participants' ability to incorporate what they have learned into their daily work practice. We have received regular feedback on the successful application of skills in the workplace, both during the courses as participants share what they've learned and have practised at their home institutions and in unsolicited post-course comments. In addition to this informal feedback, course evaluation forms specifically address this measure and have given us participant comments that indicate how the courses provide a skill set that is immediately transferable to their work. For instance, the course *Measuring Library Service Quality* has been vital in teaching participants skills they have been able to use in their home institutions through in-house measurement programmes as well as through programmes such as the hugely successful LibQUAL+^{TM} project offered via the ARL New Measures Initiative. Other prominent examples include courses on *Library Conflict Management* and *Accessible Web Design*, among others. The importance of skills transfer has been a leading force in our topic selection process, and future decisions are increasingly affected by this factor. In order to better determine if and how participants are using learned skills, however, it will be necessary to follow up with the learners to see if the knowledge has long-term relevance, likely by soliciting information through surveys several months after the courses' completion.

In addition to these measures of effectiveness, however, we also were faced with an additional unanticipated challenge that would affect the programme's success. Since its inception in 1998, the Online Lyceum has had been managed by four program officers and under the leadership of two OLMS directors. Needless to say, the programme has weathered quite a bit of transition. In the absence of stable leadership, the programme struggled with identity development (that is, branding), consistent promotions and coherent programme development. Much of the work was makeshift, only looking ahead as far as the next quarter's financial goals, rather than being guided by a long-term strategic plan.

In many organizations, technicians—people with frontline technical competence—are promoted to management positions as a reward for their skill and hard work. Certainly, the Online Lyceum manager would need to fulfil the technological requirements that are a large portion of the position, with the program officer identifying topics and seeking out experts, walking through courses to resolve errors and working with content providers on layout and with instructional designers on the best use of media to convey the intended learning objectives. Nonetheless, when looking for a manager for the Online Lyceum, technical competence was not enough. The complexity of managing the programme was such that strong leadership skills were required for the incoming program officer. The program officer has to manage the large issues related to navigating relationships with our partner, SIUC, other collaborative partners, member library leaders, online facilitators and content providers, and individual course participants. And then there are the day-to-day operational issues of budgeting, promotions, supervising support staff, writing progress reports and programme plans, and other managerial demands. But without strong communication among all these players, this infrastructure could easily change from a value-added that lets us take advantage of each player's skills and talents into a negative. Without having communication to tie everyone together to the larger Online Lyceum goals, each person could easily just focus on his/her aspect without understanding how it relates to the programme as a whole. Under stable leadership for the past 2 years, the programme has begun to establish a viable infrastructure and we now look forward to a growth phase.

The Online Lyceum has been evolving and continuously improving on many levels. The consistent leadership during the past 2 years has been an opportunity to improve communication and workflow with our partner, SIUC Library Affairs. This includes regularly scheduled conference calls to share progress reports, identify programmatic needs and address problems. There is also a growing understanding of the two institutions' mutual and diverse interests and ways to attend to those. This time has further been used to create documents that establish work policy and quality standards; to improve practices around content, course development and back-up procedures; and to examine our practices in light of current and long-term goals.

In addition to the program officer and SIUC staff, the Online Lyceum also relies heavily on working with others. Although there is only one full-time staff person for distance learning at ARL, the Director of Organizational Services provides programmatic support and OLMS's program officer for Training devotes approximately 20% of her time to facilitating and developing content for Online Lyceum courses. Additional ARL staff have also contributed time to course development and facilitation on a periodic basis. In addition, the Online Lyceum routinely works with approximately five OLMS adjunct academics and an additional ten academics from member libraries and the field.

The Online Lyceum's audience has grown in the years since it began, both nationally as it reaches a broader range of participants from a wide range of library types and backgrounds—academic, public and special— and also internationally. Participants attending our courses have done so from Asia, Europe, Africa, Australia and North America. Collaborations with non-US library associations have been fruitful, and conversations with other organizations have begun and will continue to be pursued.

Knowing that the Association of Research Libraries represents the premier research libraries in North America, and that the Office of Leadership and Management Services has long been looked to as a leader in management and leadership training for library professionals, the Online Lyceum is following in this tradition by continually reviewing its processes and courses in order to ensure that it provide a useful and high-quality distance-learning programme. Our continuous self-assessment, improvement and responsiveness to participant needs make us certain that our services will be valued and valuable.

8. Future Directions

We have learned much since we offered our first course and have met our primary goals to date. Now in our fifth year, we currently offer 14 courses and have identified topics for future development. In order to ensure that the Online Lyceum continues to grow and be an integral part of the OLMS, we have been concentrating this year on strategic planning. This has given us the opportunity to review where we are now and also to look ahead to where we want to be. As part of our strategic planning process, we are reviewing the Online Lyceum mission, taking into consideration that significant technological, distance education and professional development changes have emerged since the programme's beginning. We have also expanded our distance-learning programme to include additional means of delivery, primarily through live, interactive webcasts that highlight timely topics that are pertinent to libraries, campus academics and administrators. We will also identify goals, both short- and long-term, that are consistent with member needs, reflect customer feedback gathered over the past 4 years, and consider environmental trends.

One of our goals is to increase interaction with other ARL programmes in order to best support the Association as a whole, and to explore possibilities of expanding the content available through the Online Lyceum. The Online Lyceum has stayed true to OLMS training models and standards and now, in addition to the traditional leadership and management courses, also covers other pressing library issues. One example is the previously mentioned course *Measuring Library Service Quality*, which includes a reduced registration arrangement with the ARL New Measures Initiative to support the number of LibQUAL+™(2004) participants interested in this course. Another example is the course *Licensing Review & Negotiation*, which was developed with the Office of Scholarly Communication, based on content from the popular in-person event (it is now offered solely online via the Online Lyceum). Both of these courses have been incredibly successful, supporting our assumption that demand for continued emphasis on library-specific material is a good direction for future Online Lyceum course development. Collaborating with other ARL programmes, such as the Federal Relations Program or the Access and Technology Program, will allow us to expand the ARL distance-learning capacity beyond Online Lyceum course offerings to provide online presentations or tutorials. Therefore, additional programme crossovers are being pursued in order to offer the broadest range of services possible to the ARL membership and others.

Given our past success with blended learning, we will continue to pursue this model to create learning tracks based on complementary in-person and online OLMS workshops. This past year we offered for the first time one such programme—the Library Leadership for New Managers Program. This programme is directed towards library professionals who are new to or expect to be in management positions. It is a blend of a 3-day, in-person session led by leaders in the research library and information technology fields and an online course that supplements the in-person learning. Strategic planning will encourage us to look at our new course decisions with an eye to how the courses work with the whole catalogue of OLMS events, and what possibilities they offer for future blended learning tracks.

We also will be pursuing more collaborative institutional relationships and other possible partnerships that will enable us to broaden our portfolio and share resources. As mentioned earlier, one partnership we are currently discussing will allow us to add academic credentials to the Online Lyceum courses. This will fulfil our growing number of requests for this service and may provide us with new opportunities to work collaboratively with academic institutions.

Finally, we have begun to and will continue to look at the courses' technological environment to identify new advances to take advantage of and to assess the scalability of the system as it now stands. Some key questions we are asking as we enter our strategic planning process are:

- Will our current system still work in 5 years?
- Will our current system be able to keep up with and adapt to technological advances, such as new multimedia, different browsers and operating systems?
- As we budget for technology, do we plan for yearly, incremental enhancements, or do we seek funding for significant investment in establishing a whole new, and more advanced, learning platform?

By providing professional development opportunities to library staff, the Online Lyceum supports libraries and library professionals in providing superior service to their users and in excelling as information resources. Our continued commitment to making accessible emerging technologies, and in turn targeted professional development experiences, allows practitioners to maintain their standard of professional excellence as providers of information and preservers of knowledge.

References

Association of Research Libraries (ARL). (2004). ARL Program Plan 2004. Retrieved November 20, 2004, from http://www.arl.org/arl/pp2004/

Kolb, D. A. (1984). *Experiential learning.* New York: Prentice-Hall.

LibQUAL+™(2004). Retrieved November 20, 2004, from http://www.libqual.org/

Office of Leadership and Management Services (OLMS). (1996). Adult learning theory and model. OLMS Training Skills Support Site. ARL, OLMS. Retrieved November 20, 2004, from http://www.arl.org/training/ilcso/adultlearn.html

9.   Bibliography for Further Reading

Birch, P. D. (2002). E-learner competencies. *Learning Circuits.* Retrieved November 20, 2004, from http://www.learningcircuits.org/2002/jul2002/birch.html

Boyd, S. (2002). E-learning 1.0: Tips to make e-learning stick. *Learning Circuits.* Retrieved November 20, 2004, from http://www.learningcircuits.org/2002/may2002/elearn.html

Chapnick, S. (2000). Are you ready for e-learning? *Learning Circuits.* Retrieved November 20, 2004, from http://www.learningcircuits.org/2000/nov2000/chapnick.html

Lockee, B., Moore, M., & Burton, J. (2002). Measuring success: Evaluation strategies for distance education. *Educause Quarterly*, 25(1), 20–26. Retrieved November 20, 2004, from http://www.educause.edu/ir/library/pdf/eqm0213.pdf

Mayberry, E. (2001). How to build a business case for e-learning. *Learning Circuits*. Retrieved November 20, 2004, from http://www.learningcircuits.org/2001/jul2001/mayberry.html

Rossen, E., & Hartley, D. (2001). Basics of e-learning. *Info-line*, Training Technology 250109. Information retrieved November 20, 2004, from http://www.astd.org/astd/Publications/infoline/Training_Technology.htm

Rossett, A., & Schafer, L. (2003). What to do about E-dropouts. *T + D*, 57(6), 40–46.

Chapter 6

LEARNING TO LEARN IN NETWORKED ENVIRONMENTS: A FOCUS ON 'ORIENTATION'

Philippa Levy

1.　　　Chapter Overview

This chapter focuses on some of the themes that emerged from a practice-based, case study evaluation project exploring participants' experiences of a networked learning approach to professional development. The chapter briefly discusses the research methodology, in which action research and constructivist evaluation approaches were combined to produce a case study analysis, and then goes on to present a simplified conceptual model of experiences of 'learning to learn' on the course. The research revealed experiences of four broad, developmental processes that were associated with learning to learn, and the impact of these on the nature and quality of participants' engagement with learning tasks. These processes were: orientation, communication, socialization and organization. The chapter then presents extracts from the case study narrative on experiences of (dis)orientation, including orientation to the learning space, orientation to the information environment, and orientation to the learning design and approach. It concludes by drawing out some practical evaluation points that emerged from the research and by suggesting that practice-based research approaches such as the one described in the chapter may be of relevance not only to subject educators but also to information specialists in their new learning support roles in the networked environment, for example in relation to information design for networked environments and information literacy education.

H. S. Ching, P. W. T. Poon and C. McNaught (Eds.), eLearning and Digital Publishing, 89–107.
© 2006 *H. S. Ching, P. W. T. Poon and C. McNaught.*

2.   Introduction

Networked learning has been described as the use of information and communication technology (ICT) "to promote connections: between one learner and other learners, between learners and tutors, between a learning community and its learning resources" (Goodyear, 2002, p. 56). It is a particular approach to eLearning that draws on ideas from constructivist and situated learning theories and is closely associated with the tradition of computer-supported collaborative learning (e.g. McConnell, 2000). The emphasis in this context on dialogical interaction, collaboration and community in learning differentiates this from approaches to eLearning in which provision of access to digital learning materials and information resources takes centre stage in pedagogical design. For example, eLearning based on individual engagement with self-paced, interactive online learning packages would not be defined, from this perspective, as networked learning.

A key challenge for networked learning practitioners is to support learners to take full advantage of the range of pedagogical, social, information and technical resources at their disposal in the digital environment. This might involve developing strategies for providing contextualized information literacy support, alongside strategies for supporting the development of other 'process' capabilities required for productive engagement in networked learning. This chapter focuses upon some of the themes that emerged from a practice-based, case study evaluation project exploring participants' experiences of a networked learning approach to professional development. The research revealed experiences, in this particular context, of four broad, developmental processes that were associated with 'learning to learn' on the course, and the impact of these on the nature and quality of participants' engagement with learning tasks.

3.   Research Aims and Approach

The case study course, entitled 'Networked Learner Support in Higher Education', aimed to offer learning support practitioners from UK higher education institutions an opportunity to engage with ideas and issues associated with their changing educational roles in the networked environment, as well as to develop new technical expertise. Run over a 17-week period, with participants expected to spend between 6 and 8 hours per week on course activities, it was not designed to transmit a particular body of content. Instead, it was conceived as a resource environment within which practitioners would carry out a number of flexible tasks that would enable them to explore ideas and develop skills of most relevance to their own professional interests and circumstances. With the aim of facilitating self-directed, collaborative learning, emphasis was placed on developing new perspectives and expertise within a networked learning community, through online discussion, group-work and work-based projects with peer support. A series of tasks focusing on the experience and practice of networked learning, and involving critical reflection and discussion, were embedded into the course, and a portfolio approach to recording learning was encouraged. Access was entirely online—there were no face-to-face meetings—and the technical platform was a 'home-grown' experiment in virtual learning environment design, in that the web and a number of asynchronous and synchronous conferencing tools were used to provide integrated access to social and information resources. For all participants, this was a new type of learning experience. From the perspective of my role in developing the course design and as one of a number of course tutors, I embarked on the action research project with the aim of improving both my understanding of networked learning from the learner's perspective, and the impact and effectiveness of my own educational practice.

The practice-based research methodology, discussed in more detail in Levy (2003), blended approaches associated with interpretivist and critical traditions in educational action research (e.g. Carr & Kemmis, 1986; McNiff, Lomax & Whitehead, 1996) with those of constructivist programme evaluation (Guba & Lincoln, 1989; Lincoln, 2001)—one consideration here being that Guba and Lincoln's framework proposes a 'hermeneutic-dialectic' methodology, based on cycles of dialogical interaction amongst participants in social action, that is compatible with the epistemology and values that underpin networked learning. The purpose of this approach is to evaluate and improve educational practice and understandings through critical analysis of specific educational situations, developing knowledge that will both inform local practice and offer a resource for other practitioners working in similar settings and with similar purposes. The emphasis is on developing practical, rather than propositional, knowledge—the Aristotelian concept of 'phronesis' rather than 'episteme'—since it is practical knowledge that is understood to be the basis of professional competence. The form of theory generated through action research has been called 'living' theory (McNiff *et al.*, 1996), signalling that it is embedded in personal experience, is context-specific and is open to refinement and reinterpretation. Typically, theory building and dissemination in this context are taken forward through the development of case studies that aim to provide sufficiently 'thick' (interpretive) description of social context and action as to enable readers to judge how far these compare with their own situations, experiences and practice.

In practical terms, this project involved moving through a cycle of research activities within four main phases. These are represented in figure 6-1. In adapting the classic, problem-solving 'plan, act, monitor, reflect' action research cycle, the diagram aims to reflect the constructivist perspective that underpins the project and to point to aspects of Guba and Lincoln's (1989)

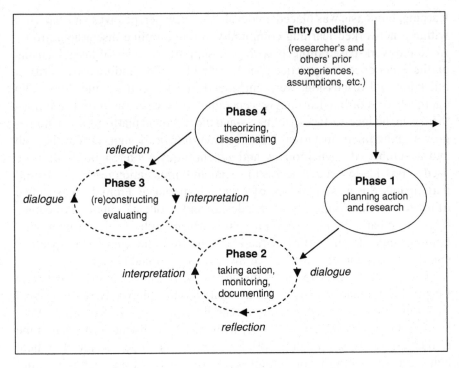

Figure 6-1. Constructivist action research cycle

methodology that were adopted. For example, the diagram highlights the iterative, participatory dimension of phases 2 and 3, the close connection between these phases and the role of dialogical 'stakeholder' interaction in data collection and case (re)construction.

A combination of online and face-to-face data collection methods were used, including participant observation and online transcript analysis, online dialogue, a post-course participant feedback questionnaire, face-to-face research conversations, peer debriefing with other tutors, reflective dialogue with a 'critical friend' and a personal research journal. The case study draws on all of these sources to (re)construct 'what happened' on the course and to explore the question 'how should this be interpreted?' in relation to (my own) educational objectives, assumptions and strategies. Since my purpose in (re)constructing this case has been to provide a basis for evaluating and improving my educational understandings and practice, its focus is on events, issues and perspectives that indicate strengths and weaknesses in the pedagogic model and its implementation. This has meant adopting a critical, 'warts and all' stance, highlighting participants' (and my own) difficulties and frustrations as well as their satisfactions and successes, and drawing attention to points of tension or contrast within the participant group, as well as to areas of common experience and viewpoint.

4.   Developmental Processes

Encouragingly, there was much that was positive in participants' responses to this course. Nevertheless, the research has revealed a fine-grained picture of diverse experiences and evaluation perspectives that highlights design and facilitation problems, and enables further refinement of the pedagogic design that was tested. One key theme to emerge from the research was the identification of four broad, interconnected developmental processes associated with 'learning to learn' on the course, as follows:

Orientation—becoming aware of, and positioned in relation to, key features of the learning environment, resources and approach. There were three main dimensions of orientation:

- orientation to the learning space: becoming aware of, and positioned within, the structure of the course website and the virtual spaces created by its computer-mediated communication (CMC) tools;
- orientation to the information environment: becoming aware of, and positioned within, the electronic information resource environment within and beyond the course environment; and
- orientation to the learning design and approach: becoming aware of, and engaged with, the nature and practical implications of the learning design and approach. This involved two stages: firstly, engaging with information about tasks and the approach, and secondly, developing a deeper understanding of the implications of these for the practice of learning.

Communication—using CMC as a means of self-expression and dialogue. There were two main dimensions here:

- communicating asynchronously, principally using the text-based conferencing system (bulletin board); and
- communicating synchronously, principally using the MOO (multi-user object oriented) environment.

Socialization—the development of interpersonal connections, relationships and community feeling within the networked learning environment. Two related themes here:

- developing connections and relationships: experiences of forming interpersonal connections and relationships with peers and tutors; and
- developing community: experiences of group or community affiliation within the learning environment.

Organization—planning, structuring, managing and directing personal and collective engagement with the networked learning environment, resources and tasks. Five main dimensions of this process were identified:

- managing communication: developing practical access and response routines for asynchronous communication, and strategies for using synchronous chat effectively;
- managing information: developing strategies for engaging with the flow of information generated within the learning environment, including for selective reading and storing information;
- managing time: allocating time to the networked learning approach to professional development in the context of working and domestic lives;
- managing flexibility: imposing personal structure and direction in relation to flexible learning tasks and the flexible mode of study; and
- managing collaboration: organizing and facilitating collaborative activity online, particularly in small, distributed learning groups ('learning sets').

Some aspects of participants' experiences in these areas were associated with the online nature of the learning environment, whilst other elements were more generic. Positive experiences contributed to productive engagement with learning environment and tasks whilst negative experiences placed constraints on productive engagement and, therefore, on learning. A combination of factors—including contextual factors external to, but interacting with, the designed learning environment, as well as factors relating to learning design and facilitation—were perceived to shape learners' experiences in these four areas, and both facilitative and constraining factors in this respect were revealed.

A somewhat different picture emerges here as compared with research that has portrayed the developmental process experienced by eLearners generically as a progression through clear-cut, sequential phases—and there would seem to be rather different implications for learning design and facilitation. For example, work by Salmon (2000) depicts eLearners' developmental experience as a stage-by-stage progression from initial entry to the environment through a sequence of practices culminating in the adoption of constructivist approaches to eLearning. The design model stemming from her research recommends a stage-by-stage pedagogical approach to support progression from one set of practices to another, whereas the findings of this research suggest the value of a more integrated, holistic approach to 'process support' for networked learning.

Reflecting these findings, figure 6-2 presents a simplified conceptual model of experiences of networked learning on the course. The diagram draws attention to the core processes of orientation, communication, socialization

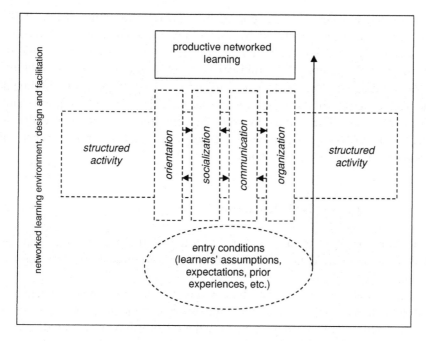

Figure 6-2. Developmental processes in networked learning

and organization as central to productive networked learning within the context of the learning environment and the implementation of the learning design. It shows these processes as parallel and interconnected, rather than as sequential phases experienced one after another, and indicates a relationship of mutual influence between process experiences in these four areas and structured learning activity (that is, activity arising out of engagement with pre-established tasks, whether these are tightly or loosely structured). The developmental dimension of learners' process experiences, in terms of improved personal awareness, relationships and practices in networked learning over time, is also highlighted, developmental progression in all four areas being facilitated in particular by opportunities for reflexive engagement with process issues over time. The impact on process experiences of variations in the 'entry conditions' for individual learners, as well as of design and implementation factors, is also signalled. However, the diagram does not show the considerable amount of variation in the speed and ease with which novice networked learners moved through these processes in developmental terms, nor does it show the potential for individuals to move at different rates through each one, despite their inter-connectedness.

In what follows, the focus is on aspects of one theme only of the case study: experiences of (dis)orientation and some implications for evaluation and practical theory building. Pseudonyms are used for individual participants, who are also designated by numerical identifier (P1 to P29). Sources of data are identified by the following conventions: OT (online transcript), QF (questionnaire feedback) and RC (research conversation). The case study points to a combination of constraining factors in relation to orientation—including designed features of the learning environment and tasks, aspects of tutoring practice, and participants' assumptions and expectations about learning—as well as facilitative factors. It also draws attention to my own developing awareness, as a practitioner–researcher, of orientation issues during the course.

5.   Experiences of Orientation

Orientation: "positioning with relation to specific directions; alignment of oneself or one's ideas to surrounding circumstances" (Collins English Dictionary, 1999).

The homepage for the first, 2-week, course Unit presented participants with a clickable image map of the Unit structure, timetable and its cycle of intended activity, illustrating graphically the relationship between individual, group and plenary tasks. Whereas some tasks were to be carried out in sequence, others were designed to run concurrently. The map was intended to show how participants should work through a cycle of activities in the Unit towards reflective 'closing round' discussion and individual portfolio work; the same format was used subsequently for all Unit maps. Participants also encountered a number of asynchronous conferencing forums and a web-based synchronous chat facility, as well as the course's Resource Base—a structured, web-based information resource comprising bibliographic references to off-line documents, annotated links to external web documents and links to a small range of materials produced specifically for the course, including guidance materials about the learning approach that suggested approaches participants might take to tasks such as learning journals, project planning and portfolios. Unit 1 included some tasks—experimenting with the learning environment technology, reading the documentation about the course, and plenary discussion about general course issues—that were intended to familiarize participants with the learning environment and its communication and information resources, and with the course objectives and learning approach. I hoped that participants would read the guidance materials and raise concerns and questions in the plenary forum, thereby initiating general discussion of learning and support issues that might extend throughout the course. Other introductory tasks, in addition to personal introductions in Arboretum, were: some additional reading in preparation for Unit 2, and personal reflection and small-group discussion on professional development interests and goals in 'learning set' forums.

5.1. *"Have I Seen Everything? Have I Been to All the Bits?"*

Most participants, using the signposting provided by the Unit map, the Technical Support area of the website and a 'technical issues' discussion forum hosted by the technical support tutor, found that they needed relatively little time in the early days of the course to identify key landmarks— designed information and communication features—of the online learning environment. Early technical concerns related to access to different areas were generally resolved quickly, and in common with the majority of others Esther later recalled that she had *"picked up finding my way around the course fairly easily really"* (P20:RC). Simon agreed: *"The web site was very easy, you knew where you were, the Units coming online in sequence, the familiarity of the site, please read overview first, that kind of thing, you could get round it easily"* (P23:RC). At the same time, it took a few participants somewhat longer to become fully aware of, and confident about, the structure of the site and the resources and facilities at their disposal, as Angela later explained: *"Looking back it is a clear structure, but I'm always a bit like that with web sites, I'm always, have I seen everything? Have I been to all the bits? So I was disorientated at first"* (P18:RC).

5.2. *"It Seemed to Go on Forever"*

In addition to finding their way around the resource environment contained within the course website, participants also needed to become oriented within the wider information landscape within which it was located. As already noted, the Resource Base, with its links to a wide range of digital resources, was introduced as an integral part of the course environment from the start. On the one hand, the richness of the web was a source of excitement, and Naomi's enthusiasm was widely shared: *"So many good information sources, and they all lead to others . . . I really enjoyed going on that resource base and going from one link to another"* (P24:RC). On the other hand, exposure to the large collection of resources in the Resource Base and beyond them, to the wider information landscape, contributed to some participants' 'information anxiety' and sense of disorientation at the start of the course—as well as to misconceptions about the role of reading within the learning design. Some later explained how coping with the 'borderlessness' of the resource environment and the seductions of hypertext could be problematic. As Lydia put it, *"One of the things I had not appreciated was that with an online course you never get to the end! When you are reading books or articles you do eventually get to the end but with links it's never-ending!"* (P27:QF). Similarly, Kate commented that, *"It was hard, being prepared for the amount of material on the web, it still seemed to go on forever even with the structured resource base you had ... I should have realized, I've had the web at home and at work for 4 years, but I felt, where do I stop?"* (P6:RC).

Some participants spent a good deal of time surfing the web as the course progressed, sometimes losing their way and becoming distracted from the purposes and focus of Unit tasks. Peter subsequently recalled, *"following links that took me literally hours to follow through and it was like somebody turning on a light bulb, you think well wait a minute, this isn't anything to do with where I started, so I got lost basically, I wasted a lot of time looking at bits and pieces that were unnecessary"* (P12:RC).

Nevertheless, as participants became acclimatized to their environment, perspectives on the course's designed information resource frequently changed, and post-course feedback indicated that the range and clearly structured presentation of the Resource Base was highly valued. Looking back, Charlotte commented that *"I wouldn't have wanted a smaller resource base in retrospect, but if you'd have asked me that 4 weeks into the course I would have said, cut it down, it's scary"* (P13:RC).

5.3.   *"Struggling to Find a Conceptual Map"*

Equally, some participants found it relatively unproblematic to assimilate information rapidly about the course's learning approach and design, the signposts provided by supporting documentation and early dialogue with tutors being sufficient to enable them to gain a clear overview of the design and its underpinning philosophy, and to understand the nature of the individual, group and plenary tasks that they were invited to carry out. Those whose prior learning experiences and expectations matched the assumptions and expectations embedded in the course design were in a better position than others in this respect. Thus, for Richard, this all seemed *"very explicit"* (P7:RC) from the start. Similarly, Frances noted that, *"There were lots of guideposts I suppose, that's what I'd say,* [the course] *was well guided to make sure you didn't get totally left behind or go off the track"* (P17:RC). They and others in a similar position tended to see the course Units and tasks as *"clearly structured"*.

However, for many the process of learning orientation proved to be less straightforward and more extended—well beyond the 2-week period of the introductory Unit. Early in the second week, a plenary discussion thread was instigated to invite questions and discussion about the way in which the course was designed, and about particular tasks that might be unfamiliar. This elicited little feedback, despite the lively exchanges that were occurring at the same time in other areas of the conferencing environment, particularly an ice-breaker thread and the technical issues forum. At the same time, it was evident that discussions in most learning set forums were not taking off as intended, despite the efforts of tutors to set a discussion task in motion there. In my research journal I noted the limits of our control over participants' activity in the online classroom, as compared with face-to-face settings, and also my ignorance about the way in which designed tasks were actually translating into activity. I felt uncomfortably in the dark about participants' responses to the course approach, including whether or not they understood and were carrying out the sequence of tasks as designed. With the following posting to the plenary forum I expressed something of my concern: "... *Maybe everyone feels perfectly clear about how it all fits together and is just busy getting on with it, which is great! But please do feel free to ask questions, make comments ... we're open to discussing any aspect of the course at all*" (OT). Again, this invitation elicited some, but relatively little, response.

Yet at this point many participants were, as Valerie put it, "*struggling to find a conceptual map to cope with the course.*" She added that, "*I usually rely very heavily on face-to-face contact*" (P28:OT). In contrast with perspectives already noted, it was common to perceive the course design as somewhat complex and fragmented at this stage, and course Units and tasks as "*unstructured*" and indistinct. Faced with a number of different tasks, participants were unsure of where the emphasis lay and which they should prioritize. Some participants would later consider that there had not been any concrete tasks at all during the early weeks of the course. Esther explained that it had been "*very difficult to realize at first what I was supposed to be doing*" (P20:RC). Ruth's first few weeks were "*very bewildering, you didn't know what to concentrate on and what to spend more time on*" (P4: RC). The result was a period of relatively directionless activity. Charlotte later recalled how she had been, "*all over the place*" (P13:RC) and Margaret that, "*I didn't know where I was*" (P21:RC).

Moreover, whilst early 'signposts' and support that were intended to support orientation to the learning approach met the needs of some participants, it was not unusual for others to fail to notice, or fully take in, early sources of information and discussions. Peter later suggested that this might be an inherent feature of the online learning environment, in that: "*people flash in and out so quick... you have to work at concentrating on a course environment like this*" (P12:RC). Margaret recalled that: "*When I looked back at the early messages that you had sent in the first two weeks, and it was like, well I know I read them but I obviously didn't take them in, and if I'd paid attention to what the messages were saying I'd have been a lot better off... the instructions were there but it was like I hadn't taken them in*" (P21:RC).

Some, like Teresa, found that getting used to the technical features of the environment tended to displace attention from other dimensions of the introductory Unit: "[the technology] *took your mind off other facets*" (P15:RC). Others found that the intensive activity in some plenary forums and the amount of information on the website, had a similar effect. In particular, attention was distracted away from activity in learning sets. Focusing in the initial and other early Units on reading and interactions in the plenary forum, some participants did not notice early information and discussion about learning sets and small-group tasks. Thus, Lydia's (mistaken) impression that, *"we weren't given anything to discuss as a group early on. It wasn't until later in the course that we were told to go away and discuss as a group"* (P27:RC) was shared by others, including Claire: *"When I went back and looked and there was something in Unit 1 that we should have got together and talked about, we just didn't do that. I must have missed that completely ... I didn't remember reading that we should get together and do that task!"* (P10:RC).

Similarly, Siobhan later commented that, *"early on we were taking in a lot of stuff and it was explained about the learning sets, so I'd read that message and just not assimilated it"* (P11:RC). And whilst early postings from tutors within learning set forums attempted to explain the intended role of groups and the potential contributions of members, it was not uncommon to fail to grasp these issues, as well as to under-estimate the intended importance of learning sets within the learning design. As Tim later explained, *"I was not altogether clear as to the exact function of the set (or perhaps convinced of their use) and so initially I had been hesitant to use it"* (P19:OT). Nor did participants always perceive, to begin with, the part that they themselves might play in establishing and developing the groups, as in Sandra's case: *"Maybe when you were asking us to work in groups I didn't fully understand what that would involve, in that it would mean I would have to take more responsibility in terms of getting it to really work"* (P8: RC).

Similarly, early pointers to, and guidance about, journals and portfolios often went unnoticed or unassimilated in the early weeks of the course, with the result that some participants ultimately decided against embarking on them. Thus, Kate later commented that: *"I must have missed that bit [...] Later on in Arboretum there were a couple of references to things we were advised to do right from the beginning, and I hadn't appreciated* [the journal]*or taken it up"* (P6:RC). Charlotte's experience was similar: *"It wasn't til a way into the course that I thought what's this* [journal]*that they're talking about, should I be doing it? Then I started trying but it was too late in the day"* (P13:RC).

5.4.   *"My Expectation was ... You'd have the Content Dumped in to You"*

More broadly, over and above the information about specific tasks, many participants subsequently came to feel that they had not been in a position to assimilate information rapidly about a learning approach that, with its emphasis on self-directedness and collaboration, was both unfamiliar and unexpected. Unused to taking a self-directed, reflexive approach to learning, they needed time and ongoing support to come to a clearer understanding of the learning approach and its implications. As Jonathon later explained: *"I didn't pick up what the model was at the start, didn't pay enough attention to it* [my]*expectation was that it was a course and you'd have the content dumped in to you . . . in the early weeks I was still expecting delivery of course content coming my way"* (P29:RC).

Participants' expectations about learning may have contributed to misconceptions about aspects of the learning design with which they felt more familiar. This was suggested by early responses to the Resource Base and to the reading and resource discovery tasks, the importance of which, in relation to other tasks, tended to be over-estimated. Some participants approached the items in the Resource Base—beyond those that were marked as 'essential'—as an indicative list, and saw its wide scope as a positive feature. As Teresa later put it, *"I didn't feel oh God I've got to wade my way through this lot, I didn't treat it like that"* (P15:RC). Her perspective matched my own intentions and expectations. However, the perception that there was a very strong emphasis on reading on the course was common, especially at an early stage when Julia's experience was widely shared: *"To begin with I was quite worried about keeping up with it all and feeling I'd have to read everything that was recommended"* (P16:RC). Charlotte later described herself as having been *"entrenched"* (P13:RC) to begin with in the same view, suggesting that this resulted from expectations derived from prior learning experiences. Moreover, as with other aspects of the learning design, not all participants were in a position readily to attend to, or assimilate, the guidance that was offered about this issue. Emma later explained that, *"*[Later on] *I was trying to read everything and several people said, well you shouldn't have done that, you should have been picking up what was relevant and of interest and not trying to do it all. But* [early on] *I wasn't sure what was expected of me, even though I'm sure you said so, I hadn't picked it up and I was trying to do everything"* *(P5:RC).*

As the course progressed, most participants found that their awareness and understanding of the various features of the learning design and its underpinning philosophy increased. With the failure of the plenary thread to encourage questions and discussion on learning issues at an early stage, and as individual participants expressed confusions and raised questions on a one-to-one basis with tutors or in learning sets, my own awareness of the developmental nature of the learning orientation process, and the importance of exploring learning issues with participants in an integrated way, alongside their activities as time went on, also increased. I also became more aware of the value of the small-group forums, as opposed to the plenary forum, in this respect.

The process of learning orientation, and in particular its second stage, therefore took place over time for many participants, facilitated by experiential engagement with learning tasks and resources, and by ongoing dialogue with both tutors and peers along the way. Thus, Julia describes how her awareness of the principles underpinning the learning design developed through involvement in learning activities and discussion: *"I think over the time you sort of developed the impression it was for you to decide which way you wanted the course to go, which I think was the aim really . . . because it was really a learning experience aimed at you rather than an examined course"* (P16:RC).

As this happened, initial perceptions of the learning design frequently changed. An approach that was at first perceived as complex and confusing came to be perceived as a coherent whole; as Siobhan put it, *"all completely integrated, there was a unity"* (P11:RC).

Nevertheless, the process of learning orientation was still ongoing as the course was coming to an end. For example, it was not until late in the course that Helen felt she came to understand the role tutors were aiming to play in support of self-directed learning: *"I realized that was your job to support us, and you'd told us often enough, but until* [then] *I don't think I really appreciated it"* (P3:RC). At a similar point, Jonathon remarked that he had only recently *"started to see how the whole course was meant to hang together . . . all that stuff about reflective practice, constructivist knowledge and active learning is beginning to make (some kind of) sense!"* (P29). Looking back after the course had finished, he confirmed that, *"It took me a long time into the course before I picked up on [the intended design] . . . it wasn't until around about [Unit 5] that I went back and read a lot of the early stuff, and I thought blimey, that's what we're doing!"* (P29:RC).

6.   Practical Implications: Supporting Orientation

The case study points to a range of issues related to the practice of networked learning design and facilitation, including, perhaps, the limits of design in a networked environment (Jones, 2002). But it draws attention in particular to the question of supporting orientation to networked learning. From an evaluation perspective, questions that arise are: how effective was this particular instance of networked learning design and implementation in this respect, and how might it have been improved?

In post-course questionnaire feedback most participants evaluated the first Unit positively—many very positively—in terms of providing an introduction to the course and its environment. The design and usability of the website and the CMC tools were highly rated. As illustrated above, most found it relatively unproblematic at an early stage to gain a clear overview of the course's learning environment and resources, and to navigate the space confidently. The quality of the technical support that was provided as an integral part of the tutoring team was widely considered to be a particularly positive feature of support for orientation within the learning space during the early weeks and beyond.

A rather less positive picture emerges in relation to orientation within the course's information environment and, especially, in relation to its learning design and approach. As the case study shows, participants often experienced a level of information anxiety and disorientation at the start of the course, and in engaging with information resources could become distracted from other aspects of the learning design. Re-orientation within the information landscape occurred over time, as participants explored what was 'out there' and came to judgements about the quality and relevance of the resources they encountered in relation to their learning purposes. At the same time, it is evident that participants did not always engage with early information, guidance and discussion about the various aspects of the learning design, and that coming to a deeper, critical understanding of the learning approach and its personal and practical implications was a developmental process for most, rather than a 'once and for all' event right at the start, facilitated by reflexive engagement in course activities and opportunities for ongoing dialogue with peers and tutors. Other research confirms that adjusting to the emphasis on self-directedness, reflexivity and collaboration in networked learning can represent a significant challenge to personal assumptions about the learning process, the self as a learner, and the roles of peers and tutors, as well as entailing the development of new skills (e.g. McConnell, 2000).

The developmental implications for learners of constructivist and critical pedagogical strategies are well known, and progression from disorientation to reorientation through 'praxis'—that is, through critically reflective action that generates personal, practical knowledge about learning—is recognized as part of the experience of becoming a 'constructivist' learner (e.g. Brookfield, 1986). In my approach to planning and facilitating this course, my intention was to take account of these considerations. A key aim during Unit 1 was to bring the learning model to the fore, and thereafter to encourage participants to revisit learning issues periodically, on both an individual and a collective basis. Participants' views on the effectiveness of support for learning orientation differed in the light of individual experiences; as the case study shows, there was considerable variation in perceptions of, and responses to, the course approach, arising at least in part from variation in participants' assumptions and expectations about learning. However, there was broad consensus that the strategies adopted for supporting learning orientation, especially in the early weeks, had only been partially successful. In particular, a need was identified for stronger emphasis on introducing key features of the learning design and approach at an early stage. Weaknesses also were identified in relation to supporting orientation to the information environment. The points that follow briefly highlight some of the practical evaluation points that emerged from the research in four broad areas of pedagogic design and practice.

6.1.   *Task Design*

Task specification at the start of the course in relation to consideration of learning issues might usefully have been more tightly structured, thereby sharpening the focus on learning orientation. The 'concerns and interests' task in Unit 1 was intended to provide early support for orientation, linked with the use of a 'general issues' plenary forum for discussion of learning issues. However, a less open-ended approach to considering learning issues at this stage—that is, through the use of a task requiring more than personal reflection and optional input to open discussion—might have been more productive; this might, for example, have been achieved through a requirement to produce an entry in personal learning portfolios, or to produce collaborative output within learning sets. At the same time, the emphasis on the use of the plenary conferencing forum meant that participants were expected to engage in a very public form of dialogue that, as the case study shows, many found daunting. The early focus on learning issues therefore might have taken place more effectively in small groups, led by learning set tutors, thereby setting the scene for further, ongoing discussion about learning issues in sets. Reducing the emphasis on plenary discussion at an early stage in favour of small group activity also would have supported orientation (and perhaps encouraged commitment) to the collaborative learning aspect of the course more rapidly than was the case.

Task complexity also was an issue at the start of the course. Being asked to carry out a number of tasks in parallel distracted attention from tasks intended to support learning orientation, and contributed to confusion about how to organize personal learning activity. Evaluation suggested that the focus on learning issues could have been distinguished more clearly from other introductory activities, perhaps as part of a more extended induction period during which there also would have been plenty of time for exploring the learning space fully. In this context, it was suggested that recommended readings in the introductory Unit could have been limited to items concerned with orientation.

Ongoing support for experiential learning, in the form of both informal opportunities and more structured tasks to encourage reflection and discussion about experiences of networked learning, proved especially effective in support of learning orientation, and could have been further strengthened. For example, 'closing rounds' at the end of each Unit offered a framework for ongoing reflection on, and discussion of, experiences of learning on the course, and were successful in stimulating interaction on issues related to the learning design and approach. However, as the course progressed, I became increasingly aware of the potential to adopt a more structured approach to following-up on learning orientation issues raised in course documentation and arising out of learning experiences, using the experiential learning cycle as a design framework within the context of periodic review phases and/or learning journals and portfolios. Other networked learning practitioners have reached similar conclusions; for example, Tallman and Benson (2000, p. 221) recommend that networked learners will "benefit from periods of reflection on their mental models of personal learning, with the goal of recognizing their needs and working toward satisfying those needs"—noting that, "at a minimum, such recognition could result in a reduction in the frustration that some students feel in online classes".

6.2.   Socio-Technical Design

More use of synchronous CMC tools early on in the course might have supported orientation more effectively, in terms of encouraging discussion between peers and tutors on orientation issues. A MOO environment (supporting synchronous, text-based communication) was introduced later in the course with very positive effects in terms of communication and socialization.

6.3.   Information Design and Resources

Information overload and anxiety were problems in the early stages of the course, and there were misconceptions about the role of reading within the learning design. Exposure to fewer pre-identified resources initially might have been helpful as part of a step-by-step process towards orientation within the broad 'information landscape' of relevance to the course. Possible strategies, as suggested by participants in evaluation discussions, might have been to defer the introduction to the full Resource Base until the second Unit, or to build up its scope incrementally during the course, perhaps collaboratively, as part of participants' independent information-seeking activity. Laurillard's (2002, p. 122) comment that "[learners] need to be protected from the tyranny of choice offered by the web" seems salient here.

6.4.   Tutoring

The research confirmed the importance of the online tutor's role in relation to each of the three dimensions of orientation. At the outset and as the course progressed, tutors supported orientation by providing clarification and guidance on technical and information resource issues, and by initiating and participating in discussion of aspects of the learning design and approach about which participants were unsure or unconvinced. However, participants' confusions or concerns in relation to learning design and approach were less likely than technical or information concerns to be voiced in public forums, and without opportunities for small group or one-to-one interaction, could be missed by tutors. At the same time, some participants did not rapidly become aware of, or engage with, early guidance about the learning design, either in the form of course documentation or plenary and small-group discussion. Evaluation feedback confirmed that there had been a need for more intensive, personal contact with tutors in the early stages of the programme in particular to monitor their awareness of specific facilities and resources at their disposal in the learning space, and to initiate discussion about learning issues and concerns.

7.   Concluding Remarks

Learning experiences are situated in particular contexts of social action. In developing educational and learning support practice within the networked environment, we need to gain a holistic understanding of our learners' experiences and the effects on them of the ways in which we design and support learning in this context. In this chapter, I have aimed to share something of my own learning, through practice-based inquiry, about key dimensions of learners' experiences on a networked learning course and about the impact of aspects of my own practice. I have pointed to some implications in terms of the development of my own practical knowledge, or 'living' theory, about support for networked learning. Whilst action research is of necessity highly context-specific, the findings of this project may point to more general considerations for networked learning design and facilitation, and be relevant to practitioners with similar purposes, especially in terms of implications for support for 'learning to learn'.

The action research approach to developing new practice may also be of relevance to information specialists in their new roles in learning support. In the changing educational environment, library and information professionals are working increasingly closely with colleagues from different professional backgrounds—including learning technologists, information technologists, educational developers, skills support specialists as well as academic staff—on the development, delivery and support of new modes of blended and distributed learning. As they become more involved in designing, developing and supporting eLearning, for example in the information design aspects of networked environments and as information literacy educators, practice-based research approaches of the type described in this paper potentially offer valuable opportunities for exploring learners' interactions with digital learning and information resources within specific educational contexts. They also offer a framework both for the development and dissemination of good practice, and for the important contribution that these professionals potentially have to make, alongside other practitioners, as "co-researchers in the pedagogy of online scholarship" (Laurillard, 2001).

Acknowledgements

I would like to thank course participants for their involvement in this research, and colleagues (including course tutors and others) for their support during the process.

References

Brookfield, S. D. (1986). *Understanding and facilitating adult learning.* Milton Keynes: Open University Press.

Carr, W., & Kemmis, S. (1986). *Becoming critical: Knowing through action research.* London: Falmer Press.

Goodyear, P. (2002). Psychological foundations for networked learning. In C. Steeples & C. Jones (Eds.). *Networked learning: Perspectives and issues* (pp. 49–75). London: Springer Verlag.

Guba, E. G., & Lincoln, Y. S. (1989). *Fourth generation evaluation.* London: Sage.

Jones, C. (2002). Situation, learning and design: contexts for educational use of computer networks. In A. Williamson, C. Gunn, A. Young & T. Clear (Eds.). *Winds of change in the sea of learning* (pp. 309–318). Proceedings of the 19th annual Australian Society for Computers in Learning in Tertiary Education 2002 conference, UNITEC Institute of Technology, Auckland, New Zealand, 8–11 December. Retrieved January 24, 2005, from http://www.unitec.co.nz/ascilite/proceedings/papers/101.pdf

Laurillard, D. (2001). Supporting the development of scholarship skills through the online digital library. Paper presented at SCONUL Autumn Conference, November 2001. British Library, London. Retrieved January 24, 2005, from http://www.sconul.ac.uk/event_conf/egm2001/Laurillard.ppt

Laurillard, D. (2002). *Rethinking university teaching: A conversational framework for the use of educational technologies.* (2nd ed.). London: RoutledgeFalmer.

Levy, P. (2003). A methodological framework for practice-based research in networked learning. *Instructional Science, 31,* 787–109.

Lincoln, Y. S. (2001). Engaging sympathies: relationships between action research and social constructivism. In P. Reason & H. Bradbury (Eds.). *Handbook of action research: participative inquiry and practice* (pp. 124–132). London: Sage.

McConnell, D. (2000). *Implementing computer-supported co-operative learning* (2nd ed.). London: Kogan Page.

McNiff, J., Lomax, P., & Whitehead, J. (1996). *You and your action research project.* London: Routledge.

Salmon, G. (2000). *E-moderating: The key to teaching and learning online.* London: Kogan Page.

Tallman, J., & Benson, A. (2000). Mental models and web-based learning: examining the change in personal learning models of graduate students enrolled in an online library media course. *Journal of Education for Library and Information Science, 41*(3), 207–223.

PART TWO

FOCUS ON DIGITAL PUBLISHING AND ELECTRONIC CONTENT

Chapter 7

TRENDS IN ELECTRONIC PUBLISHING

Chennupati K. Ramaiah, Schubert Foo and Heng Poh Choo

1.   Chapter Overview

The parallel development of information and communication technologies, and the pervasiveness of electronic information fuelled by the Internet, has provided electronic publishing with new explosive growth opportunities. Electronic publishing (EP), from its initial mainly text-based stand-alone publication base, is fast transforming into a resource set of interactive publications endowed with rich multimedia that can be packaged in many ways and disseminated in various forms across different networked environments. The whole publishing chain is changing as the distinction between author, publisher, reader or user, and library are being blurred.

The fast changing landscape in EP has resulted in many issues that need to be addressed, developments that are worthy of mention, and emerging trends that need to be understood. These include tracing the development from print to EP; various publishing models for eContent; various distribution models for eContent; emerging and defacto document formats and file formats used in EP; new file sharing technologies for EP; authoring and reading eContent; policies and legislation; combating piracy and concept of fair use; EP business models; growth and impact of the EP market in both developed and developing countries; and the latest EP trends and future technologies.

This list is by no means exhaustive. It is intended to highlight several pertinent areas of EP development. This chapter attempts to cover and summarize a number of these areas by highlighting contributions along these various aspects, thereby providing an up-to-date overview of EP. They not only reflect new EP developments and research trends but also reflect the continuation of this body of rich EP literature from the past.

H. S. Ching, P. W. T. Poon and C. McNaught (Eds.), eLearning and Digital Publishing, 111–131.

2.   The Potential of Electronic Publishing

Electronic publishing (EP) refers to the application of computing software by a publisher to information content created and packaged for a specific audience, and the distribution of the final product through electronic means. As such, publishing is an integrated process aimed at providing information in different quantities and with different qualities to different categories of end-users.

Initially, ePublications were stand-alone publications distributed through storage media such as diskettes and CD-ROM. Later, ePublications became multi-dimensional when multimedia technologies enabled sounds, moving images and occasionally even smell to be incorporated. Advances made in networking technologies has resulted in EP increasingly being used to refer to information content distributed over network environments such as the Internet (Ludwick & Glazer, 2000; Burk, 2001). EP can therefore be categorized broadly into offline and online publishing. Offline publishing utilizes different types of storage and delivery media such as CD-ROM, CD-I, DVD, memory card, and diskettes, while online publishing uses communication networks such as the Internet, intranets and extranets as the delivery platforms. Many types of ePublications exist. These include all kinds of information resources, educational aids, games and other kinds of entertainment products.

Electronic and networked information creation and dissemination has created new opportunities for the distribution of the information products and new varieties in the kind of information that could be made available. The whole publishing chain is changing and the distinctions between author, publisher, reader or user, and library are being blurred (Peek, 1994). With the advent of the World Wide Web and its transformation into a graphical medium, new possibilities for EP were created.

ePublications offer the potential of enhancing information with additional dimensions in a cost-effective way and thus enabling the information to reach a wider audience of users compared to paper-based print publications (pPublications). EP offers a number of advantages and benefits to publishers, readers and users, libraries and organizations. Publishers can potentially: benefit from decrease in publication costs, increase the amount of information that can be included in a publication, and implement new approaches to the organization and presentation of information. Users are given the opportunity and ability to interact, customize and create individual pathways and information layers; include simulations and experiments; and to visualize the impact of full-colour figures and video.

The major information owners and providers that engage in EP are commercial publishers, corporate organizations, government organizations and information publishers. Commercial publishers are concerned with creating a marketplace for EP products and devising viable business models for the new medium. This is closely linked with the concept of value-added publishing, whereby the expertise and experience of publishers are put to good use to package and produce electronic information products that suit the targeted users' needs. Corporate organizations have developed EP technology solutions for the efficient management of information as a functional aspect of a core business. This in turn enhances the bottom-line of these organizations. Typical applications are technical documentation, in-house publications and product description brochures. Government organizations have adopted EP technologies as the better management of information can improve the efficiency of the bureaucracy and support decision-makers' need for sufficient information. Information publishers such as financial information services and bibliographic database services have a long history in EP due to the demand for market information that is volume-dependent or time-dependent. Finally, the academic and research community benefits from EP through cost reduction and functionality enhancement through machine search and retrieval capabilities.

3. Developments in EP

Until recently, the only means of publication was through the medium of printing and paper distribution. The high cost involved in paper publications meant only written work that is able to appeal to a fairly large audience was published due to the economics of print runs and first copy costs. The cost of pPublishing and the associated distribution and marketing costs also meant authors had no other viable alternative to relying on professional publishers to publish their work. The developments in information technology since the early 1990s offered the possibility of online communication and electronic distribution of research findings more cheaply, timely and equitably than pPublications. At this point the academic and scientific community was ready to embrace and experiment with the new medium.

3.1. *Publishing Models of eContent*

EP is a very broad term that includes a variety of different publishing models, including digital content or shorter length content, electronic books (eBooks), electronic newspapers (eNewspapers), electronic magazines (eZines), eJournals, email publishing, database publishing and courseware publishing. These models are different with each of them having its own set of distinguishing characteristics, features and functions.

Digital content generally refers to the electronic delivery of fiction that is shorter than book-length, non-fiction documents and other written works of shorter length. Publishers of digital content deliver shorter-sized works to the consumer via download to handheld and other wireless devices.

eBooks are electronic versions of books that are delivered to consumers in digital formats. The potential market for eBooks and shorter length digital content is large; widespread acceptance and usage is expected with the ability to download rich multimedia content eBooks directly from the Internet (Rao, 2004).

eNewspapers are the online accompaniments of established newspapers where news articles and the latest updates are published on the web. The paper version from the printing press is still the mainstay but the electronic version is where the most up-to-date developments are found.

eZines are equivalent to eNewspapers but published by established print magazine publishers. Many magazine titles such as The Economist, Times, National Geographic, and so on, have also established online websites. On the other hand, there are others that exist solely as electronic entities such as ZDNet (http://www.zdnet.com), Slate (http://slate.msn.com), and others. There are also not-for-profit, self-publishing eZines that first appeared as text-only publications distributed via email, Usenet and Gopher servers (McHugh, 1996).

eJournals are electronic versions of journals, publications used extensively by the scientific and academic community to disseminate research findings. The online medium can facilitate the anonymous peer refereeing process. The prospect of interactive publications with peer commentaries and spontaneous refereeing options can be explored because of the online medium ability to publish timely critiques of fellow scholars and researchers (Harnad, 1996; Ashcroft, 2002).

Email publishing or newsletter publishing is a growing medium due to the ease of delivery and production of email newsletters and its popularity among readers for the ease of receipt. A variety of formats, styles and topics are evident among the large number of email newsletters, mailing lists and discussion lists available. Some email newsletters are similar to printed newsletters or mini-magazines, functioning like small eZines, which are delivered to subscribing readers. Some email mailing lists are discussion lists that resemble an ongoing virtual conversation with messages delivered to all the subscribers.

Database publishing requires information contents to be stored as document components in databases. These document components could then be reused for the production of new publishing products when the databases are queried by the publishing system to extract and combine information to produce professional looking documents. Database publishing tools allows selected fields to be applied with particular styles and printed. Such tools are invaluable for publishing catalogues that require regular updating, for example the yellow pages, directories and catalogues of parts.

Courseware publishing refers to publishers reusing information content in databases to create customized texts for particular audiences. An early example of courseware publishing systems is McGraw-Hill's Primis (Lynch, 1994), a dynamic information database designed to meet the individual course needs of teachers and professors at all levels of education. Top professional societies like IEEE and ACM also use courseware publishing to provide electronic contents to students who cannot afford the price of the printed periodicals or textbooks.

3.2.   Distribution Models for eContent

As in the many forms of eContent, the concept of EP embodies a variety of different distribution models, including Internet bookshops, digital publishing on print-on-demand basis (POD), direct publishing on the web and wireless Internet publishing on wireless/mobile handheld devices.

Internet bookshops, such as Amazon.com and barnesandnoble.com can offer up to 40% discounts off the cover price of a book to customers due to having distribution costs which are lower than a conventional book chain. Of course, costs such as postal charges and overhead costs still exist (Vitiello, 2001).

Print-on-demand (POD) publications are hybrid publications that reside in cyber space until they are printed on special digital printing machines (Vitiello, 2001; Jensen, 1998). POD book production process can now be done on a fully automated vending machine shortly after an order is placed on the Internet (Rose, 2001). The POD model is especially useful for publications in minor languages, academic publishing which is a relatively small market, and non-commercial content. However, POD is still a method that uses paper and so cannot be delivered as cheaply and quickly as eBooks.

Direct publishing on the web: HTML is still the most widely used web programming language but XML is making headway and is regarded as the future direction of the Internet. XML is useful because it allows publishers to create content and data that is portable to other devices, such as handheld reading devices. Developments such as Britannica's system of content distribution on a subscription model is making publishing more similar to television broadcasting than to traditional publishing (Vitiello, 2001).

Wireless Internet/web publishing: Wireless Internet publishing opens another avenue for the distribution of time-sensitive and compact content. This form of publishing relies on the widespread availability and continuing growth of mobile phones, PDAs and other wireless devices; these now have multimedia capabilities, including the ability to retrieve email and access information from the Internet. Wireless Internet publishing focuses on the provision of information content and value-added services in demand by wireless users who are on the move, namely the delivery of timely information and the ability to conduct transactions and inquiries with pinpoint information access from a small screen.

4.   Production of eContent

The decision about which format to adopt is closely related to the issue of access to content authoring and reading. Access to content and software development tools is important for the growth of ePublishing and eBooks as this allows traditional publishers, ePublishers and self-publishers to generate and sell content. Some companies choose to make the authoring tools freely available to encourage adoption and usage of corresponding reading devices or eBook file formats while others choose not to support the easy creation of content due to piracy concerns and business models that focus on selling content to readers.

eBook reading devices are potentially very useful for in-the-field situations but their adoption is affected by issues such as the current pricing of electronic content and eBook reading devices. For example, Anderson (2001) found that potential users were put off by high prices of reading devices and felt that an eBook should not cost more than a paperback. The fact that commercial electronic titles are usually restricted to specific reader hardware is another hindrance (Quan, 2000). There are basically three types of reading devices: dedicated hardware devices, multi-purpose PDA type devices, and desktop or laptop PCs. A Seybold survey at the turn of the century (Runne, 2001) listed readers' preferred reading platforms for eBooks and ePublications as, firstly, desktops or laptop PCs, followed by dedicated hardware reading devices (when these are readily available) and lastly, multi-purpose PDA type devices. The situation has not changed in recent years.

4.1.   New File-sharing Technologies for EP

New file-sharing technologies provide new ways and alternatives for distributing information without relying on expensive centralized web servers. These systems could make the Internet even more immune to government censorship and promote self-publishing to a greater extent by making it possible for anyone with a computer and an Internet connection to publish a document electronically without the need for a web server or a central catalogue. From the point of view of publishers, these systems are the enablers of unlimited content piracy. The future of peer-to-peer (P2P) file-sharing is intertwined with copyright law as copyright owners are targeting both makers of file-sharing clients like Napster and Scour, and providers of products that rely on or add value to public P2P networks, such as MP3Board.com and its web-based search interface for the Gnutella network.

4.2.   *Document and File Formats*

There are a number of proprietary and open standard document formats currently being used for ePublication. Each of these has a different approach to document layout and document content. Document layout refers to the original design of a document that gives a publication a distinctive look and feel, while document content refers to the actual information contained in the document. The different types of document format can be classified broadly into three categories, namely, content-only formats, layout-oriented formats and mark-up formats (Miller, 1996). Often, eBook formats are specific to each particular reading system with content creation and viewing restricted to the usage of particular software(s) and hardware(s) (Gandhi, 2000), limiting the success of eBooks (Harrison, 2000). The different file formats for eBooks could be classified broadly into three categories, namely, OEB compliant formats, proprietary formats, and hardware specific formats (Randolph, 2001).

5.   Policies and Legislation

Access to information is the new frontier for legislators and policy makers of the information society. On one hand, it is important that the protection and enforcing of intellectual property rights in the electronic environment is addressed adequately by legislation. On the other hand, it is equally important to protect and ensure that there is free flow and access to information in the electronic environment in order to facilitate the course of education, scholarship, free rights to comment on current issues, or for other societal goals (Vitiello, 2001). In general, there is a need to balance the rights of content providers or owners with the rights of content users so that users are not unfairly disadvantaged in the electronic environment (Stefano, 2000).

5.1.   *Content Users' Rights in Licensing Agreements*

Licences are negotiated between the copyright owner (the licensor) and the organization that wishes to exploit the material (the licensee). Among the different types of arrangements are: selling the work up front to the user, the user buying a subscription for an unlimited number of uses without ownership, the user paying for each use of copyright-protected works, or the user paying for use of a work at a particular site.

Publishers are experimenting with these different business models to secure payment before reading and thus there are changes in the way information is sold and owned, with serious implications such as the difference between pBooks and eBooks ownership. For example, a reader could buy a paper copy novel and then lend it to her friends or give it away. However, she is unable to do so when she buys an encrypted title from Barnes & Noble as no one else can read it unless she lend her friends her laptop or PC also. Another example is when a reader pays a subscription to a website for accessing and reading online. When he stops paying the subscription, he loses all access to the content, although when he stopped subscribing to a printed magazine, he still had the old back issues.

The displeasure of readers and users might force publishers and distributors to rethink the ways they use technology to deliver content but there is also a need for governments to put in place legislation that protect the rights of consumers to information and content that they have purchased and paid for.

5.2.   *Legitimate Users' Rights in Copy Protection*

Publishers and authors have been using copyright and the courts to protect their print investment and are relying on the same concept to protect ePublications and works. This is problematic as copy protection is more like putting a lock on each copy then selling a key with each locked eBook. The attempt to equate intellectual properties with tangible properties or rights on tangible properties is too limiting and cumbersome, generating legal expenses and causing annoyance to legitimate users.

Established precedents and code of practice that do not short-change users have evolved after each introduction of a new technology such as the printing press, photocopiers, cassette tapes, video tapes, etc. The same needs to be established for the online environment and electronic content (Lagenberg, 2000). Governments need to put in place legislation that determine the nature and manner of intellectual property rights copy protection which address the legitimate concerns of readers and users and do not hamper the conduct of easy searching and collating of information.

5.3.   *The Concept of Fair Use*

The concept of fair use permits copying or excerpting of copyrighted material in the course of education, scholarship, commentary, advancing learning or for other societal goals (Harper, 2001; Besek, 2003). It has been said that the principle of public access can only be safeguarded and not limited by the exclusive rights given to authors and producers when the existing practices in libraries are also valid in the electronic environment. This is the underlying framework on which the Council of Europe/ EBLIDA Guidelines on Library Legislation and Policy in Europe suggested that "Governments should establish a legal position for libraries in copyright and neighbouring rights" (art. 9.i) and that "copyright exemptions that apply to printed materials should, as far as possible, also apply to digital materials" (art. 9.ii). Governments are making attempts to do this to a certain extent but issues such as distance learning usage and inter-library loans have not been not addressed because of a lack of consensus (Henry, 2003).

The 1998 Digital Millennium Copyright Act (DMCA) anti-circumvention clause (section 1201), which prohibits the creation and distribution of methods for getting around copyright controls, has raised public concerns about the adverse impact on fair use and other copyright exceptions (Cave, 2001). The anti-circumvention clause has already been used to indict the Russian programmer Dmitry Sklyarov for explaining, in a publicly presented technical paper based on PhD research, how one eBook encryption system works. An online magazine has also been prohibited from posting or even linking to DeCSS, a program that decrypts DVDs and allows the digital videos to be watched on computers running the Linux operating system (Cave, 2001). Such developments are disturbing because there is no room for fair use and the rights of legitimate users such as owners who would want to watch their purchased DVD on their PCs.

In general, governments should regulate the application of copyright provisions in libraries and other educational and cultural institutions in order to ensure the general public, scholars and students can have free access to electronic copyright content. It is important to continue the tradition of making knowledge (in all forms or mediums) universally accessible to all members of society. This is especially needed in this digital age with a widening income range and the digital divide determining who are the haves and have-nots in society (Hundley *et al.*, 2000; Clark, 1996).

5.4. *The Scope of Legal Deposits and Public Access*

Legal deposits have been legislated and established for printed documents and have been extended to audio-visual documents, films, microfilms and other categories of non-print materials. The same should be done for ePublications. Many websites that provide valuable information move or delete information (or parts of it) when it is no longer current. As it is, many articles make reference to ePublications that do not exist anymore (Anderson, 2004; Bolman, 2003; Booth, 2004; King, 2004). The deposit of ePublications is needed to ensure the availability of electronic communication.

However, the mere act of depositing would be meaningless if the public does not have access to these materials. Legal deposits legislation should cater for the public to be allowed access to deposited electronic materials, for example, having unrestricted local access to ePublications at public institutions. Since national repositories assume the burden of maintaining full deposited collections, remote access could be selective.

6.   Business Models for EP and Growth of the EP Market

The development of eCommerce and ePublishing on the web requires the development of viable business models. So far, three basic business models have emerged in the form of selling space, selling subscriptions and selling goods or services. Selling space, or space sales on the web are similar to a conventional advertisement but with the addition of a 'link' that allows customers to click and go to the advertiser's own site for more information or further interactions. The web is important to advertisers because it offers them the potential to target their sales pitch on the group of users or consumers who are most likely to purchase their products or services. Subscription sales usually offer some 'teaser information' to the web audience while restricting access to the core of the site to users who have already registered and or subscribed to the site's services. In the last category of selling goods or services, product and services sales are sought by eRetailers through the concept of Internet shopping and by providers of financial information, such as Dun and Bradstreet. It is common to find a combination of the three basic business models being employed to generate revenue streams from ePublications.

With the use of such business models (Carpenter, Joseph & Waltha, 2004), we have seen a steady growth of ePublishers in the market. It has been estimated that fewer than 1% of the manuscripts sent to New York print publishers are published (Ludwick & Glazer, 2000). This means that there is a huge supply of potentially high quality original electronic literature waiting to be published by ePublishers. Top ePublishers like Hard Shell Word Factory, Online Originals, DiskUs Publishing, Dead End Street Publications and the Internet Book Company are able to offer book lists in a range of genres including romance, science fiction or fantasy, Westerns, mysteries, horror and thrillers titles. Niche ePublishing is another development with companies selling eBooks in genres as specific as short science fiction (FictionWise), Christian social commentary (Xulon Press), graphic novels (Duck Soup Productions) and fiction by women (DLSIJ Press).

Major trade publishers such as Simon & Schuster, Random House, Penguin Putnam, Harper Collins, St. Martin's Press and Time Warner Trade Books are issuing more of their front lists in electronic form. With Stephen King's *Riding the bullet* in March 2000, Simon & Schuster became the first New York publisher to release a work by a best-selling author exclusively in eBook form. Simon & Schuster followed up in June 2000 with *The class of 2000*, an eBook-only supplement to a CBS News broadcast about the experiences and attitudes of graduating high-school students. Simon & Schuster later launched a new electronic-only series of Star Trek novels.

Time Warner launched iPublish.com, the company's ePublishing arm in 2000; it has steadily grown since that time. Environments where customers can download published eBooks and eAuthors can submit and discuss their own work are likely to build a loyal online community of readers and writers.

Random House launched its own electronic imprint, @Random, in 2000 and shook up the industry by offering a 50% royalty on net revenues to eBook authors, creating a way for niche websites to sell Random House eBooks directly, thus exposing the publisher's traditional book selling partners to competition. @Random imprint has since stopped but Random House is still committed to eBooks and intends to continue distributing eBooks among its other imprints. Major publishers are expected to continue experimenting with new eBook business models as they compete with booksellers, electronic-only publishers, and self-publishing authors for direct access to readers.

7.   The Impact of EP

The introduction and adoption of EP in recent years have made tremendous impact on various constituent groups including publishers, retailers and readers (Jantz, 2001). Rawlins (1997) highlighted the difficulties commonly faced by all publishers in the pre-EP era and the impact of today's EP in the publishing industry. Publishing is a difficult business as the economics of paper printing and distribution means titles have to be produced in large print runs to be profitable but there is no guarantee that a book will sell its print run. Large print runs tie up capital in a product for a long time, leaving less capital to buy new titles or to promote current ones. Other related costs are: warehousing, transportation, salaries, delay times, backordering, competing for scarce outlet shelf space, overestimating demand and having to destroy the remainder, underestimating demand and having to lose business or annoy customers, and writing off depreciation in capital due to decay or obsolescence. Publishers allow retailers to return unsold copies in order to encourage retailers to carry their titles; however, sometimes as much as half of a mass-market fiction print run of 500,000 copies is returned.

With the introduction of EP and electronic distribution, outlets will no longer have to keep as many copies of each title as they think they can sell; they only need one copy or a few copies for promotional use. This can increase the diversity of titles that outlets can offer. Eventually, distribution costs to publishers might be negligible since the retail model has shifted from publishers supplying products to readers acquiring products. Additionally, publishers would not lose revenue to used-textbook stores as the most recent version could be instantly and cheaply available to students.

Moving into eBooks and electronic distribution on demand eliminates printing and its costly consequences. Production would involve only editing, reviewing and developing acceptable projects. Printing and distribution costs would be very much reduced, allowing more resources for acquisition and marketing. Publishers in the subscription scheme would also have large stable incomes over a period of years, making it easier to attract venture capital for start-up or expansion, to plan and to reduce risk.

As for retailers, the electronic media allows retailers to choose from a melange of distribution schemes to reduce risk and increase profit. For example, bookstores might have half their stock as compact discs, thereby increasing shelf space for more titles to be displayed. eBooks are more flexible than paper books and this quality might attract more customers to retailers. For readers not comfortable with browsing electronic systems, there will always be bookstores similar to those existing today to serve them. However, these bookstores could carry hundreds more titles than they carry today because they would need only one copy of each. Customers could browse through the copy as they do today and then have an electronic copy delivered to them when they decide to buy the publication.

With eBooks, readers could have instant and online access. Readers could also have instant updates and revisions and electronic contact with all the other readers of a book, thereby sharing ideas and reactions more rapidly and with more people. eBooks also need not go out of print and might be cheaper and less bulky than paper books. Instead of several expensive books, thousands of books could be stored on one small and light memory device.

eBooks could contain electronic bookmarks and cross-referencing. They can have all the advantages of paper books such as handwritten annotation, highlighting with coloured markers, underlining, post-it notes and bookmarks through software on small portable pen-based computers. Unlike pBooks, eBooks can be multimedia and thus aid the blind, sight-impaired, illiterate or busy users. eBooks could also be customized for their readers and need not be an exact copy. eBooks would become increasingly lifestyle-targeted with the global information economy and the corresponding increased knowledge of consumer tastes and competition (Bar-Ilan, Peritz & Wolman, 2003; Cochenour & Moothart, 2003).

8.   EP Trends in Developed and Developing Countries

Developed countries have been in the forefront of EP developments and much has been done, studied and written on EP. Generally, these countries are wired societies with populations of highly computer-literate and Internet-savvy citizens. EP interest is not just limited to the academic, scholarly and library communities (generally the early adopters) and is actively pursued by commercial publishers.

In a survey conducted by the UK government's Department of Trade and Industry (DTI) in 1998, UK-based publishers were then in the midst of switching to EP. In 1996, only 40% of them had electronic products but by 1998, 65% were still into EP and 82% expected to become more involved. The proportion of publishers expecting to receive revenue from eProducts has also improved from 32% in 1996 to 46% in 1998 though these figures still reflect difficulties in persuading customers to pay for ePublications. Paper-based products are still seen as having the best opportunities for growth but Internet and online publication is seen as almost as good an opportunity area, well ahead of CD-ROM. Moreover, 83% of the UK-based publishers already have an Internet presence with Internet activity being profitable for 27% of the respondents. The profitability was expected to increase to 49% of publishers by 2000. Publishers felt that customers were willing to access their products electronically and had both the equipment and the skills to do so, though they thought that customers were unwilling to pay high prices for eProducts. Part of the reason for this complaint was the high cost of maintaining parallel print and electronic versions. At the same time, there was a feeling that ePublications provide an opportunity to improve their products. Paradoxically, there was no feeling that parallel ePublication reduces the sales of the printed product, nor was the possibility of non-commercial competition, such as from Ginsparg's electronic preprint server, seen to respondents to be a significant threat. There was a consensus that the EP industry needs the collection, by government or trade associations, of better market statistics (Williams, 1999; Rowland, 1999).

In terms of the Internet being used as the delivery mechanism, 60% of the publishers thought the Internet was too slow. Almost 70% of the publishers were worried about copyright infringement, while 60.5% were concerned about unknown legal liabilities in the EP environment. There was much concern about staffing for EP. Publishers felt that there were insufficient trained staff, training costs were too high, skilled people could not be recruited at reasonable salaries and that poaching of experienced staff by competitors was a problem. There was also a feeling that senior management did not understand the EP business adequately (Williams, 1999; Rowland, 1999).

The findings from another study on the children's multimedia publishing industry in the UK found publishers who had entered into the multimedia market in the 1980s and 1990s to be facing several challenges in order to adapt to the changes in the publishing industry. It is recognized that publishers' business models must be re-engineered to adapt to the changing market conditions in the EP industry. Several factors were identified as critical to the success of publishers. The factors were modification of corporate culture, internal structures and processes, branding of the company's chosen multimedia identity, focusing on the added value element of multimedia products, promotion of organizational learning, innovation and creativity within the company and sourcing of necessary skills effectively (Anthoney, Royle & Johnson, 1999).

Nonetheless, EP still has a long way to go even in the more favourable and conducive conditions of developed countries. For example, Peurell (1999) found that POD would be a complement to the existing book market and not in competition with traditional book printing and publishing in Sweden. In Sweden, POD is a medium for non-mainstream writers, for titles that are not economically defensible for a traditional publisher to keep in stock and literature written by authors whose first language is not Swedish. The demand for POD titles is not at the expense of traditionally printed and published titles because POD titles are so specialized in nature.

Problems encountered included the need to educate and market the concept as all things concerning web publishing, POD, and how to find and purchase POD titles were still not common knowledge. There was also the need to build up a considerable list of titles to sustain interest in POD titles, and for the digitally stored backlist of classic literature to be authoritative editions that could be relied on by teachers (Peurell, 1999). POD was also seriously considered for the publication of academic literature, such as scientific reports and possibly Swedish dissertations by PhD students as the grants to students for the printing of dissertations was no longer supported by the Swedish system. Peurell contended that the POD technique needed to become much cheaper and have many more titles before it could be an alternative for the ordinary book reader. Meanwhile, POD could be utilized to keep more titles in stock, single titles that are asked for repeatedly but not in any large quantity each time, and titles of experimental fiction and poetry that have a consistent but not large readership (Peurell, 1999).

In a somewhat expected scenario, EP developments in developing countries have been hampered by technological and financial limitations so that access to ePublications is generally limited to a very small percentage of the population. EP initiatives are limited to governmental and academic circles as there is generally no commercial market for ePublications due to lack of consumer purchasing power and demand. Technological and financial limitations have prevented many developing countries from reaping the benefits of the Internet. Before EP could be given serious considerations, the technology must become available and affordable. Nonetheless, developing countries are making some progress in EP through whatever resources and expertise are available.

Upadhaya (1999) related the difficulties of establishing IT networks in countries in which the government maintained a monopoly on telecommunication facilities, such as Nepal, and how these difficulties were overcome to set up a platform for ePublishing and information sharing. This was made possible through contributions of international agencies, non-government organizations (NGOs) and volunteers contributing funds, equipment, expertise and content. This platform could then be duplicated across the country at low cost so as to establish a nationwide network of information publishing and subsequently to connect this information structure to the Internet. At the same time, the information flow could be redefined from one that is limited to producers of information from the top and accessible only to a privileged few to one that is established and accessible to all irrespective of status and background. Widespread geographical access across Nepal and access to information at grassroots' level would then allow the people to be mobilized locally to enter into the world of electronic information publishing and access.

Packer (1999) related the cooperative publishing of scientific and technical eJournals in Latin American and Caribbean countries through initiatives such as SciELO—Scientific Electronic Library Online Project (http://www.scielo.br) that has already been established in Brazil, Chile, Colombia, Cuba and Venezuela. By the end of 2004 more than 130 journals existed under the SciELO Model throughout Latin America and the Caribbean. The SciELO Model aimed at the operation of electronic libraries of scientific journals on the Internet. This is realized through the technical cooperation among national and international related organizations in order to rationalize scarce national resources in the creation and development of electronic collections. With the adoption of the SciELO Model by several Latin American and Carribean countries, regional cooperative programmes could be established.

Nechitailenko (1999) highlighted EP developments in Russia, especially online eJournals. Nonetheless, the state-of-the-art ePublications in the field of planetary geophysics developed by the Geophysical Centre RAS in cooperation with the American Geophysical Union (http://eos.wdcb.rssi.ru), the Russian counterpart of Earth Interactions (http://EarthInteractions.org), still have print-on-paper versions of the eJournals. This was due to a number of reasons, including authors' preference for paper as a basic tool for dissemination of scientific results, archiving systems that were still highly oriented towards traditional publications and copyright concerns about the lack of proven, agreed upon and reliable systems for ePublications. Nonetheless, EP was still viewed as providing new possibilities for authors, publishers and readers alike.

However, in other developing countries, EP has not been embraced. Nasser and Abouchedid (2001) found that EP has not appealed to the academic community in the Arab and Middle Eastern society and remained in a dormant state despite the many advantages of ePublishing and the fact that universities budget were highly constrained in Arab countries. In many Arab countries, including Lebanon, print was associated with authority and power (McDowall, 1983). Communities were divided explicitly by their religious identities but implicitly by technological expertise as the communities with the technological advantage of print were able to use the media for the perpetuation of their political cause and cultural traditions. Initially, it was thought that the economic, social and political crosscutting cleavages between communities in the Arab world would be bridged by equal access to technology such as the Internet. However, technology seemed to have deepened the divisions based on social and economic dimensions. There are three distinct groups in the Arab society. The first group is the rich ruling elite of the population who has become richer, allowing them to buy and use technology easily and providing them with multiple advantages in their professional lives. The second group is the poor and rural majority of the population who are completely alienated from the knowledge structures supported by technology and much in need of technological assistance in terms of hardware, software and training. The third group is the middle class population who is preoccupied with the cultural and social influences of globalization and cautions the adoption of Western technology, regarded by them as an extension of the colonial past.

The lack of priority and funding for IT can be seen in the Lebanese University, which does not subscribe to ePublications services and, in 2001, did not have its various campuses across the country connected by a network. None of its campuses had access to the Internet or the equipment to access CD-ROMs, microfiche or microfilm. The lack of basic infrastructure means there was a lack of awareness of the advantages of EP and the abundance of free journals and quality content available on the web. This lack of awareness in turn contributed to a lack of regard for eJournals and ePublications. Nasser and Abouchedid (2001) found that Arabic academics were pragmatic about the use of information technology; however, almost half felt that EP undermined academic rigour, more than 60% valued print as opposed to EP, and few have published in any form of ePublication. The lack of interest towards EP could also be attributed to the fact that many wrote in Arabic or had an indigenous approach that the web does not serve or accommodate. Moreover, the political regimes wanted to control the privileges of publishing in the Arab world and discredit any form that might compete with or supersede the current Arab model.

9.   Latest Trends and Future Technologies in EP

Recent developments in information and computing technology have enabled higher bandwidth to be made available to support online multimedia applications. Wireless networking allows online access to information and content by mobile users on the move or in the field. Cheaper and higher capacity storage technology provides a means to contain large amounts of multimedia content. Written, audio and visual works are no longer a book, a record, a film, or a television programme when transmitted through the Internet but instead they become 'content' or 'knowledge'. This is the consequence of the convergence of media forms in EP, which blurs the previous distinction among works created with different media.

EP is expected to create an environment where authors can circulate their works widely, producers can see their investments rewarded by high profits and distributors (information providers and librarians) can make cheap information widely available to all. It is estimated that the eBook market will grow to $US 2.3 billion by 2005 (Association of American Publishers, 2000), with the figure for scientific, technical and medical publications predicted to be between 20 to 30% of ePublications. However, many publications are still being produced conventionally and in conventional formats. Where electronic products do exist, they complement rather than replace print, resulting in few benefits because publishers, distributors and users must sustain both the printed and the electronic forms of production, distribution and use.

Nonetheless, producers have taken advantage of the Internet capabilities to market their content and profitably penetrated institutional markets and households. Every player in the publishing chain has benefited from the technological revolution. It is expected that by 2005, 28 million people will use electronic devices for reading eBooks (Wiesner, n.d., early 2000s). So, it is likely that eBooks will dramatically change the publishing industry in the next few years. eRetailers and publishers such as Amazon.com, Bertelsmann and Britannica.com are just some prominent examples who have managed to penetrate the market of ePublications. Meanwhile mergers and alliances are reshaping the existing information and communication industries. Some examples are the conglomerates formed by the mergers of America Online and TimeWarner, or Vivendi and Vodaphone.

eInk and ePaper is expected to be the future for EP. eInk combines the look of ink on paper with the dynamic capability of an electronic display (Sheridon, Howard & Richley, 1997; Desmarais, 2003). eInk displays are being designed for many applications, including handheld devices, outdoor billboards, eBooks and eNewspapers (McKernzie, 2001). In future, it is expected that eInk will allow almost any surface to become a display, bringing information off computer screens and into the world around us. Companies such as E-Ink, Phillips Components, Xerox and Advanced Display Systems are working on products for eInk and ePaper, though progress has not been as rapid as early enthusiasts hoped.

Current handheld devices with LCD displays are expected to be replaced by a new generation of mobile devices with eInk displays and highly graphical mobile applications using 3G technologies that are lighter, thinner, more readable and yet require much lower power consumption. Prototype eInk displays with bright paper-white backgrounds, readable in most lighting conditions, and flexible paper-thin displays have existed for some time

(McDonough, 2001); however, widespread use in commercial handheld devices has not yet occurred.

10.   Conclusions

Developments in computing, telecommunications and networking technologies have brought EP to the current stage of online delivery to users. Much experimentation and progress had been made with this form of delivery, including concepts such as eJournals, POD, eBooks, customized courseware publishing, Internet bookshops, and so on. Although many EP products are produced for display on PC or laptops, there is a move to produce EP products for dedicated reading devices and mobile devices as this area is regarded as a potentially high growth market. However, before ePublications can become as prevalent and accepted as pPublications, copyright and technical issues need to be resolved in order to allow readers or users a reading experience as good as, or better than, pPublications. Likewise, the convergence of formats and emergence of standards are essential to provide uniformity and to allow the constituents of publishers, authors and readers to adopt ePublications on a wide scale. In this respect, the development of eInk and ePaper may be important in EP's future.

References

Anderson, A. (2001). High prices stifle e-book market. Retrieved February 12, 2005, from http://www.nua.ie/surveys/index.cgi?f=VS&art_id=905356459&rel=true

Anderson, B. (2004). Open access journals. *Behavioral & Social Sciences Librarian, 22*(2), 93–99.

Anthoney, A., Royle, J., & Johnson, I. (1999). The UK children's publishing house—Adapting to change for the multimedia market. In J. Smith, A. Ardö & P. Linde (Eds.). *Electronic publishing '99. Redefining the information chain—New ways and voices* (pp. 21–30). Proceedings of an ICCC/IFIP conference held at the University of Karlskrona/Ronneby, Sweden, 10–12 May. Washington D.C.: ICCC Press.

Ashcroft, L. (2002). Issues in developing, managing and marketing electronic journals collections. *Collection Building, 21*(4), 147–154.

Association of American Publishers (2000). Your standard e-book. Retrieved February 12, 2005, from http://www.artsjournal.com/issues/epublishing.htm

Banks, Peter (2004). Open access: A medical association perspective. *Learned Publishing, 17*(2), 135–142.

Bar-Ilan, J., Peritz, B. C., & Wolman, Y. (2003). A survey on the use of electronic databases and electronic journals accessed through the web by the academic staff of Israeli universities. *The Journal of Academic Librarianship, 29*(6), 346–361.

Besek, J. M. (2003). Copyright: What makes a use 'fair'? *EDUCAUSE Review, 38*(6), 12–13. Retrieved February 12, 2005, from http://www.educause.edu/ir/library/pdf/erm0368.pdf

Bolman, P. (2003). Open access: Marginal or core phenomenon? A commercial publisher's view. *Information Services & Use, 23*(2–3), 93–98.

Booth, A. (2004). The politics of e-access and e-funding in the library environment. *Serials* *17*(3), 257–261.

Burk, R. (2001). E-book devices and the marketplace: In search of customers. *Library Hi Tech,* *19*(4), 325–331.

Carpenter, T. A., Joseph, H. & Waltha, M. (2004). A survey of business trends at BioOne Publishing partners and its implications for BioOne. *Portal: Libraries and the Academy,* *4*(4), 465–484.

Cave, D. (2001). Copywrong? Retrieved February 12, 2005, from http://www.salon.com/ tech/feature/2001/08/31/dmca_report/index.html

Clark, C. (1996). The copyright environment for the publisher in the digital world. Joint ICSU Press/UESCO Expert Conference on Electronic Publishing in Science, 19–23 February 1996. Retrieved February 12, 2005, from http://www.library.uiuc.edu/icsu/clark.htm

Cochenour, D., & Moothart, T. (2003). E-journal acceptance at Colorado State University: A case study. *Serials Review, 29*(1), 16–25.

Desmarais, N. (2003). E ink and digital paper. *Against the grain, 14*(Dec–Jan), 88–90.

Gandhi, S. (2000). E-books-the future of reading and ultimate book publishing. *Journal of Educational Technology Systems, 29*(1), 49–66.

Harnad, S. (1996). Implementing peer review on the Net: Scientific quality control in scholarly electronic journals. In R. Peek & G. Newby (Eds.). *Scholarly publishing: The electronic frontier* (pp. 103–118). Cambridge MA: MIT Press.

Harper, G. K. (2001) Copyright endurance and change. *The Journal of Electronic Publishing,* *7*(1). Retrieved January 19, 2005, from http://www.press.umich.edu/jep/07-01/harper.html

Harrison, B. I. (2000). E-books and the future of reading. *IEEE Computer Graphics and Applications, 20*(3), 32–39.

Henry, G. (2003). On-line publishing in the 21st century: Challenges and opportunities. *D-Lib Magazine, 9*(10), Retrieved February 12, 2005, from http://www.dlib.org/dlib/ october03/henry/10henry.html

Hundley, R. O., Anderson, R. H., Bikson, T. K., Dewar, J. A., Green, J. D., Libicki, M. C., & Neu, C. R. (2000). The global course of the information revolution, political, economic and social consequences: Proceedings of an international conference. Retrieved February 12, 2005, from http://rand.org/cgi-bin/Abstracts/ordi/getabbydoc.pl?doc=CF-154

Jantz, R. (2001). E-books and new library service models: An analysis of the impact of e-book technology on academic libraries. *Information Technology and Libraries, 20*(6), 104–113.

Jensen, M. (1998). Developing the appropriateness matrix. *The Journal of Electronic Publishing, 4*(1). Retrieved February 12, 2005, from http://www.press.umich.edu/jep/ 04-01/jensen.html

King, D. W. (2004). Should commercial publishers be included in the model for open access through author payment? *D-Lib Magazine, 10*(6), Retrieved February 12, 2005, from http://www.dlib.org/dlib/june04/king/06king.html

Lagenberg, D. (2000). Electronic publishing and the evolving intellectual property regime [On-line]. *Conference Proceedings for ICCC/IFIP Conference on Electronic Publishing 2000.* Retrieved February 12, 2005, from http://www.albertina.ru/elpub2000/abstracts.html

Ludwick, R., & Glazer, G. (2000). Electronic publishing: The movement from print to digital publication. *Online Journal of Issues in Nursing, 5*(5). Retrieved February 12, 2005, from http://www.nursingworld.org/ojin/topic11/tpc11_2.htm

Lynch, R. (1994). Electronic book publishing on demand-McGraw-Hill's Primis electronic database publishing system: A case study in the development, implementation and management of on-demand publishing. In B. Blunden & M. Blunden (Eds.). *The electronic publishing business and its market* (pp. 119–121). London: IEPRC/Pira International.

McDonough, B. (2001). Think 'e-ink' if you like paper. Wireless Newsfactor. Retrieved February 12, 2005, from http://wirelessnewsfactor.com/perl/story/10301.html

McDowall, S., Ford, G., Rice, B. A., Richardson Jr., J., Stevens, N., Petru, W. C., Mann, A., Knox, J., Leach, A., Rumble, M., Ainsworth, J. W., Bagley, D. E., Apted, S., Stevenson, G., & Jones, E. (1983). The JAL guide to new books and book reviews: Library services. *Journal of Academic Librarianship, 9*(2), 108–111.

McHugh, M. P. (1996). From e-zines to mega-zines. *Networker, 7*(2). Retrieved January 19, 2005, from http://www.usc.edu/isd/publications/archives/networker/96-97/Nov_Dec_96/zines.html

McKenzie, M. (2001). Electronic paper still on the horizon, but getting closer. *Seybold Report Analyzing Publishing Technologies, 1*(6), 4–6.

Miller, A. (1996). Electronic publishing: Examining a new paradigm. Retrieved January 19, 2005, from http://www.ddg.com/LIS/CyberHornsS96/amiller/EP.html

Nasser, R., & Abouchedid, K. (2001). Problems and epistemology of electronic publishing in the Arab world: The case of Lebanon. *First Monday, 6*(9). Retrieved February 12, 2005, from http://www.firstmonday.dk/issues/issue6_9/nasser/

Nechitailenko, V. (1999). Integrated electronic publishing environment. A case study. In J. Smith, A. Ardö & P. Linde (Eds.). *Electronic publishing '99. Redefining the information chain—New ways and voices: Proceedings of an ICCC/IFIP conference* (pp.187–193). University of Karlskrona/Ronneby, Sweden 10–12 May. Washington D.C.: ICCC Press.

Packer, A. L. (1999). SciELO-An electronic publishing model for developing countries. In J. Smith, A. Ardö & P. Linde (Eds.). *Electronic publishing '99. Redefining the information chain—New ways and voices: Proceedings of an ICCC/IFIP conference* (pp. 268–279). University of Karlskrona/Ronneby, Sweden 10–12 May. Washington D.C.: ICCC Press.

Peek, R. P. (1994). Where is publishing going? A perspective on change. *Journal of the American Society for Information Science, 45*(10), 730–736.

Peurell, E. (1999). Print on demand in Sweden: Four projects and their products, problems and prospects. In J. Smith, A. Ardö & P. Linde (Eds.). *Electronic publishing '99. Redefining the information chain—New ways and voices: Proceedings of an ICCC/IFIP conference* (pp.179–186). University of Karlskrona/Ronneby, Sweden 10–12 May. Washington D.C.: ICCC Press.

Quan, M. (2000). E-book industry faces standards, copy-protection issues. *EE Times*. Retrieved January 19, 2005, from http://www.eetimes.com/article/printableArticle.jhtml?articleID=18304585&url_prefix=story&sub_taxonomyID=

Randolph, S. E. (2001). Who would choose to read an e-book rather than a printed book? *Information Outlook, 5*(2), 22–28.

Rao, S. S. (2004). Electronic book technologies: An overview of the present situation. *Library Review, 53*(7), 363–371.

Rawlins, G. J. E. (1997). Publishing over the next decade. The new publishing: Technology's impact on the publishing industry over the next decade. Retrieved February 12, 2005, from http://www.roxie.org/papers/publishing/index.html

Rose, M. J. (2001). Twelve-minute book delivery. Wired News. Retrieved February 12, 2005, from http://www.wired.com/news/culture/0,1284,45228,00.html

Rowland, F. (1999). Two large-scale surveys of electronic publication in the United Kingdom. In J. Smith, A. Ardö & P. Linde (Eds.). *Electronic publishing '99. Redefining the information chain—New ways and voices: Proceedings of an ICCC/IFIP conference* (pp. 131–136). University of Karlskrona/Ronneby, Sweden 10–12 May. Washington D.C.: ICCC Press.

Runne, J. (2001). Why ebooks are sputtering. Retrieved January 19, 2005, from http://www.entrepreneur.com/article/0,4621,288261,00.html

Runne, J. (2001). Why ebooks are sputtering. Retrieved January 19, 2005, from http://www.emarketer.com/analysis/ecommerce_b2c/20010314_b2c.html

Sheridon, N., Howard, M. & Richley, E. (1997). Gyricon displays and electric paper. Proceedings of SID, May 1997. San Jose, California: Society of Information Display.

Stefano, V. (2000). The 'cyber-newspaper' and the European Community law—The law of information in the Internet era (an example of technical, sociological and legal analysis of e-publishing). ICCC/IFIP Conference-ELPUB2000. Retrieved February 12, 2005, from http://www.albertina.ru/elpub2000/abstracts.html

Upadhaya, G. R. (1999). Indreni—the Nepali Intranet: A platform for electronic publishing and information sharing in Nepal. In J. Smith, A. Ardö & P. Linde (Eds.). *Electronic publishing '99. Redefining the information chain—New ways and voices: Proceedings of an ICCC/IFIP conference* (pp. 169–178). University of Karlskrona/Ronneby, Sweden 10–12 May. Washington D.C.: ICCC Press.

Vitiello, G. (2001). A European policy for electronic publishing. *Journal of Electronic Publishing*. Retrieved January 19, 2005, from http://www.press.umich.edu/jep/06-03/vitiello.html

Wiesner, K. S. (n.d.). Electronic publishing: the definitive guide and weave your web. Retrieved February 12, 2005, from http://www.angelfire.com/stars4/kswiesner/nonfictionreviews.html

Williams, P. (1999). *The advance of electronic publishing*. London: Department of Trade and Industry.

Chapter 8

'COPY AND PASTE' OR SCHOLARLY COMMUNICATION? CHANGING THE BALANCE POINT

Hsianghoo Steve Ching and Lai Chu Lau

1.   Chapter Overview

Constructivist teaching pedagogy advocates open learning environments whereby students can develop the ability to conduct research, and exchange ideas with peer students and teachers. However, many students these days are prone to copying and pasting other's information rather than doing their own individual work. It is simply because information technology has made it easier to retrieve full-text articles. Websites offering student papers for sale are easily accessible.

Students' plagiarist behaviour can be explained by utility theory. Students are assumed to act rationally and make choices about the risk of being detected. They weigh up several factors about the costs and benefits of being dishonest, and the good factors associated with being honest. Simply installing a detection mechanism and increasing the punishment is not sufficient to deter plagiarism. A more effective approach is to honour student's legitimate hard work.

The authors, who are both information professionals, propose a library–teacher–student partnership model. Operated on a course basis, the model is made up of three stages, namely content creation, content collection and content publishing. During stage one, librarians co-partner with the academic teachers in designing curriculum experiences. Librarians coach the students throughout the learning journey, equipping them with information retrieval, information evaluation and writing skills. In stage two, academic teachers recommend quality student papers to be deposited in the institutional repository maintained by librarians. In stage three, students are invited to publish their quality papers as eBooks. Librarians organize authorship training and

H. S. Ching, P. W. T. Poon and C. McNaught (Eds.), eLearning and Digital Publishing, 133–149.

collaborate with the academic teachers to refine and edit the eBooks. The library develops and maintains a digital publishing platform and forms a consortium with others in order to share resources. As the project grows, the publishing tasks can be outsourced to a commercial vendor.

More student papers will be available on the Internet as a result. But this is not just another paper mill; valuable intangible benefits will be created too. Not only will the students turn away from plagiarism; they can also become lifelong learners to some extent. By having the published items, academics will have a wider spectrum of materials to choose for teaching purposes and their teaching effort can be more systematically measured. After such a transformation into the digital era, librarians can deliver teaching and learning support more directly and effectively. Finally, the professional community can enjoy an outstanding academic database at a more affordable price.

2.   Background

In the past, universities provided a secure and closed learning environment. Teachers played the role of the knowledge organizer, transmitter and depositor. Students patiently received and memorized the information, which was organized, homogenized and customized by their teachers. However, in the context of today's emerging open learning environments, updated technology tools and a wider acceptance of constructivist theories of learning have led to a variety of new student-centred teaching and learning settings and approaches. There is also a huge investment in large-scale information infrastructure and the collection of electronic resources to support these new modes of learning. Teachers have redefined their roles as facilitators and learners are no longer seen as passive participants. One of the goals of education is that students, with the guidance of teachers, should develop the ability to conduct research using comprehensive learning resources and tools, articulate outcomes, and join learning communities to exchange ideas with peer students and teachers. With the Internet and electronic resources, it is now much easier than a decade ago for students to search and access information anywhere and anytime. However, is the quality of their work better than before? Are the concepts of open learning environments assisting students to take more responsibility for learning, and supporting teachers as facilitators of that process?

Students are now more comfortable with fast, nonlinear and non-sequential modes of reading and thinking. The problem is that the easier and quicker it is to retrieve full-text articles, the greater is the temptation for plagiarism. Many teachers have experienced 'copy and paste' student work and find that student plagiarism is on the rise, and is also increasingly sophisticated (Wood, 2004).

We are living in a free-market economy and it is not surprising that some businesses and individuals have developed new web-based information services to meet our students' demands. Such businesses play a dual role in the new market economy: they are the suppliers of students' essays, term papers and research papers, as well as the buyers of these students' works. One can easily locate many commercial sites on the Internet offering writing services to students. Using databases, the papers, book reports and theses on these sites are organized by category and by subject. Customers can browse through them or carry out searches of information at different levels of sophistication. In the United States, the website, EssayTown.com (http://www.essaytown.com/) provides a variety of services to suit student's various time frames and financial situation.[1] A term paper costs from $27.99 per copy to $38.00 per page (in $US). On the European continent, the UK-based Essays-r-Us (http://www.essays-r-us.co.uk/) sells as well as buys papers. On the demand side, students can browse through 144 broad topics, from accounting to welfare law. A readily available paper is priced at £50. There is a service for brand new papers too and each item seems to be costed differently. On the supply side, a student can sell her/his own essay for £50 each, and can even join the company as a writer, specifying the hourly rate expected. In addition to the trade in student works through web-based essay mills, many student essays are advertised on eBay or other auction sites for sale.

Unlike the traditional scholarly communication environment, these content creators are not aiming at wide exposure and are only concerned about someone paying money for their work. Conversely, these content readers do not care about the pre-selection and quality control of content; they just want to obtain an article with sufficient appropriate content to fulfil their assigned assessment task. In this knowledge-based digital era, scholarship and information ethics have become fragile entities.

3.   Plagiarism Behaviour and Deterrence: An Economic Analysis

Behind these 'copy and paste' actions and paper–purchase transactions are the decisions made by individual students. Students decide whether to devote more time or less time to intelligent work. Utility is the term most commonly used by economists to describe the satisfaction or benefit derived from a particular action.[2] For each student, the process of decision-making involves attaching an expected value of this utility (called the expected utility[3]) across different outcomes. Students commit plagiarism because the utility derived from such action is greater than the utility obtained from doing the study her/himself. Each plagiarist faces a risk of detection which must be balanced against the perceived degree of punishment upon detection. The plagiarist will assess the probability of detection against the degree of punishment. If plagiarism is detected, her/his academic development (grade being a fail grade or a reduced pass grade; student being expelled or suspended, etc.) or even future career will be affected.

Many institutions are now reviewing and redrafting their plagiarism policies and using anti-plagiarism software to scan and detect whether any part of a student's work has been copied from the Internet.[4] In conjunction with the assessment of the benefit of cheating, the potential plagiarist also must assess the benefit of not cheating, and actually doing the study or the work on her/his own. By doing the work honestly, there may be positive feelings of achievement and pride. This feeling of moral integrity may override the benefit of dishonest behaviour. For example, even if the probability of detection was nil and the benefit of cheating was great (for example, a higher mark or more time for leisure), some students may still elect not to cheat. They may do this because they wish to have a sense of higher moral integrity and a clear conscience, thus avoiding guilty feelings which can arise from dishonest behaviour. Alternatively, they may be interested in the topic and derive pleasure and satisfaction from their own research and learning.

The aforementioned description of students' decision-making behaviours can be explained by Robert A. Becker's economics analysis (Becker & Boyd, 1997; Eide, 1994). The fundamental assumption of the analysis framework is that students act as if they are a rational utility maximizer. Students are assumed to act rationally in accordance with the choice between the risk of being detected, and an assessment of the costs and benefits associated with the act. The student's expected utility, $E[U]$, is the expected value of the student's utility from committing plagiarism or cheating. $E[U]$ can be defined as:

$$E[U] = p \times U(Y^P - Y^L - c) + (1 - p) \times U(Y^P - Y^L)$$

where $U(\cdot)$ is the student's von Neumann–Morgenstern utility function,[5] $E[U]$ is the student's expected utility, p is the probability of being detected, Y^P is the monetary and non-monetary benefits from plagiarism behaviour, Y^L is the monetary and non-monetary benefits of non-plagiarism behaviour, and c is the monetary and non-monetary direct costs of plagiarism.

A student will take the risk and commit a plagiarist behaviour on her/his assignment if $E[U]$ is positive, and will not if $E[U]$ is negative. Institutions install anti-plagiarism software to raise 'p', and increase the severity of punishment for plagiarism to raise 'c'. The changes in the probability and the cost will alter students' expected utility and choice behaviour. Somehow, if institutions have a new regulation or tool, smart cheaters might have a measure to circumvent detection. Institutions will then have to respond and search for another new tool for plagiarism deterrence, in a vicious cycle. Conventional wisdom suggests that the 'stick' is less effective than the 'carrot' in moulding one's behaviour. What we are suggesting here is that it is better to focus on nurturing serious and honest students by providing them with real incentives and motivation, rather than threatening them with harsh deterrents. Because non-original academic work is so readily available and increasing difficult to detect, it is increasingly important in the academic setting to foster or encourage the traditional values of academic honesty or integrity, and to reward and encourage students for original work.

4.   A Practical Solution to Rebuild Information Ethics

Teachers should not be detectives. Teachers should be interested in helping students develop learning skills and coaching the students' learning journeys. A successful teacher does not merely disseminate information but also teaches the student to learn. Traditionally, the delivery of scholarly information associated with students' learning was assumed to be a one-way, linear and non-recursive relationship. The intellectual output from teaching and learning was disseminated only within the classroom, disappearing soon after the class.

Few libraries have adapted to the changes in student learning behaviour driven by student-centred approaches. Students are the readers and consumers of scholarly information, but they might also be the authors and contributors of scholarly information at the same time. Teachers may not be the only point of quality control for the dissemination of scholarly information in the classroom; for example, students can review and comment on fellow students' work via a learning management system. In the electronic and Internet age, scholarly information created by students can be rapidly published and distributed at substantially lower costs than the traditional methods of publication of academic work. The output of scientific information from students' work can result in new flows of scholarly materials that might recursively feedback to the inputs for new teaching and learning activities, and could therefore be accessed and retrieved more widely and easily.

Scholarly communication has been represented as the process of disseminating scientific information and research results, and the major players in this process have always been researchers and academics in the higher education sector. Publishing adds significant value to authoring. Scholarly authors do not write primarily for direct cash compensation, but to obtain readership and recognition from which indirect compensation may follow. The scope and parameters of scholarly communication have been broadened during the past two decades or so due to the development of information technology and new teaching pedagogy. Scholarly communication in the present day is no longer the exclusive preserve for research results contributed by researchers and academic teachers. Teaching and learning have also figured prominently in this process of scholarly communication and have indeed become an integral component of it. If librarians and teachers could work with students to provide publishing services and thus give students a real audience to write for, then a demonstrable value of performing hard intellectual study work could be elicited and enlarged. In terms of the student expected utility formula, the value of Y^L will increase. Given the probability of being detected and the direct cost of plagiarism, the relative benefits from plagiarism behaviour against the benefits of serious study will also change students' expected utility and choice of behaviour.

5.   The Conceptual Framework of the Proposed Approach

To respond to the explosion of information and continual changes in the means of accessing information, universities are turning their education goals to teaching the skills of lifelong learning and enhancing research methodology (Hull, 2001). Libraries are developing many information literacy tutorials to integrate information retrieving skills into the curriculum (e.g. Roldan & Wu, 2004). Both teachers and librarians are increasingly interested in the development of a scholarly communication system for higher education by taking advantage of the power of eLearning and digital publishing. In addition to (and hopefully instead of) innovative plagiarism detection and harsh punishment, teachers and librarians can now also coach students' learning in a collaborative process (Harris, 2004). By encouraging students to publish their work (even if the work is not widely distributed), teachers and librarians are giving them incentives and possibly physical rewards (or returns) for undertaking serious study and research. Publishing will also deter plagiarism because the probability of detection is higher with the dissemination of the work.

The system consists of three major stages—creation; collection and management; and, finally, publishing. The role of the actors, intelligent output created, and information technology system involved in each stage are described in figure 8-1.

5.1.   *Creation of Knowledge and Contents*

Academic teachers initiate the learning journey by designing the curricula. As teaching becomes more an exercise of designing learning experiences and coaching rather than just delivering lectures, librarians can become good consulting partners in curriculum design (D'Angelo & Maid, 2004). Librarians can point out to the teachers the sources to be used for particular learning tasks. To tackle problem-based assignments, students must have the skills to locate relevant information sources. A collaborating librarian can coach the students by giving appropriate training at different periods of time, for instance, an information retrieval workshop in week 1, information

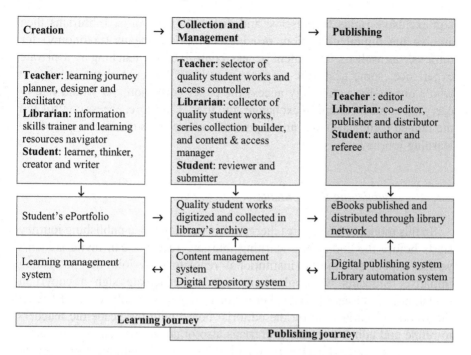

Creation	→	Collection and Management	→	Publishing
Teacher: learning journey planner, designer and facilitator **Librarian**: information skills trainer and learning resources navigator **Student**: learner, thinker, creator and writer		**Teacher**: selector of quality student works and access controller **Librarian**: collector of quality student works, series collection builder, and content & access manager **Student**: reviewer and submitter		**Teacher** : editor **Librarian**: co-editor, publisher and distributor **Student**: author and referee
↓		↓		↓
Student's ePortfolio	→	Quality student works digitized and collected in library's archive	→	eBooks published and distributed through library network
↑		↑		↑
Learning management system	↔	Content management system Digital repository system	↔	Digital publishing system Library automation system

Learning journey
Publishing journey

Figure 8-1. Learning journey empowered by the scholarly communication system

evaluation workshop in week 6, and information organization and citation training in week 10 (Spence, 2004). In this problem-based/case-based/collaborative learning mode, the teacher exchanges ideas with the students and the students exchange ideas among themselves on the learning management system. The learning experience and learning objects collected are deposited in the student's ePortfolio. An ePortfolio reflects a student's development over the course of education and is used as an academic assessment as well as career development tool. Librarians can use their expertise to help students organize and digitize the various items in the ePortfolio (Mason *et al.*, 2004).

5.2.   Content Collection and Management

At this stage of the learning journey, teachers grade the students' work. Students will be invited by the teachers to review the work of their peers via the learning management system. Teachers then recommend quality papers to be included in the university's institutional repository which is maintained by librarians. After teachers' recommendations, students submit digital copies of their work to the institutional repository. Librarians clear copyright of the works by getting students to sign a declaration, granting the university non-exclusive rights to preserve and distribute the works. Librarians then archive the digital collection, provide appropriate means (taxonomy) for retrieval, as well as implement access control. Since teaching is a private experience, some academic teachers may have concerns about letting the whole university community access the paper collection, yet would like to carry out some meaningful exchange activities. Therefore, access control and the related technical issues are important matters. This marks the end of the learning journey.

5.3.   *Publishing the Contents*

In this model of library–teacher–student partnership, a publishing journey starts before the end of the learning journey. Teachers can invite students whose papers are in the institutional repository to join the publishing initiative. Students who voluntarily opt to participate sign a copyright declaration, granting the publisher exclusive rights to publish and distribute the works. Librarians sit on the editorial board with the academic teachers to refine and edit the works. Librarians also organize workshops with other departments (such as the Department of English and Communication, Student Development Services, etc.) to equip students with basic authorship concepts and skills, such as peer review methods and writing styles. The end product is primarily an eBook, with a supplementary print version for each title. EBooks can be disseminated and archived on a digital publishing system developed and maintained by the library. If ten paper copies are produced via print-on-demand per title, then students, academic teachers and libraries could receive, say, five, two and three copies respectively.

To leverage the operating costs and to achieve resource sharing, a consortium of libraries can be formed to undertake the publishing. Consortium members share the same vision and mission as set out here. They become the founding members of this publishing initiative. Each member university then invites the other local universities to participate. The latter participate by contributing their institutions' outstanding student papers. The founding members remain as the governing body. Figure 8-2 is a projection of the growth of the consortia eBook collection.

Figure 8-2 simplifies the real life situation for illustrative purposes and demonstrates the effect of growth. The publishing initiative starts out with one member in each region. As it gains the momentum, more members can join in a respective region. On the eBook side, during the initial stage, one university can only produce eBooks for one or two programmes (or for a defined number of courses in those programmes). After the skills are developed and more connections established, more programmes can be handled in the subsequent years. As the number of eBooks produced and the number of sharing titles from

No. e-books produced Members		Year 1	Year 2	Year 3
Region 1	Member A	Program i: 5	Program i: 5 Program ii: 5	Program i: 5 Program ii: 5 Program iii: 5
	Member B	Not joined yet	Program i: 5	Program i: 5 Program ii: 5
	Member C	Not joined yet	Not joined yet	Program i: 5
Region 2	Member D	Program i: 5	Program i: 5 Program ii: 5	Program i: 5 Program ii: 5 Program iii: 5
	Member E	Not joined yet	Program i: 5	Program i: 5 Program ii: 5
	Member F	Not joined yet	Not yet joined	Program i: 5
Region 3	Member G	Program i: 5	Program i: 5 Program ii: 5	Program i: 5 Program ii: 5 Program iii: 5
	Member H	Not joined yet	Program i: 5	Program i: 5 Program ii: 5
	Member I	Not joined yet	Not joined yet	Program i: 5
No. of eBooks added in a year		15	45	90
Cumulative eBooks produced	Year 1	15		
	Year 2	60		
	Year 3	150		

Figure 8-2. Projection of the growth of the consortia eBook collection

collective efforts among libraries increases, the average developmental cost of each eBook for individual member libraries will be reduced significantly.[6]

As the database grows, the publishing and marketing tasks can be outsourced to commercial eBook distributors. This can utilize the technical and professional expertise of the publishing industry and offload the burden from the librarians. The commercial distributors would be required to provide services such as marketing, sales and billing, storage, access control, search engine, copyright monitoring, and cataloguing (MARC record delivered with each eBook title).

For this business model, it is proposed that both the founding and contributing members have free access privileges while others have to pay to use the database. Subscription fees can be charged on a cost-recovery basis. Through a review of the various digital scholarly communication initiatives, different models of recovering operating costs can be found. Massachusetts Institute of Technology's DSpace project provides the public free access to MIT's digital research repository. Other institutions which adopt the software to develop similar databases are expected to open up those databases for free also (Barton & Walker, 2002). MIT recovers DSpace's costs from associated libraries' operating budgets and donations. The Berkeley Electronic Press (http://www.bepress.com), which is the University of California at Berkeley's

digital scholarly publishing project, contains academic works by scholars at
UC and all over the world. Some of the publications are free while some
require payment for access. The free publications include the 'Monograph &
Newsletters' and 'Working Papers' sections. Subscription fees are charged
on the 'Journal Collection'. The model proposed here is simple and
straightforward. Universities which submit papers to the database have already
paid by contributing their time and effort in editing and reviewing. Therefore,
the database should be open to them for free. It is just fair for the others to
pay to use those value-added student papers.

6.   A Viable Approach to Follow?

The authors propose this approach for a good cause, but are the results
worth the effort, or are we just creating another, perhaps better, paper mill for
students to use for plagiarism? Will this approach really solve the problems
facing academics and students mentioned earlier? Can it substantiate itself?
Does this approach work across the board for every academic and every
university course? How are the universities going to get the funds required to
pay the costs? A cost–benefit analysis may help solve some of these queries.
Figure 8-3 lists all the possible costs involved and the outputs to be produced.
The costs part is quite self-explanatory and will not be elaborated here. The
outputs do not just include the number of items created in the institutional
repository and the number of eBooks produced, but also intangible benefits
which will be explained in detail next.

6.1.   More than Just Another Paper Mill

The student papers collected in the institutional repository and the eBooks
published are only the physical output. We should also take into consideration
the intangible benefits. The total benefits should be equal to the value added
to the students ($\sum_{i=1}^{l} VA1_{Si} + \sum_{j=1}^{m} VA2_{Sj} + \sum_{k=1}^{n} VA3_{Sk}$), the value added
to the universities ($\sum_{j=1}^{m} VA2_{Ij} + \sum_{k=1}^{n} VA3_{Ik}$) plus the value added to the
professional community ($\sum_{k=1}^{n} VA3_{Ck}$).[7]

6.2.   Benefits to the Students

In a particular course, the total number of students do not only possess
their ePortfolios and papers. Those who have submitted their papers to the

		Creation	Collection and Management	Publishing
Costs	Salaries including benefits – all affected staff and new dedicated staff as required	Subject librarians: Co-design curricula with teachers Reference librarians: Deliver library training	Subject librarians: Negotiate with teachers to collect papers IT librarians: Upload quality papers and maintain institutional repository	Subject librarians: Negotiate with teachers to collect & edit outstanding papers IT librarians: Provide platform for dissemination Library support staff: Desktop publishing & graphical work
	Direct expenses – staff travel, conference fees, office supplies where necessary	Required at all three stages		
	System equipment (hardware and software)	Nil	Depending on the IT platform chosen, separate hardware and software may be required	Depending on the IT platform chosen, separate hardware and software may be required
	Service charges levied by commercial eBook vendor	Nil	Nil	Payment method and charge level to be worked out with the vendor selected
Outputs — Tangible		Student papers, ePortfolios	Student papers of good quality	eBooks produced from the outstanding papers, print copies (10 for each title)
Outputs — Tangible and intangible	Value added to students	$\sum_{i=1}^{l} VA1_{Si}$	$\sum_{j=1}^{m} VA2_{Sj}$	$\sum_{k=1}^{n} VA3_{Sk}$
	Value added to institutions		$\sum_{j=1}^{m} VA2_{Ij}$	$\sum_{k=1}^{n} VA3_{Ik}$
	Value added to professional community			$\sum_{k=1}^{n} VA3_{Ck}$

Figure 8-3. Costs incurred and outputs produced

institutional repository will not just get an entry in there. And those who decide to have their papers publish will not merely get an entry in the eBook database and the five print copies. The value added to the total number of students, $\sum_{i=1}^{l} VA1_{Si}$, includes also better information seeking, analysis and problem-solving skills; correct attitudes towards intellectual property; and pride in their legitimate work. The value added to the students whose papers have been selected for the institutional repository, $\sum_{j=1}^{m} VA2_{Sj}$, includes also review and editing skills gained as well as recognition by their teachers. The value added to the students who finally proceed to the publishing journey, $\sum_{k=1}^{n} VA3_{Sk}$, includes the authorship skills acquired, the recognition by the larger academic community and, quite possibly, better career development. The demonstrable value of doing hard intellectual study work (Y^L) is enlarged; the relative monetary and non-monetary value of plagiarism (Y^P) will be reduced. According to the student-expected utility formula, with everything else being constant, a increase in Y^L will lower the value of $E[U]$. And students will refrain from plagiarist behaviour when $E[U]$ becomes negative. Although the portion of the students who can attain this high value VA3 is small, the number of students who enjoy the lower values VA2 and VA1 is much larger. Thus, the summation of the VA1 and VA2 may be higher than that of VA3. In other words, the benefits this approach brings extends to the total number of students who take part in this project. To differing extents, these students should turn out to be more independent and information-ethical lifelong learners.

6.3.   Benefits to the Universities

To the universities, there is not only an increase in the size of the institutional repositories and free access to a quality eBook collection, but also intangible benefits for the teaching staff and librarians. The value added to the institutions is equal to $\sum_{j=1}^{m} VA2_{1j} + \sum_{k=1}^{n} VA3_{1k}$. As more and more students move away from plagiarism and become independent, academics can concentrate more on teaching rather than detecting. The academics will have a wider spectrum of course materials to choose from when the quality papers and the eBooks feedback to the university. Academics spend a great deal of time on teaching, yet career evaluation focuses on research activities. There are several reasons for this. "Research is visible to colleagues at other institutions, whereas teaching is not" (Hind, 1974). Student judgment normally does not carry much weight as it is not considered to be up to professional standards. By having the student papers included in the institutional repository, published and later cited in other scholarly publications, teaching effort has a way to be systematically measured. Academics can include in their yearly reports the number of items published under their supervision and, possibly, the number of times each of those items is cited. For the librarians, this approach creates a formal channel, by which they can work with academic teachers. It is through this channel that librarians can provide better, and more direct, teaching and learning support. By assisting students to archive their digital papers and organize their ePortfolios, librarians can demonstrate that their traditional roles can be successfully transformed into the electronic era.

6.4. Benefits to the Professional Community

To the professional community, there is not only the birth of a new eBook collection. The total benefits are equal to $\sum_{k=1}^{n} VA3_{Ck}$. Without this knowledge management effort, all the innovative and valuable ideas of the students would have been buried. Mainly to recover costs rather than to make profit, this eBook collection should be priced at a reasonable level and should be more affordable to the professional community. These graduates who join the workforce may be more receptive to lifelong learning. In different ways, all this can help to rejuvenate the professional community.

6.5. Flexible Handling of Operational Issues

As can be seen from figure 8-3, a series of costs is required to start and maintain this project. One source of funding could be the money saved from the cancellation of the print subscriptions. As more and more electronic journals become available, the print counterparts are dropped. The subscription fee and binding fee thus saved could be used to recover part of the operating costs. The space freed up from downsizing of the print serials can be innovatively used to display outstanding student papers. This kind of public recognition will certainly help reinforce honest behaviour as well as boost a university's image.

The success of this project hinges a great deal on the trust and support gained from the academics. Academic teachers' concerns must be directly addressed. Librarians need to assure them that they will not be overloaded with new duties. Not every course is required to follow this approach. It is those with in-built research elements (for example, with case study analysis or research projects as assignments) that would be initially targeted. As teaching is a private experience, the decision of some teachers (and their students) not to share their quality student papers must be honoured. The access control system will need to be able to cope with this.

Unlike the practice of detecting and punishing plagiarism, the approach proposed here will fundamentally alter learning attitudes and behaviours, which commercial paper mills do not set out to achieve. Under this library–teacher–student partnership model, learning experiences can be capitalized and turned into tangible assets for universities and the professional community. One of the library's traditional functions has been to acquire resources and make them readily available. This role should be extended to capturing knowledge created from within an institution and capitalizing it as an asset. Teaching and learning should be, and will continue to be, an integral part of scholarly communication. Librarians have an important role to play as facilitators in this process.

7.   The Future in Perspective

The emergence of easily disseminated information technology gives unprecedented freedom for individuals to distribute information widely and cheaply either via informal 'blogs' or via more formal and structured electronic information repositories. Librarians as well as academics must respond to this new technology in creative and constructive ways by seeking to utilize this technology for learning purposes. Merely responding to this technology in a 'knee-jerk' fashion by seeking new anti-plagiarism technologies, or in a negative fashion by increasing punishment, is not sufficient. A 'carrot and stick' approach can be used simultaneously.

A library does not operate in a vacuum. Even though our primary function remains bringing users and information together, our role is constantly evolving over time. Karyle Butcher, a US library professional, has written about how academic libraries have changed in the last two decades. She concludes her article by saying that "librarians have become more engaged in teaching and research to serve the needs of students, faculty and the profession better. Finally, librarians are crossing campus boundaries and entering wholeheartedly into the political process to insure that libraries have a role in the redefinition of the information access" (Butcher, 1999, p. 353). Her view is very much echoed here. With the emergence of the digital era and growing focus upon the concepts of open learning, we are moving away from a top–down information dissemination process. With the rapidly declining cost of digital information technology and deep collaboration among libraries across institutions and regions, students have an opportunity to be facilitators and learners at the same time. They are being presented with the opportunity to be potential authors. On the one hand, authorship will instil in students the skills of sound research, respect for work of others as well as knowledge learned. On the other hand, these student works will enrich the traditional reading materials such as textbooks, journal articles and course reserves. Disseminated through a worldwide library network, this new type of academic writing will benefit not only the existing students of the same institution, but also students of other institution, as well as students of the next generation. As students reading these works are also potential authors, there may be an amazing synergistic result beyond the potential of deterring plagiarism. Knowing that serious study attitudes and scholarly devotion can be honoured, students may drive through their learning journey with happiness, inspiration and innovation. The role of the library is constantly evolving and the library has the opportunity to be a bridge between generations of current and future students by providing information exchange via an institutional dissemination process. Such a process has benefits for the students, the university and the professional community.

7.1.   *A Pilot of this Library–Teacher–Student Partnership Model*

In order to work how to strike an optimal balance between the librarian, teacher and student under this approach, the Run Run Shaw Library of the City University of Hong Kong has initiated a pilot project together with mainland China's Tsinghua University and Taiwan's Feng Chia University as partners. With sponsorship from the City University's Academic Exchange Fund, academics and librarians of these three institutions met together in Hong Kong at the end of January, 2005, for a 2-day workshop. The participants exchanged their views on the appropriate courses to be targeted, academic paper selection criteria, librarian and teacher roles, information technology, dissemination control and copyright issues. An action plan was formulated for phase 1 of the project. Each participating library aims to collect at least 10 quality student papers and make them available on an appropriate information technology platform by the end of August 2005. The project will then proceed to the next phase after a thorough review and we will share our experiences with the different issues in a separate paper. It is imperative to keep in mind that the primary motive for this project is the benefit to the student. Although the benefit to the majority of the individual students may be perceived as small, the total benefit is the aggregate benefit spread amongst all students. Therefore, the benefit to the students should be more than the benefit to the university or the professional community. Although the enhancement of knowledge is always a goal of universities, it is without doubt that teachers and librarians are primarily in this business for the benefit of students.

7.2.   *Concluding Comments*

The digital era allows the dissemination of information widely and cheaply and provides tempting sources of information for students to pass off as their own work. Just like students who try to find a balance in their lives between studying and other activities, and thus decide whether (or not) to cheat so as to enable them to put their energy or resources towards other activities, educators too must strike a balance between detecting and punishing wrongful behaviour, and teaching and encouraging honest scholarly work. Librarians also have tough choices to make. Under stringent financial situations, libraries need to decide whether to put resources into acquiring ever more expensive publications (print and electronic) or to devote more effort on coaching students' learning and capitalizing quality student works into an institution's own asset base. A carrot and stick approach can and should be utilized. We all should not fear new information technology but should embrace it and find ways to creatively use this technology to actively encourage electronic publishing of work to both bolster learning and provide a further disincentive to the present trend of 'copy and paste' work by students.

References

Barton, M. R., & Walker, J. H. (2002). MIT Libraries' DSpace business plan project. Final report to the Andrew W Mellon Foundation. Retrieved 21 February, 2005, from http://libraries.mit.edu/dspace-mit/mit/mellon.pdf

Becker, R. A., & Boyd, J. H. (1997). *Capital theory, equilibrium analysis and recursive utility.* Cambridge: Blackwell.

Butcher, K. (1999). Reflections on academic librarianship. *Journal of Academic Librarianship, 25*(5), 350–353.

D'Angelo, B. J. D., & Maid, B. M. (2004). Moving beyond definitions: Implementing information literacy across curriculum. *Journal of Academic Librarianship, 30*(2), 212–217.

Eide, E. (1994). *Economics of crime: Deterrence and the rational offender.* Amsterdam: North-Holland.

Harris, R. (2004). Anti-plagiarism strategies for research papers. Retrieved 21 February, 2005, from http://virtualsalt.com/antiplag.htm

Hind, R. (1974). A theory of evaluation applied to a university faculty. *Sociology of Education, 47*(1), 114–128.

Hull, B. (2001). Libraries: Deliverers of lifelong learning. *Adult Learning, 12*(6), 20–22.

Mason, R., Pegler, C., & Weller, M. (2004). EPortfolios: An assessment tool for online courses. *British Journal of Educational Technology, 35*(6), 717–727.

Roldan, M., & Wu, Y. D. (2004). Building context-based library instruction. *Journal of Education for Business, 79*(6), 323–327.

Shamdasani, R. (2004, September 30). University tackling exam cheats head on: Chief. *South China Morning Post,* p. C3.

Spence, L. (2004). The usual doesn't work: Why we need problem-based learning. *Portal: Libraries and the Academy, 4*(4), 485–493.

Wood, G. (2004). Academic original sin: Plagiarism, the Internet, and librarians. *Journal of Academic Librarianship, 30*(3), 237–242.

8.   Endnotes

1. For a term paper, students are offered these options. Service 1: Paying a flat rate of $US27.99 to have a paper delivered the same day. Service 2: By paying a higher price, students can use a different search engine to find another lot of papers and download one instantly. Service 3: To order a brand new paper by paying an even higher price, ranging from $US18 to $US38 per page.

2. In general, the concept of utility is applied to a consumer's choice or decision about work and leisure, and the allocation of expenditure on different goods, resulting in a market demand curve.

3. Students are assumed to maximize their expected utility. The expected utility of an action is the utility associated with each possible outcome of action multiplied by the probability of its occurrence.

4. In UK, Joint Information Systems Committee (JISC) has licensed 'Turnitin' to use in every university and college. In Hong Kong, after expelling two, and suspending another two, law students for plagiarism in 2004, the University of Hong Kong considered asking the students to submit assignments with declarations that they have not plagiarized the works of others (Shamdasani, 2004).

5. A von Neumann-Morgenstern utility is a function which describes the expected utility property: an expected utility maximizing student's choice is invariant for additive or linear transformations of the utility function.

6. By way of example, assuming an average developmental cost of $1,000 per title for the first copy of an eBook, Member A, D & G in Year 1 will spend $5,000 each (5 × $1,000) to obtain 15 eBooks and the average cost will be $333 per eBook title. At the end of Year 3, Member A, D & G have spent a cumulative amount of $30,000 each to produce 30 eBooks but has access to 150 eBook titles for an average cost of $200 per eBook title. This average cost per eBook title will continue to decrease as participation increases.

7. Definition of l, m, n in the formula: l: the total number of students registered for a particular course; m: the number of students in a particular course whose good quality papers have been selected to be included in the institutional repository; n: the number of students who opt to have their papers published. Definition of VA1, VA2, VA3: VA1: value added to each individual student in the course; VA2: value added to each student in a course who has been invited to submit a paper to the institutional repository; VA3: value added to each student in a course who has created an eBook. For each individual student, VA3 > VA2 > VA1.

Chapter 9

BELIEVING SIX IMPOSSIBLE THINGS BEFORE BREAKFAST: ELECTRONIC RESOURCE COLLECTION MANAGEMENT IN A CONSORTIAL ENVIRONMENT

Arnold Hirshon

Alice laughed. . . . "One can't believe impossible things."

"I daresay you haven't had much practice," said the Queen. "When I was your age, I always did it for half an hour a day. Why, sometimes I've believed as many as six impossible things before breakfast." Lewis Carroll, *Through the looking-glass*

1. Chapter Overview

As the electronic information environment evolves and as libraries move forward with their consortia, there are critical factors that must be considered in developing an effective electronic information collection management programme. This chapter first discusses some current major developments in the information industry that are affecting electronic resources and library consortium collection development. Thereafter, the paper explores six 'impossible things' that are essential for an effective consortial electronic collection development programme: (1) understanding the nature of the collaborative consortial environment to enable electronic collection management; (2) understanding the underlying economics of prices, funding and cost-sharing of electronic resources; (3) development of collaborative collection selection programmes; (4) methodologies for the evaluation of consortial electronic collection development effectiveness; (5) techniques for integrating print and electronic resource collections; and (6) strategies for marketing of consortial electronic resources.

H. S. Ching, P. W. T. Poon and C. McNaught (Eds.), eLearning and Digital Publishing, 151–171.
© 2006 *H. S. Ching, P. W. T. Poon and C. McNaught*

2.   The Information Environment Today

To appreciate the collection management issues facing any library and their consortia today, it is first necessary to have a sense of from where we have come, where we are today, and what changes currently underway in the information industry are likely to affect us in the near future.

There are a number of factors that make collection development quite different in the electronic world than they were in the print world. At its most elemental level, collection development in the print-based environment involved only three major steps: (1) each library would identify (or select) the content that it wished to purchase; (2) the library would send an order for that item to a vendor; and (3) the library would acquire and receive the item, and process it for user access. Of course, for print journals this was a bit more complicated since each separate issue had to be received and a claim processed if it did not arrive.

Today, the situation involves more decisions and potentially more partners in the decision-making process. While the basic three steps noted above still apply, collection development in the electronic information world involves at least two complicated new steps. The library must decide whether it will acquire the material in print only (in which case the acquisition steps are the same as described above), or whether it will acquire the item either in electronic format only or in a combination of print and electronic formats. While not exclusively true, the concern of most consortial collection management is primarily with electronic, and not print, resources. Thus, for electronic purchases, most libraries explore whether they can realize a better price, terms or conditions if they acquire the item through a consortium. In this process, there are a number of ways in which a consortial purchase can require greater coordination on the part of both the consortium and its member libraries. Furthermore, if the library is acquiring a print version concurrently, the library may also employ the resource's vendor (such as a serials agent), and this may require additional coordination among the library, the consortium and the vendor.

3.   Information Industry Trends and Transitions

The information industry is in great turmoil today, and the signs and portents concerning the future are unclear. During the past few years, an economic slowdown that affected many countries has resulted in reduced library spending, either through permanent budget reductions or through reallocation of their current funds.

Another factor is the push for publications to become electronic-only, but without there being a worldwide trusted and reliable third-party archive.

While electronic-only is very attractive in terms of price and collection management in general, the long-term implications of such actions are unclear because long-term or persistent access in a live archive is not yet guaranteed. Projects such as LOCKSS (Lots Of Copies Keep Stuff Safe, a prototype of a system to preserve access to scientific journals published on the web; see http://lockss.stanford.edu/) are helping to resolve the dark or semi-dark archiving issues, but these solutions are intended to be implemented in worst-case scenarios, such as when a publisher ceases to exist. More problematic issues in the electronic journal world include provision of real-time access and retrieval of electronic journals when a library chooses to stop subscribing to a publication, or when the publisher chooses to keep only a limited backfile.

Even the acceptance of electronic books is still not fully clear. While electronic reference books are being used widely, the acceptance is not as great for electronic scholarly monographs or for trade books. The latter has not yet taken hold in part because of the state of the technology relative to the application. However, overall there is no doubt that electronic books have yet to garner the same size audience as electronic journals.

This is not to say that the future of the electronic scholarly journals is perfectly clear. Perhaps the most troubling development has been the large-scale merging and consolidation of commercial scholarly publishers into near monopolies. This has been particularly true in the fields of science, technology and medicine (STM), as well as in law. The benefits to the publisher for this consolidation are clear; it has been estimated that the publisher will save at least 16% in production costs if it can eliminate the print product (MorganStanley Equity Research, 2002). There are also substantial economies of scale to be gained, so that the larger the publisher's base of titles the more marketable its products become. Certainly the largest publishers have seen substantial operating profit percentages over the past few years. And this is likely the tip of the iceberg; as this chapter was being prepared, BertelsmannSpringer was in the process of selling its Springer titles to Kluwer. According to a press release from Kluwer about the purchase, "the combination of Kluwer Academic Publishers and Springer will result in the creation of the second largest scientific publisher in the world". The one to whom they would be second is Reed Elsevier.

The trend toward consolidation is troubling for at least two reasons. First, there is a demonstrated direct correlation between increased consolidation and rising scholarly journal prices. Susman and Carter (2003) provide several examples of this correlation; for example:

Harcourt's purchase of Churchill-Livingstone and Mosby in 1997 and 1998, as well as Wolters Kluwer's purchase of Plenum Publishing, Thomson Science and Waverly in 1998, resulted in average prices for the journals in each of the two new combined portfolios that were six percent higher than their pre-merger levels. Analysis suggests that the merger activity over the past decade has been a significant factor in explaining the inflation in STM journal prices. As a result, if mergers continue unabated, it is likely that subscription prices will also continue their commensurate climb (Susman & Carter, 2003, p. 19).

Second, a variation on Gresham's Law seems to be at play here; it is not that the big publishers are driving out the small ones—they are simply buying them and eliminating the competition. It has been posited by more than one person that within before too much longer it is likely that there will be only two major scholarly publishers left who will dominate the vast majority of the market; the smaller players will be left to fight over the remains (Poynder, 2001).

Perhaps even more troubling is that these major companies are not only buying the information content—they are purchasing the entire information chain, from content through distribution. When the only way a library can acquire the publisher's content is to purchase a subscription to purchase web access from that company, then the library no longer has a means to provide its customers with access via alternative means. When significant price increases, the library can no longer differentiate the cost of the information technology infrastructure from the cost of the content itself.

This scenario might be acceptable if access to information were to be limited solely to the scholarly content, but it is not. In addition to the many publishers and publishers' content that Reed Elsevier has bought over the past dozen years (including Mosby, Pergamon, Academic Press and Harcourt health sciences), they also own the aggregator Lexis-Nexis and a local library system, Endeavor. Similarly, Kluwer (whose majority shareholders are the equity firm of Cinven and Candover) has acquired not only the publishers Lippincott, Plenum, the parts of Harcourt not purchased by Reed Elsevier, and important titles from Thompson and Waverly (Susman & Carter, 2003, p. 18), but they are also acquiring other key components of the information chain, including two major third-party abstracting and indexing (A&I) services, Ovid and SilverPlatter.

In addition to these changes, there are others within the information industry that affect library consortia even more directly. A few years ago, Academic Press began to market what has become known as the 'Big Deal', offering all members of the consortium full access to any title to which at least one member of the consortium subscribed. For a while, other publishers also adopted this model, including major publishers such as Reed Elsevier. However, the current marketing strategy is to make consortial cross-access as expensive and as limited as possible, and thus to fragment the market back into individual customers. While publishers will no doubt continue to bundle their portfolio of titles into subject-based packages for library purchase, it is likely that the Big Deal as we have known it will be dead within a few years.

4. **Impossible Thing # 1: Consortium eCollection Management: Understanding the Collaborative Environment**

Collection management is a programme that must be seen within the broader context of the consortium as a whole. To do this, it is important to understand the various organizational factors upon which the consortium is founded, and to understand the implications in terms of collection development. In other writing, I have divided these organizational factors into three levels (Hirschon, 2001):

*   *Strategic.* This level encompasses issues such as the consortium's mission, sponsorship and funding; membership composition; and the geographic boundaries within which it will operate.
*   *Tactical.* This level defines the programmes, services and enabling technologies of the consortium.
*   *Practical.* This level involves issues such as the governance structures, staffing, and fee and payment structure for the consortium.

There are strong implications within each of these levels for a consortium collection management. For example, if the primary service provided by the consortium is to secure a better purchase price for electronic resources (a 'buying club'), the funding and governance structure of the consortium can have an important effect on the negotiating power of a consortium to secure an effective electronic resource offer, both in terms of the price of the product as well as the terms and conditions of the licence. A government-funded programme, whether funded by a state or by a country, often has both more financial resources to command the attention of publishers and vendors. It may also be able to invoke the clout of the government to secure terms that might otherwise be unavailable to an independent self-sustaining organization. By contrast, if there is no central source of funding, the consortium will need to look for a sustainable source of funds to support the licensing operations.

Another key strategic issue is the composition of the membership. When negotiating a licence, will the consortium purchase the product by or for all members of the consortium, or will each member of the consortium ultimately act independently on each offer? Clearly, the ability to secure good offers will depend not only upon the size of the consortium, but also upon the willingness of the membership to partake of the offer once it is on the table.

The tactical-level decisions a consortium reaches will heavily influence the state of development of the information services it provides. If the consortium limits the scope of its work solely to negotiating licences for electronic resources that are to be purchased separately by each member library, then the consortium may not need to develop a collection management plan at all since each member library will be making its purchase decisions independently. The funding for resources may also be affected. For example, unless the consortium is a government agency (or heavily funded by a governmental body), sustaining the organization generally requires some type of dues or fee structure. The consortium must then decide whether all libraries will have a large contribution to pay for common support of all programmes, or higher membership dues but with lower transactional fees based upon actual use of each service. Since electronic resources are likely to be a core programme of the consortium, the method of cost-sharing to purchase the resources (such as through a surcharge) is directly related to the consortium's other sources of income.

4.1.   Strategic, Tactical and Opportunistic Approaches
to Collection Management

Building upon this three-part model, there are also at least three modes in which to develop a collection management plan: strategically, tactically, or opportunistically. The strategic approach asks the long-term questions. For example, what is the mission of the consortium and how will this affect the collections that the member libraries wish to build? What would the libraries like their collections to look like in 3–5 years? For example, does the consortium want to create a core collection, or simply provide each member library with options for purchase? Do the members of the consortium, and does the consortium as a whole, have sufficient funding to accomplish its goals? Most importantly for the member libraries, what will the effect of consortium collection building be on the member institutions, and how will the members coordinate their activities with those of the consortium?

The tactical approach to consortial collection management stresses the practical issues to move the collection management programme from one of theory to reality. It poses questions such as how will the needs, abilities and expectations of our users affect our collection development decisions? Will the consortium need an information technology infrastructure to support cooperative collection development? What process will the consortium use to decide among competing offers from different publishers and vendors?

Finally, opportunistic collection management is epitomized by the answer Indiana Jones gave when, while in a scrape, he was asked by his compatriots, "what's your plan?" To this, Jones replied: "I don't know. I'm making it up as I go along." In collection development terms, the opportunistic approach calls upon collection managers to respond to opportunities as they are presented. For example, how would the consortium respond if a publisher or vendor approached with a 'great deal' for an electronic resource, but the deal is available only if the consortium were to act immediately? Would the consortium pursue the offer even if it did not necessarily fit the plan the consortium outlined in terms of the types of resources or the subject areas in which the consortium had an expressed interest? If the consortium did choose to pursue the offer, what would the consortium (or its members) need to do to afford the offer? What would be the implications if the consortium passed on the opportunity to purchase this resource?

Recognizing these three alternative approaches, which one is best? The answer is clear: all of the above. The consortium must plan ahead but must also be sufficient agile to employ different methods at different times to achieve the maximum effect. Effective consortial collection management requires not only a clearly articulated strategy, and a predictable and reliable tactics to gain the maximum benefit of that strategy, but also a constant readiness to act upon unpredictable and unique opportunities that may otherwise not have fit within the existing plan.

5. Impossible Thing # 2: Understanding the Economics—Prices, Funding and Cost-Sharing

In the print environment, the economics behind the purchase of library materials was rather straightforward: the library requested the materials, and the vendor or agent quoted those materials at the list price. The list price was then discounted for books or perhaps surcharged for serials to pay for the added value services that were provided (such as claiming, statistical reports and centralized payment of bills). As noted earlier, the electronic world is quite different. Libraries generally are paying for a licence to access, not to purchase materials that they will own. The price is not a single price for the content, but rather it is usually a variable price that is based upon the expected use. To understand how to build an effective collection development consortial management plan, it is important to have an understanding of the economics of electronic resources.

The first building block in this foundation is the pricing of the resources. At present there are a number of approaches employed by product vendors and publishers. The pricing mechanism used by these companies can often affect the way in which the consortium receives either discounts or is compensated for the services it provides to its members. Although there are numerous variations on these themes, the following are the major product pricing methodologies:

1. *Full-time equivalent (FTE) with unlimited access.* This is most commonly found in the North American market. In some countries (such as in the UK) the actual number of FTE may not be known, but tiers may be used

to give an approximate sense of relative sizes of different institutions. Another common variation on the FTE approach is to charge based upon the 'weighted FTE', for example, charging a public library for only a portion of the population of a city.

The FTE pricing method is often used for services such as abstracting and indexing databases, and electronic books and journals. In particular, smaller institutions tend to benefit because the price per FTE multiplied times the small number of FTE makes the product affordable. However, for a consortium the negatives can be that it may be difficult to assemble the population data, and size is not always an accurate reflection of the complexity of a member institution or its actual activity. For example, some intensive research universities may actually have rather small user populations but a very large amount of use.

2. *Per simultaneous user (SU)*. In this method the library or consortium pays for the number of computer ports—or concurrent accesses—to the system. The SU pricing is often used for products such as electronic reference books, and occasionally for abstracting and indexing services. The advantage to simultaneous user pricing is that it can allow the consortium to aggregate its use and purchase fewer ports, and the consortium can expand its purchase based upon actual need or use. There is also the opportunity for the consortium to establish the maximum amount that it will allocate to a purchase versus the FTE-based pricing, which provides unlimited use but at a cost fixed by the publisher or vendor. One disadvantage is the difficulty in gauging the initial number of simultaneous users that are necessary to serve a population adequately. If the consortium estimates incorrectly, it will be the user who will suffer because they will not be able to gain access to the product. When this occurs, the user may incorrectly assume that the product is defective, rather than understanding that it was the library or consortium that was responsible for the under-configuration. A further disadvantage of SU pricing is that at some point it can become as (or more) expensive than unlimited access.

3. *Subscription-based pricing*. This model is most frequently employed for electronic journals, with the price based upon the cost for each member library to subscribe to print-based materials, with a minimum price established for libraries that previously had low bases of print subscriptions. Subscription-based pricing certainly has the advantage of fixed and predictable costs. However, this pricing scheme also usually comes with little or no opportunity to reduce the base charge (that is, to cancel subscriptions); the inflation factors can be substantial; and it bundles the cost of the content, access and archiving into a single charge.

4. *Per transaction* (also known as 'pay by the drink'). This type of charge may be used to purchase articles from electronic journals (particularly for access to titles for which the library has no subscription) or for document delivery services. While a library can set an arbitrary limit as to how many articles it will purchase in a single year, on a practical basis the cost is not fixed because there is usually an unpredictable quantity of transactions that may be requested in a year. The member library or the consortium must also decide whether to pay for the transactional charges or whether to pass those charges onto the user. Should the library or consortium choose to pay without limits, this can amount to creating a virtual 'open cheque book' of costs. If the cost is passed on to the user, the system must have a method in place for the user to make payments (such as deposit accounts or acceptance of credit card transactions).

5. *Per title pricing.* This type of pricing is most used for electronic books, including some reference works. The pricing clearly is based upon the similar practice in the print environment. However, given that electronic books usually also carry both a fee for the content and for access, the title is usually not owned but merely licensed for a prescribed period of time.

5.1.   *Consortial Purchasing of Material*

For consortial collection management planning purposes, probably the most important decision is how the consortium will fund its purchase of materials. In this regard there are to diametrically opposed approaches: (1) each institution purchases separately from its own funds, but purchases through the consortium to receive a better price; or (2) there is a central source of funds (such as from the government or a grant) to pay the cost. A variation on the second option is when the consortium members decide in advance to pool a certain amount of funds to purchase one or more known resources, and thereby create a firm customer base. In addition to these two basic options, there is a hybrid model in which the consortium pays part of the cost and each participating member library matches or shares the expense to cover the remaining cost.

The first of these models, in which each institution pays from its own funds, is often referred to as the 'buying club model'. Here, the consortium and the member library reach their collection management decisions independently. The consortium negotiates the potential offers, and then each member library decides independently whether to purchase that product. For example, if the consortium negotiates five different offers, one member library may choose to purchase all five products, a second library may choose to purchase only one or two, and a third library may purchase none.

In the second model, in which there is central funding, the consortium works with its member libraries to determine the purchasing priorities, and then the consortium negotiates with the publisher or vendor for the licence. Since all payment is made centrally and at one time, the costs for the publisher or vendor are generally lower, and they usually pass those savings on to the consortium. Under this model, all members of the consortium receive access to all centrally-funded electronic resources. Therefore, it is important for the consortium members to reach consensus on what they want to purchase. If funding is sufficient, the consortium may also establish a collection goal to create a balanced core collection of resources. Therefore, central funding requires that there be a strong alignment of collection development goals between the consortium and its member libraries.

The advantages of the central funding model are clear. In essence, this is often 'new money': whatever funding is received to purchase central funding is in addition to whatever the individual libraries may have to spend. This model works well as long as the central funding agency decides to dedicate funds to this purpose. However, as funding priorities change, electronic resources may suffer, particularly in difficult economic times. In such situations, the large collective price to fund electronic resources stands as an easy target for budget cutting.

Another advantage of the central purchasing model is also a potential disadvantage. When the member library and consortium collection development goals are in alignment, this system can work very well. Indeed, any purchases made from the central funds frees up funds that the member library may reallocate for another electronic resource. However, it is also possible that the collecting goals of the member library and the consortium may come into conflict. For example, some member libraries may wish to concentrate on purchasing only generalist materials, while others may be seeking specialized resources. For the consortium to succeed, these viewpoints must be brought into alignment. If they are not, the viability of the entire consortium can be threatened.

In the hybrid model, the consortium may have some but not all of the funds it needs to purchase the product, and offer to fund centrally only a part of the purchase if the member libraries will fund the remainder. The consortium will do all of the negotiation and payment, the libraries will get a part of their cost borne from these extra-institutional funds, and they will only have to pay for those resources that they consider to be of significant value. A variation on this model—when member libraries commit to purchase a resource if they can come to agreeable pricing and terms and conditions of use—can still be very effective in leveraging the collective purchasing power of the member libraries.

The hybrid model (and its variations) raises the question as to how the cost will be shared. At the simplest level, how much of the cost will be borne centrally versus by the members? On a deeper level, given that all participating member libraries may not benefit equally, what method should the collection management policy employ to apportion the cost among the members? Typically, this is done in one of four ways:

1. *Size of the institution*, with each library paying according to the size of its user population. This methodology works particularly well when the product is priced on a per FTE model, provided the FTE count turns out to be a reasonable predictor of activity. However, it is possible that a library may have a low FTE count and high usage, or vice versa. If, after a year or more of analyzing statistical activity, FTE counts are shown not to be a good predictor of activity, then the consortium may need to look at other alternatives, such as option 2 below.

2. *Actual usage*, with each library paying according to its actual usage of the particular electronic resource. The easiest and most reliable way to implement this strategy is to use the usage statistics from the previous year, and to apportion costs to each library based upon its total activity. For example, if the consortium as a whole conducted 10 million searches or 750,000 downloads of full text, and if Library A conducted 1 million searches or downloaded 75,000 downloads, then the cost apportionment for Library A would be 10%.

   There are at least two limitations to this approach. First, statistics on activity from the previous year may not be an accurate reflection of the coming year, especially if new members are coming into the consortial agreement each year. However, over time this factor generally should be mitigated as each library begins to pay its costs in the subsequent years. The other limitation is what to choose as a measure of activity. Should it be number of searches? The number of downloads? What if there is not a close correlation between the two in some of the member libraries? To avoid inter-consortial squabbling later, it is best to agree upon the measure before the actual activity begins to occur.

3. *Ability to pay*, with each library paying according to a standard measure, such as the size of its annual library materials budget. A variation on this model, particularly for the purchase of electronic journals, is to base the cost upon the amount that each member library has been paying for its print-based subscriptions. While member institutions with lower levels of funding may believe that there is a social responsibility for their better-funded colleagues to pay a larger part of the burden, this discussion can rapidly devolve into a 'haves and have nots' dispute in which no-one ultimately wins.

4. *Equal share*, in which case all libraries (regardless of size, mission or complexity) pay an identical amount. This method can work well if all members of the consortium are relatively homogenous. However, this is much less effective as the membership becomes more heterogeneous (such as differing types or sizes of libraries).

Which of these cost-sharing methods works best ultimately will rest upon the mission, goals, sponsorship and governing structure of the consortium. A key factor to consider is the extent to which members may already be paying for consortium services through dues or other fees.

6.   Impossible Thing # 3: Collaborative Collection Selection Programmes

Effective collaborative collection selection is not a single event, but actually a series of interrelated steps, including at the least the following: (1) identify the consortial decision-making group; (2) engage in general education of the decision group; (3) develop appropriate collection selection evaluation criteria; (4) create a consortium collection development policy; (5) establish the consortium budget for purchasing; (6) develop effective communications mechanisms for decision makers and other key staff of the member libraries; (7) identify electronic resources for potential purchase; (8) determine the purchasing priorities from among the available choices; (9) establish a database of membership profiles; (10) negotiate the licensing agreement; (11) generate orders for the selected resources; (12) engage the vendor or publisher and the consortium and library staff in product training and support; and, (13) continuously assess the effectiveness of the selected electronic resources. Given the general nature of this paper, only some of these steps will be discussed in greater detail here.

6.1.   *Step 1: Identify the Consortial Decision-making Group*

No step is more important than knowing that the task has been delegated to individuals who will be highly effective in keeping the consortium's collection development programme on track. It is also vital that the group size be kept reasonable, which ideally would be no more than six to ten people. If the total consortium has more than this number of members, the consortium should probably consider a representative collection management group rather than one in which every member has a delegate. The individuals assigned to the group should not only be experienced collection managers, but they should also have significant collection development decision-making authority within their own institutions. In addition to being knowledgeable about library collections, the individuals must be flexible and be collaborative by nature, so that they can work effectively with others to achieve compromise and consensus.

6.2. Step 3: Develop Appropriate Collection Selection Evaluation Criteria

The process and criteria for electronic resource selection is a complicated subject that clearly could be a paper in itself, but there is space here only for a few brief observations. For consortia that are building core collections, the process for developing the selection criteria should begin with a gap analysis to identify the current core strengths and weaknesses of the consortial collections, as well as the key opportunities and threats for building new and strong collections. As part of this process, the consortium should consider benchmarking itself against other consortia. This will help both to identify both successful and unsuccessful electronic resources based upon experiences in similar environments.

In addition to the gap analysis, consortia may also wish to develop a checklist of criteria for evaluating the key areas of concern, such as the content, access systems, interfaces, technology requirements, user support, relative cost. The selection process will also include trials of the resources that the consortium is most interested in pursuing.

6.3. Step 4: Create a Consortium Collection Development Policy

Closely related to the selection evaluation criteria is the creation of a collection development policy. Through this policy, the consortium can articulate not only its basic operating methods, but also its principles for collection and selection. The policy may articulate principles on a wide range of topics, such as fair use expectations, minimum licensing requirements and electronic archiving requirements. The consortium also may wish explicitly to endorse or adopt general guidelines that have been developed concerning best practices for the purchase of electronic resources, such as those developed by the International Coalition of Library Consortia (1998, 2001a). In addition, some consortia, such as the Northeast Research Libraries (2003) and the California State University (2003) have extensive licensing principles to inform their members and to alert publishers and vendors as to those principles that they believe are most critical in their electronic resource licences. These statements can be particularly valuable if the consortium updates them regularly to ensure that they remain sensitive to changes in the information industry.

6.4.   *Step 5: Establish the Consortium Budget for Purchasing*

Cooperative collection development can be successful only if the members are realistic about the financial resources that are available. The consortium will not be able to pursue every possible resource, and should not waste the time of the consortium, or of vendors and publishers, in engaging in trials for products that the consortium is unlikely to be able to afford.

There is an important caveat about budgeting: one of the worst approaches to electronic resource collection management, and one too often taken by consortium members, is to ask for licences to be negotiated and for price quotes to be provided for numerous products, but to hold back on making a purchase commitment only until after the final price is known. This might work if the process were as simple as calling up a publisher and vendor and asking for a price. However, as with any negotiation, the process is far more complicated. It typically takes at least a few months (and often longer) to negotiate the licence. It is a waste of time to develop agreements with numerous vendors only to find that there is not enough of a core constituency for any one product to make the licensing agreement viable. The consortium and its member libraries must avoid getting caught in a vicious cycle, with the library saying "tell me the product cost and I will tell you whether I am interested", while the consortium is saying "tell me how much you are willing to spend and I will let you know whether I can realistically achieve that goal". While opportunistic collection development is one way to building a collection, overuse of any methodology is inadvisable. The consortium should have a general sense of what its members want, and should actively pursue only those items that fit the criteria. Since the consortium will have a maximum amount that it can afford to spend in any 1 year, it should also set a limit as to how many resource licences it will pursue in the year.

6.5.   *Steps 7 and 8: Identify Electronic Resources for Potential*
          Purchase, and Determine Purchase Priorities

The identification of purchase priorities from among the available choices includes the generation of rank-ordered lists of resources for further consideration. While this process will be governed by the selection criteria described above, there are likely to be far more products that qualify under the criteria than the consortium can actually afford to licence. To set its priorities, the consortium will likely want to survey the consortium membership to determine which resources are already held by consortium members, as well which of the available products are most desired by the consortium members. Such surveys should encompass not only the members of its immediate consortium decision-making group, but the survey method can be augmented with interviews with key members, focus groups or other nominal group exercises.

Having gathered the general preference data, the political part of the process begins as different members of the committee make the case for certain resources. For those products that make this semi-final round, the typical next step is to schedule vendor demonstrations and free trials. The purpose of a free trial is to make an assessment of the product. This usually requires only a matter of weeks or a couple of months.

Having assessed the available products, the consortium should then generate an action plan and timetable for each resource that is to be pursued. For example, the consortium should establish when the licensing process will be completed, when the invoice will be paid, when the training for the product will be available, and when the product will be available to the general public.

6.6. Step 10: Negotiate the Licensing Agreement

Achieving an effective licensing agreement takes time, skill in negotiation and the willingness to compromise by both the consortium and the publisher. Too often consortia will establish and then adhere unflaggingly to a mandatory (and sometimes arbitrary) condition. Only later do they realize that they probably would have been more successful if they had identified key negotiable variables and attempted to reach a compromise. Knowing the potential variables can be critical to a successful negotiation. For example, when negotiating pricing for electronic journals the publisher's price may be based upon a number of different variables, including: (1) the subscription price basis or the price basis for subject collections of titles within the publisher title list; (2) the charges for the content fees; (3) the charges for the electronic access fees; (4) the allowance for cancellation of subscribed titles; (5) the provisions for cross-access to titles to which one (but not all) members of the consortium subscribe; (6) the provisions governing resource sharing (interlibrary loan), downloading, or other fair use provisions; (7) the length of the agreement; (8) the annual cost inflation factor; (9) the willingness of publisher to reduce the cost (particularly for a country in transition); and (10) the other general terms and conditions governing use. In the negotiation process the publisher may indicate that it is unwilling to negotiate one or more of these items, but it will rarely place all of these variables off-limits for discussion. Therefore, rather than holding fast to a single point that the publisher may have set as its only non-negotiable position, it may be best to explore other options that will still enable the consortium to reach its overall goals. If the consortium knows at the beginning of the process what the consortium membership will ultimately accept and, if the consortium has established its 'fallback positions' at the beginning, it will be in a much better position to gain the needed compromises through alternative strategies.

7.   Impossible Thing # 4: Evaluating Consortial eResource Effectiveness

Selecting and implementing an electronic resource should be the starting point for effective collection management, not the end point. One of the key differentiators between print and electronic resources is that evaluation of the use of the former was cumbersome and elusive. By contrast, there is usually a wealth of information about electronic resource usage, particularly in statistical form. It is incumbent upon all consortium collection managers to know which resources are being used, whether that usage is sufficient given the price of the product (that is, its return on investment), and the relative cost per use.

To ascertain this information, it is first necessary to establish general evaluation criteria. Many of these criteria will be the same as those used to decide about purchasing the resource in the first place, such as the quality of the content, the ease of use of the product, or the extent to which the resource meets the needs of most or all of the consortium members. However, after the product has been purchased, implemented and been in place for a period of time (usually at least 6 months), the consortium should evaluate the product to ensure not only that it meets the initial goals, but also that it is being well received by the members.

User satisfaction with a product can be established through surveys or focus groups, and the product effectiveness can be evaluated through feature checklists. However, the most effective single tool is to analyze the statistical data provided by the publisher or vendor. While the thought of statistics can instantly induce boredom, the analysis of data is essential for effective collection development because statistics provide the most reliable source of information about usage that is available. Electronic resource statistics can help a consortium understand the current use of resources, compare data across the membership to determine which libraries may be using the resources more cost-effectively, and help in the planning of technology infrastructure expansion.

The fact that statistics can provide such invaluable planning information makes it all the more regrettable that too few consortia seem to regularly review their statistical data concerning members' use of electronic resources. Through such analysis, the consortium can generate comparative data on the relative cost per use in each member library, or in the consortium as a whole. It is also possible to develop comparative benchmarks as to the cost per use of different products to which the consortium subscribes. Longitudinal data can also be compiled so that individual libraries in the consortium, or the consortium as a whole to measure growth in use and value of a product.

Statistical data can be used not only to establish the cost-effectiveness of different products (or of different member library's implementation of an electronic resource), but it can also be used for marketing purposes. For example, by showing a steady decrease in the unit cost of the information provided, the consortium and its individual members may be able to go to funding sources to demonstrate the value of the programme and to generate request additional funds. It is also possible to demonstrate how each member library—and the consortium as a whole—is receiving far more value than each member purchasing the resource separately. A particularly compelling marketing statistic concerning electronic journals is to show the cost if the library had to subscribe to each of the journals that it accessed during the year, or to purchase articles from those journals to meet the needs of their clients.

Until recently, one of the greatest concerns about statistics is that there has been no standardization on the data or the format in which it is available. Each publisher or vendor provided different data that required a great deal of massaging to yield useful comparative information. Although this problem is by no means solved, great progress has been made through publisher and vendor adoption of the guidelines on statistics for electronic resources that were promulgated by the International Coalition of Library Consortia (2001b). More recently, Counter (Counting Online Usage of Networked Electronic Resources, 2002) has been developing an information-industry-wide solution by developing not only standard statistical output and reports, but also a method to audit the compliance of any publisher or vendor who wishes to assert that its statistics are Counter-compliant. The first code of practice is now available for use and the second code is available for comment.

8.   Impossible Thing # 5: Integration of Print and Electronic Materials

One of the most difficult collection management problems that libraries have had to face is how to develop their collections during a period of transition in which they must simultaneously collect information in both print and electronic form. Clearly there are many ways in which the collection management problems are the same regardless of format. For example, there must be an effective collection management policy and plan regardless of format. In addition, the library or consortium needs reasonable funding to make purchases, and they require criteria and a system to evaluate the cost-effectiveness of the resources. Since no library in the world has enough money to buy all of the electronic or print resources that it might desire, there must also be a system to place potential purchases into a priority order.

While the two formats share these concerns, there are also ways in which the collection management issues are different. For electronic materials, it is necessary to evaluate not only the content, but also the quality of the technology-based infrastructure, such as the access (search) systems, the user interfaces and the statistics-generating systems. Furthermore, while the price for print resources was rarely negotiable, the price of electronic resources often is negotiable, particularly if consortial purchasing is employed. With print resources it was possible to negotiate the discounts that a book agent might provide to a library, or the surcharges that a serials agent might assess; however, this is different to negotiating a different cost for the content as is possible with electronic resources. In most cases, purchase of print materials through a consortium was rarely an option, but this is a highly valued tool for purchasing electronic information. Through the efforts of the consortium, libraries can collectivize their funding and perhaps their technology infrastructure in order to receive more services for less money.

There are other key ways in which the two formats differ. As noted above, electronic resources generate more reliable usage data available than was ever possible for print resources. While print resources were accessible only when the library building was open, electronic information is accessible anytime, anyplace and anywhere. Therefore, it is important to measure the effectiveness of each resource against the ability of the resource to meet these expectations. Finally, consortial purchasing of electronic resources is far more complicated than the purchase of electronic resources. Not only must the consortium or library agree to the licensing terms for use of an electronic resource, but in the consortium environment there are many more decision-makers involved as each member library seeks to have input into the purchasing process.

Knowing that these differences exist, it is important to develop policies and plans that enable the consortium to have the most effective possible implementation of the electronic collections. One method for ensuring strong integration is for the consortium to take a role in portal development. For example, if the consortium has a union catalogue, it will want to develop a uniform interface to both the catalogue information and each of the electronic resources it provides. For example, by employing broadcast search software to enable searching of multiple resources simultaneously, or by using federated search software to enable cross-linking of URLs across databases, the consortium can go a long way in helping its clients create a virtual integration of the collections, and to measure the use of those collections.

9.   Impossible Thing # 6: Marketing Consortial Resources

Probably the most important step in the electronic resource collection development process is one that is often not recognized as such—marketing.

While often seen as 'someone else's responsibility', in fact the marketing is an essential element for collection managers because an electronic resource can only be valuable if users know that it exists and are able to use it effectively. As each new electronic resource becomes available, it is important to develop a standard marketing approach (such as a standard checklist of implementation steps) to publicize its availability to the user community. For example, the consortium might do the following:

1. *Train the member library staff on the effective use of the resource.* There are a number of resources that require no special training for use, but there are others in which maximum benefit will be realized if the library staff are fully trained and prepared. However, it is probably more important to get the resource as quickly into the hands of the end-users than it is to ensure that the librarians have been exhaustively trained in the use of the resource. Unfortunately, there seems to be a global malady of librarians to hold back user access to a resource until the librarians themselves fully understand how to use it. The problem with this approach is that while the librarians are educating themselves, the library may be paying for a resource for many months before it receives any use. After the resource is available for a year the actual use statistics may look very low because member libraries may not have released the resource until after three or 6 months have transpired.

2. *Develop online materials.* The most effective materials for online resources are online. If the library or the consortium has a portal to its resources, then the portal home page should include announcements about new resources. It should also point the user to information about that resource, such as a basic description about the resource, training materials, help screens, simple 'how to get started' information on how to gain access to the resource, and how to use the resource effectively.

3. *Develop publicity materials.* The consortium will be most effective if the group comes together to develop and provide common publicity materials, such as brochures, or newsletter or public relations announcements. The publicity materials need not (and should not) be developed separately by each member institution. The core materials should be developed as common publicity materials by the group. If desirable, these materials may be customized by the individual institutions, such as to co-brand the materials so that both the name of the consortium and the local library appears as the sponsor of the resource on any marketing materials.

4. *Provide training.* For more complex products, the consortium may wish to coordinate the provision of training for its user community as to how to make best use of the resource. The consortium should be responsible for

coordinating the effort with the publisher or vendor to determine whether the training will be live or self-paced online learning units, printed training materials, or some other format.

10.   Summary: Believing the Unbelievable

Cooperative collection management in an electronic resource environment can seem a daunting—and sometimes impossible—task. However, it is possible to believe in achieving impossible things by breaking the process into its component steps, and by assigning responsibility for each component to an appropriate individual or group within the consortium. The key is to develop a holistic understanding of what the consortial electronic resource collections, and to continuously update that base of information. With this consistent source of information available, the consortium can move ahead to develop effective pricing, funding and cost-sharing strategies that will advance collaborative collection selection.

After the consortium has put some electronic resources in place, it is essential to assess regularly the consortial use of the electronic resource collections by analyzing the statistical data available at both the individual institutional level as well as the collective data for the entire consortial community. Use of this data will be important for the consortium to help its users to develop multiple strategies so they can make an effective transition from the print to the electronic environment.

Finally, the consortium has an essential role to ensure the success of the resources that it has helped to select and implement by working with its members to develop and implement an effective programme for marketing both the programmes of the consortium and the electronic resources that it makes available. If the consortium takes a consistent and steadfast approach to all of these issues, it will be possible to realize many believable benefits for its members, and to 'believe as many as six impossible things before breakfast'.

References

California State University. (2003). Principles for CSU acquisition of electronic information resources. (May 2003) Retrieved February 2, 2005, from http://seir.calstate.edu/acom/ear/docs/principles.shtml

Counter. (2002). Code of Practice, release 1 (December 2002). Retrieved February 2, 2005, from http://www.projectcounter.org/codeofpractice.pdf

Hirshon, A (2001). International library consortia: Positive starts, promising futures. *Journal of Library Administration, 35*(1/2) 147–166.

International Coalition of Library Consortia (ICOLC). (1998). Statement of current perspective and preferred practices for the selection and purchase of electronic information. Retrieved February 2, 2005, from http://www.library.yale.edu/consortia/statement.html

International Coalition of Library Consortia (ICOLC) (2001a). Statement of current perspective and preferred practices for the selection and purchase of electronic information: Update No. 1: New Developments In E-Journal Licensing. Retrieved February 2, 2005, from http://www.library.yale.edu/consortia/2001currentpractices.htm

International Coalition of Library Consortia (ICOLC). (2001b). Guidelines for statistical measures of usage of web-based information resources. (November 1998; revised December 2001) Retrieved February 2, 2005, from http://www.library.yale.edu/consortia/2001webstats.htm

MorganStanley Equity Research (2002). Scientific publishing: Knowledge is power. (September 2002) Retrieved February 2, 2005, from http://www.econ.ucsb.edu/%7Etedb/Journals/morganstanley.pdf

Northeast Research Libraries (NERL). (2003). Principles for electronic journal Licenses. (June 2003). Retrieved February 2, 2005, from http://www.library.yale.edu/NERLpublic/EJrnlPrinciples.html

Poynder, R. (2001). Are Reed Elsevier and Thomson Corp. Monopolists? *Information Today, 18*(6), p. 1, 58.

Susman, T. M., & Carter, D. J. (2003). Publishers Mergers: A consumer-based approach to antitrust analysis. Washington DC: Association of Research Libraries. Retrieved February 2, 2005, from http://www.informationaccess.org/WhitePaperV2Final.pdf

PART THREE

IMPLICATIONS FOR THE GROWTH OF KNOWLEDGE AND SCHOLARLY COMMUNICATION

Chapter 10

DIGITAL PUBLISHING AND
THE KNOWLEDGE PROCESS

Colin Steele

1.   Chapter Overview

The digital information environment has ensured that the twenty-first century will be a global watershed, like that of the fifteenth century in the Western world, for changes in the creation of, access to, and distribution of knowledge and information. Changes, however, are not being adequately reflected in the formal frameworks of scholarly publishing. In the digital information environment, the challenges will be significant, ranging from information overload to a multimedia non-linear access to information. Developments in the public and private web reflect the tensions of initiatives and consequent challenges, such as those currently being experienced between the increasing aggregation of multinational publishers on the one hand, and open access initiatives on the other.

Globally, 'publish or perish' pressures have increased on researchers, with the need for publication becoming the pathway to success in the all-important research assessment exercises which lead to tenure and promotion. The book and the article are no longer intrinsically a means of distributing knowledge. Depending on one's viewpoint of the 'Faustian bargain' between authors and publishers, the scholarly publishing environment has been in crisis for a number of years.

While this has been particularly reflected in the debates on serials, many humanities scholars have experienced declining sales of their monographs and a lack of appropriate outlets for their research publications. While many traditional university presses have been closing down or losing money for a number of years, new models are emerging with different philosophies and capitalizing on new electronic settings. User studies have indicated that

H. S. Ching, P. W. T. Poon and C. McNaught (Eds.), eLearning and Digital Publishing, 175–193.
© 2006 *H. S. Ching, P. W. T. Poon and C. McNaught.*

print-on-demand (POD) is universally seen as an essential requirement of output in these models.

Open access initiatives have seen the creation of a number of ePrint repositories which in turn have organically led to the establishment of ePresses. Future scholarly publishing patterns will be heavily influenced by author attitudes to ePublishing. Major programs of scholarly advocacy in the context of scholarly communication processes will need to be implemented if scholarly authors, their institutions and their research output are to benefit from the new digital frameworks.

2.   Background

Before examining current trends in digital publishing, an historical framework needs to be provided, however briefly, of the nature of knowledge access and the patterns of textual publishing. The contemporary sources of knowledge in contrast to the past are now multiple, multi-dimensional and often non-textual.

First we must reaffirm the well-known adage that information is not knowledge and knowledge is not wisdom. In historical terms, access to knowledge was essentially oral in the first millennium. For much of the second it was textual, following the introduction of the printing press in the fifteenth century in the Western world by Johannes Gutenberg. By the year 1500 there were nearly 1,500 print shops. Eight million volumes had been printed comprising 23,000 titles (Eisenstein, 1979, p. 44). A major shift in the ability to disseminate knowledge and information had occurred.

We now need to examine the nature of authorship and readership. In the medieval era, scholars were often indifferent to the original creator. Copying and, what might be termed explicit or implicit plagiarism, went hand in hand and it was thus often difficult to ascribe particular passages to particular authors. Textual integrity was enforced in a generic sense by the state and ecclesiastical authorities in order to ensure orthodoxy. It is ironic in this context that the authority of the Catholic Church in the sixteenth century was severely challenged by the European Reformation of Martin Luther and John Calvin. The message of dissent was propagated and accelerated through the printed book revolution.

In a less obviously revolutionary context, a variety of supplementary organizational knowledge devices appeared in the sixteenth and seventeenth centuries which now we take for granted; examples are indexes, numbered pages and bibliographies, although not all of these appeared simultaneously. Examining the printing of Shakespeare's First Folio (1623) reveals the various textual variations of print production and the nature of 'best text' at that time. The ubiquity of web sources will impact on textual veracity in the twenty-first century. The eighteenth century Enlightenment was a period in which the storage and communication of information accelerated with the developments of the encyclopaedia, learned societies, and scientific and literary salons which led ultimately to the late nineteenth century movement for bibliographic organization and public domain documentation. Metadata standards are directly related to this latter process.

The intellectual strands of today are derived from the historical models of yesterday. Thus, in the Middle Ages, every monastery was its own publishing house and a monk with a desk, ink and parchment was almost his own publisher because of the individual nature of creation, although the output was clearly 'branded' in an ecclesiastical framework. A sixth century monk exhorted his colleagues "he who does not turn up the earth with his plough ought to write the parchment with his fingers".

Today, every writer on the Internet can be his or her own publisher, admittedly with qualifications as to the authoritativeness of the text. The web makes it possible for instant lodging of material but self-publishing on the web at its base level is vanity publishing. There has to be, all agree, a credentialing of knowledge in the digital environment, but whether it needs the costs imposed by the large multinational publishers is a matter of significant contemporary debate. The nature of the robustness of a digital text refers not only to the physical environment of the text in a web setting, but also to the need to re-establish varying modes of textual authority and then, ultimately, to the process of exploring what it means to create and disseminate knowledge.

3.   Global Knowledge Shifts

The World Wide Web has undoubtedly caused major cultural shifts in terms of access to and dissemination of information at numerous levels. New ways of writing and reading may well come about in new multi-dimensional environments, for example through hypertext links and non-linear approaches to knowledge. Explicit or implicit navigational tools will increasingly offer pre-ordained pathways or the opportunity for unlimited serendipity. Issues with the semantic web are leading to new constructs in the underlying text infrastructure with alternative 'meaning functions' being produced.

Elizabeth Daley, the Executive Director of the Annenberg Centre for Communication at the University of Southern California, has argued that we require an expanded definition of literacy in the twenty-first century (Daley, 2003). The multimedia language of the screen constitutes the current vernacular and provides the opportunity to construct complex meanings independent of text. Many students today often have more exposure to multimedia sources such as television, computer games and the Internet rather than the textual reading of books and newspapers. Thus, shared experiences in their context are often derived from images and sounds. To extend into the research environment, multimedia and grid computing applications are enhancing inter-disciplinary developments and changing the nature of what we might term 'publishing'.

Berners-Lee has noted that the 'semantic web' will transform access to information and foster greater productivity, especially in science and inter-disciplinary research (Berners-Lee, 2003). The semantic web, Berners-Lee argues, will be created when tiny standardized tags—universal resource identifiers—are added to pieces of data on websites and databases. The tags in turn point to machine-readable vocabularies and a set of definitions which allow computers to 'understand' the data. The semantic web developments have much in common with other emerging web technologies and grid computing.

Tony Hey, Head of the UK eScience program, has commented about the current 'data deluge,' which refers to the flood of scientific data from eScience experiments, simulations, sensors and satellites (Hey & Trefethen, 2003). For the exploitation of this material by relevant search engines and data mining software tools such data needs to be archived and stored in appropriate formats with relevant metadata. Hey (2004) has argued that librarians should be playing a vital role in eScience preservation as they are metadata experts and digital curators. Hey believes they are neglecting this role, which he implies is at their peril in terms of their maintaining relevance.

Another interpretation of the changing models comes from Joseph Esposito who has contrasted the printed book of history, the 'primal book' with the 'process book' (Esposito, 2003). The impact of text in a structured networked environment allows for modifications in the act of knowledge creation. Esposito says this has at least five aspects: as a self-referencing text, as portal, as platform, as machine component, and as network node. This allows for flexibility in access and distribution which will enable different societal patterns of knowledge utilization. The whole act of reading could be deconstructed from linear models and publishing could become segmented—which, incidentally, at the student level is becoming increasingly the norm as students use search engines to seek instant electronic gratification.

The digital age essentially creates the framework of two contradictory paths of knowledge access. Firstly the ghettoization, or the compartmentalization of knowledge (like only talking to like), can have significant repercussions in terms of reinforcing values or prejudices. Secondly, as Chartier (2001) has argued, this can lead to overwhelming global conformities with the destruction of cultural or indigenous diversity, an example of which is the Murdochian amphitheatre of global television and newspaper publishing, with its almost uniform editorial practices. At a very simplistic level, one can see this in a decline in indigenous languages and the overwhelming importance of the English language in the global village as defined in the public web debate. In the scientific publishing industry English is a sine qua non for publishing, particularly in the context of distribution and bibliometric citation patterns.

James and McQueen-Thompson (2002) argued that "the dominant form of knowledge production is becoming more abstract, even if the dominant content of knowledge follows a strangely contradictory path of an abstract obsession with technical application to 'concrete' outcomes" (James & McQueen-Thompson, 2002, p. 183). To illustrate this they contrasted what they call the "traditional modern cataloguing" of nature in Linnaeus' Systema Naturae (1735) to "late modern mapping" of the human genome.

They identified five key trends in the contemporary production of scholarly knowledge. The first is that knowledge production has become increasingly rationalized; publishing output is used in a quantifiable sense for academic performance measures. This will undoubtedly become even more important, rightly or wrongly, in the future as methods for research assessment. Secondly, knowledge has become increasingly commodified. A clear example is the way that university education is often viewed primarily as an economic process in the recruitment of overseas and full-fee paying students. Thirdly, knowledge has also become increasingly codified and information is broken down into information bits. The electronic process of digital file information storage has only accentuated this process. Fourthly, James and McQueen-Thompson argued that knowledge production has become increasingly mediated by technological frameworks. In the information context one can see this represented not only in 'scholar' portals but also in flexible delivery of course content. Fifthly, technological mediation relates to the more generalized process of extension, and new methods for networked communication in a post-Gutenberg era. The collective framework here of knowledge creation and distribution will lead to new forms of social relationships.

In the digital publishing transition we need to be aware of the exact impacts on knowledge dissemination. Examples here are new kinds of information transmission such as text messages and PDAs in the bio-medical area, the developments of information repositories, new methods of data mining, and the emergence of different commercial business models. In the wider perspectives of information creation transfer we need to ask much more profound questions about the nature of information access, motivation, knowledge synthesis and outputs.

4.   Scholarly Publishing: Digital Dreams or Nightmares?

Science publishing in its printed origins in the seventeenth century had the principal aims of protecting intellectual property and ensuring the communication of scientific knowledge. Various email lists in 2003 and 2004 have seen arguments propounding the pros and cons about whether science publishing in its early years was essentially not-for-profit or commercial publishing. Michael Mabe of Reed Elsevier has argued for the early commercialization of scientific publishing, while Guedon (2001) has argued the case that scientific publishing remained for several centuries significantly in the hands of learned societies and institutions with motivations being driven more by research dissemination ideals than profits.

Commercial multinational publishers, particularly in the second half of the twentieth century, have without doubt significantly changed the commercial landscape of scientific, technical and medical (STM) publishing with increased numbers of journals, high level price increases on an annual basis, and the offering of aggregated packages. This has impacted in general on scholarly communication patterns and, in particular, on the volume of purchasing of material by libraries from smaller publishers and learned societies, and on monograph publishing.

The term 'crisis in scholarly publishing' has been with us for so long as to almost nullify the term crisis. Indeed the Librarian of Harvard University stated in 1898 that the rising cost of books and serials could not be sustained into the twentieth century! I recall my first meeting in 1976 of the Council of Australian University Librarians when a motion was proposed that Australian university libraries should cease purchasing journals from Elsevier in order to protect declining library budgets for other priorities. Plus ça change ...

Cox (2002) outlined the rise of Robert Maxwell and the Pergamon publishing empire which was eventually incorporated into what is now Reed Elsevier. In 1951, Elsevier was a purely Dutch company before becoming the largest STM publisher in the world by the end of the twentieth century. Cox noted "where would we have been without the US market?" (Cox, 2002, p. 276). This basically reflects the fact that the profits of the major multinationals depend significantly on sales to libraries of universities and research institutions on the North American continent. Solutions to the 'serial crisis' may only result by action in North America where 65% of STM sales occur.

The recent downturn of the US dollar could, however, provide a significant catalyst for change. It is somewhat ironic for those in countries whose currencies had depreciated during the 1990s against the US dollar, for example Australia, Canada, New Zealand and South Africa, to hear the cries of American anguish in 2003 and 2004. What has been beneficial, however, from the American experience is that their universities, as well as complaining about the serial crisis, have delineated strategies for scholarly communication change which involve their faculties.

5.   Scholarly Communication Patterns

University and institutional researchers create a large part of the world's knowledge base. Researchers, unless they are tied into institutional policies of copyright protection, or are prudent with their licensing, tend to give away their intellectual output free of charge to publishers. In many instances their work is refereed by other academics free of charge. Academics become 'editors in chief' or sit on editorial boards for minimal returns as part of a misguided belief in academic collegiality. Editors in chief usually orchestrate peer review and provide frameworks for manuscript publication. The academic community currently handles free of charge for commercial publishers a significant proportion of the intellectual infrastructure of journals.

The UK ALPSP (2002) report, Authors and electronic publishing, found that fewer than 1% of academics considered direct financial reward to be their primary publishing objective. What attracts authors is the ability to communicate with their peer group (33%) and career advancement (22%) which comes primarily from publication in highly regarded and, even more importantly, highly cited journals. This latter point is somewhat worrying as the Institute of Scientific Information (ISI) citation rankings are not infallible and need to be taken into account with other metrics in terms of research assessment.

The Faustian perspectives on the publishing cycle are generally meant to relate to the giving away by scholars of their research output to multinational publishers in return for the branding and accreditation which results from publication. Parks (2001) observed "that the actors in the academic publishing game have little or no incentive to stop publishing in the current journals". Moreover, it is interesting that by the time their work is published, academics no longer consider the published printed journal to be the primary mode for knowledge facilitation; they have often already disseminated the contents of their work by email to their global peer groups; or their product has been 'mined' by other interested academics in the web environment through email alert services and/or web searching.

There is, thus, an almost schizophrenic nature (the Jekyll and Hyde syndrome) to an academic as author of an article or book, who is not overly concerned about her or his intellectual property as long as it is branded and accredited, and the academic as reader, who complains about the high cost of journals for the library and increasingly prefers electronic free access to material. The academic is both the creator and consumer of knowledge but is acting dysfunctionally if viewed in theoretical terms of the scholarly communication of knowledge.

In Frank Capra's award winning 1946 movie, It's a wonderful life, Clarence the angel shows George Bailey what life would have been like in the small American town if he had not existed. We all make a difference in some way but, according to Schnoor (2003), publishers and, by implication academics, have taken this idea to a new level by trying to quantify the impact of everybody's research on everyone else, for example, by counting citations and publishing impact factors.

6.   Research Assessment and Implications for Publishing

The Australian Government funded research project, Changing research practices in the digital information and communication environment, reflected this dysfunctionality in scholarly communication processes and recommended that a much more holistic understanding of the dynamics of the whole scholarly cycle (Houghton, Steele & Henty, 2003).

New opportunities in scholarly publishing have, however, to be placed within historical frameworks such as the need for performance measurement and research assessment. We need in terms of research assessment, to establish a more complex set of citation indicators to establish new publishing paradigms. Rowlands (2003) foreshadowed that we need a broader range of indicators.

At present, the increasing dominance of quantitative research assessment procedures and citation analyses plays into the hands of multinational publishers, particularly in the northern hemisphere, and particularly citation sources such as those operated by the ISI. There is increasing evidence that authors are switching to the aggregated commercial publishing outlets because of their impact factor in such areas as citation listings (Oppenheim, 2004). Such processes also affect new researchers, multi-disciplinary researchers and those who publish in 'smaller' journals.

Authors are thus encouraged by their departments or institutions, because of research assessment practices, to seek out publishers who are included in the Institute of Scientific Information (ISI) citation rankings. There is also evidence that journals are changing their practices to obtain citation increases. In an ISI website description of leading journals, the editors of one journal reported that in order to seek maximum citations they changed editorial practices by accelerating the editorial review process, moving to theme-based issues, reducing the size of the editorial board and increasing the rate of submissions (which also increased the rate of rejections) (Jeste, 2003). It is clear there are major issues at stake and that the process will need to change in the publication arena to match the required outcomes. Publishing has to be seen within the totality of the research process.

Citations in themselves should not be seen as sacrosanct in a policy-making context. For example, in the higher education sector we need to consider a whole range of inputs that facilitate knowledge production, outputs, and downstream research impact and quality measures. In research assessment exercises, for example in the UK and New Zealand, there is considerable emphasis on standard metrics, particularly publications within the ISI citation indices. There are some predictions that publications indexed by ISI provide sufficient metrics for analysis so that these articles do not need to be read for assessment processes. This is known as 'peer review by peer review', meaning that assessors do not need to review publications again which have already been allegedly peer-reviewed by branded journals.

7.   Peer Review Issues

There has been concern expressed about the efficiencies of peer review particularly as the demands increase on academics in terms of their time. Peer review done properly takes considerable time and earns the reviewer little 'kudos' except for the warm feelings of (misguided?) collegiality. A recent study for the Cochrane Collaboration provided somewhat damaging evidence about the inefficiencies of the peer review system in improving the quality of published bio-medical research (Jefferson, Alderson, Davidoff & Wagner, 2003). While their conclusions have been vigorously debated, most agree that there are relatively few comprehensive analyses of the peer review process, particularly if viewed historically. The Cochrane study was based on 21 studies of the peer review system chosen from a literature survey of 135 studies. The well-accepted practice of concealing the identities of peer reviewers appears to have little impact on the quality assessment process. Anecdotal evidence often indicates the exercising of academic rivalries within the peer review process when blind refereeing is the norm. There also seems to be a confusion at times between elements of copy editing and peer review processes.

Garca-Berthou and Alcaraz, researchers at the University of Girona, reported that 38% of a sample of papers in Nature and a quarter of those sampled in The British Medical Journal, two of the world's most respected scientific journals, contained one or more statistical errors (Garca-Berthou & Alcaraz, 2004). While not all of these 'errors' led to wrong conclusions, the authors believe that 4% of the errors may have "caused non-significant findings to be misrepresented as being significant". We undoubtedly need more research into editorial peer review. If only a fraction of the money that has gone into scholarly publishing had gone into analyses of the peer review process we might have a clearer picture of the cycles involved and assertions perceived or understood. This is similar to the spending of billions of dollars on the acquisition of knowledge but relatively few studies on its use once the material has been acquired.

8.   Copyright and Open Source Issues

Another area like peer review which is seen as sacrosanct, but is often the cause of academic misunderstandings, is the issue of copyright. Drahos and Braithwaite (2002), in their publication *Information feudalism*, have argued for the major importance of intellectual property rights in the modern knowledge economy. They take their title from the European medieval period when feudalism became a system of government and the majority of the working class had to live with the arbitrariness of ultimate power. They argued that it was the loss of the Roman Empire's capacity to protect its citizens that provided an important pre-requisite for the feudalization of its social relationships. We now need to protect citizens from knowledge monopolization imposed by ruthless digital rights management systems.

When governments set intellectual property rules they start to interfere in markets in information. This action is only justifiable if the costs of deregulated information markets outweigh the benefits. Drahos and Braithwaite (2002, pp. 2–3) suggested that governments rarely take a cost–benefit approach to intellectual property and standards, which today are largely the product of the global strategies of a relatively small number of companies and business organizations that have realized the value of intellectual property sooner than anyone else. The situation in scholarly publishing reflects some of the dialogues in the computing industry between Microsoft and open source providers. It is important to keep pressure on commercial providers by judicious consideration and evaluation of open source offerings, while recognizing the need also for open standards.

Protection of the ownership of original creation, which is vested in the creator, is a pre-requisite, at least in theory, for knowledge access and distribution. The retention of electronic rights by creators of knowledge in universities is an essential process in terms of scholarly communication in the twenty-first century. In monograph publishing some trends in commercial eBook offerings are leaning towards 'imprisoning text'. This tendency needs to be balanced against the global distribution of ideas by the Academy in the most effective manner, given that financial reward is not a prime motivation for the academic author.

Lawrence Lessig of Stanford University has argued the creation of a 'Creative Commons' as a common intellectual space. Lessig (2003) defined four categories for licensing or authorizing the use of creative and intellectual work:

- attribution (author shares work, but requires right of attribution);
- non-commercial (author shares work but only for non-commercial use);
- derivative (author allows distribution but disallows derivative work); and
- copyleft (share and share alike).

Lessig has extended this into the Science Commons, a new project of Creative Commons, which will be launched on 1 January 2005. Its mission is to encourage scientific innovation by making it easier for scientists, universities and industries to use literature, data, and share their knowledge with others. Lessig has said, "my view is that the law has, for unintended and intended reasons, radically changed the burden on creators and producers of knowledge who wish to share and make their work available to a larger public...my objective is to work to find ways to reduce that burden" (Lessig, 2004).

The work by project RoMEO (Rights MEtadata for Open archiving) in the UK, now assumed by SHERPA (Securing a Hybrid Environment for Research Preservation and Access), has established a base listing by publisher which documents the ability or not to place material in institutional repositories. This is an essential framework for those wishing to adopt advocacy programs within their universities. The development of the Creative Commons licences and the issues arising out of open access initiatives also constitute major developments in the increasing availability of open networked research.

9.   The Academic Monograph

Much of the debate on the so-called crisis in scholarly communication has focused on the article, particularly in science, technology and medicine but few have analysed in depth issues relating to the future of the academic monograph. Monograph sales have been declining globally in the social sciences and humanities, while many university presses are either closing down or are in dire financial straits (Steele, 2003). The monograph is still the prime instrument of research output for many scholars in the humanities and social sciences, although again, as with articles, the end product is often seen more as a prerequisite for tenure and promotion rather than for an effective mechanism for the dissemination of knowledge.

Cronin and La Barre (2004) revealed that, despite rhetoric to the contrary by many universities, the publication of a monograph remains the essential prerequisite for tenure and promotion in the humanities, even though many markets for traditional publishing are drying up. Within the monograph sector, it is clear that the brand name of an institutional press, such as Cambridge University Press or Stanford, is itself enough to be a major factor in promotion and tenure unless reviews are severely critical.

New models based on existing institutional infrastructures are emerging through open access initiatives and institutional repository developments. Two strands, namely the 'decline' in university presses and the 'rise' of university libraries/repository centres, are now beginning to intersect and could allow the rebirth of the scholarly book in a significant way. Digital publishing technologies, linked to global networking and international interoperability protocols and metadata standards, allow for an appropriately branded institutional output to serve as an indication of a university's quality and also as an effective scholarly communication tool through visibility, status and public value.

10.   Institutional Repositories

Institutional repositories have received very good press but the reality is, at the time of writing, that many repositories are under populated. The issues in populating them are in fact cultural and political rather than technical (Steele, 2004b). It is clear, however, that ePrints and open access repositories/activities have not yet entered the consciousness of many researchers and that there are a number of issues that need to be addressed, particularly in the context of copyright, peer review and long term utility.

Often academics, particularly in the sciences, do not see a need to deposit in their institutional repositories, as they already deposit in global subject repositories or they are 'catered for' by the multinational publishers. Nonetheless their publications, if they have been deposited in subject repositories, can be relatively easily harvested back to their own institution's repository. Younger scholars are often reluctant, at say the post-doctoral level, to deposit articles although, on the other hand, the digital publication of theses in the social sciences and humanities provides a publication opening which is rapidly disappearing in traditional publishing markets.

The need for an institutional repository is something that requires commitment at a number of levels within the institution. The university needs to provide a coherent administrative structure to support trusted digital repositories and individual authors have some responsibility to deposit material. Institutional repositories can also be relatively easily incorporated into existing library and IT structures within universities. Experience has shown that the effort and organizational costs required to address academic concerns regarding publishing, copyright and scholarly communication issues in general have tended to far outstrip the technical requirements.

Scholarly advocacy, preferably on a one-to-one basis, is the key to scholarly communication change. The movement to deposit material in institutional repositories often needs a one-to-one dialogue or dedicated departmental meetings to explain to academics that depositing in their own repositories will not impact upon their output in traditional journals; indeed, such deposits often increase global access to their publications. The process of populating repositories will no doubt be incremental and modular, and will require institutional backing at local and national levels. Lynch (2003) sees institutional repositories as the essential infrastructure for scholarship in the digital age. In his opinion, they allow "universities to apply serious, systematic leverage to accelerate changes taking place in scholarship and scholarly communication".

The Australian National University (ANU) ePrint repository (http:// eprints.anu.edu.au) has been one of the more successful repositories, perhaps by concentrating on internal faculty publications—'guild literature'—and not so much on the STM post-printed article. By March 2004 the repository held just over 2,000 'documents'; these cover material from pre-prints to refereed articles, and from conference papers to books. By May 2004 these ePrints had also been included in the ANU's D-Space Repository, which has a wider role in terms of inclusion of material such as art and archival images. A number of universities are now examining the wider scope of defining, populating and supporting digital repositories. In this latter development publishing is seen in a much wider context, for example, databases of various complexions such as statistics and astronomical sky charts. Scholarship has become data-intensive and we are now looking at appropriate cyber infrastructures for the larger end of science research. It is not the purpose of the current paper to examine and document dataset repositories and technical infrastructures, but we do need to recognize that institutional repositories have a wider remit than simply textual frameworks.

11.   ePress Initiatives

Australian university libraries were amongst the first in the world to move to electronic versions of serials and to relinquish print copies. Similarly, Australian universities are pioneering access to electronic monographs through new ePresses (Steele, 2004a). ePress developments have been accelerated because of the lack of suitable global markets for most Australian material and, secondly, a decline in the number of local outlets for scholarly monographs. Major scoping and benchmarking activities led to the establishment of the ANU ePress in early 2003. The ANU ePress has a focus on monographs, while the Monash University ePress, founded at roughly the same time, has an initial focus on serials.

Production implements XML standards and the facility to view via HTML, with PDF as the main print output format. Material is free of charge on a website, (the cost of printing being the responsibility, if required, of the reader at their home site) or is priced to maximize purchase. It is interesting that the University of California eScholarship monographs are monitored for PDF downloads in terms of consideration for eventual traditional publishing outlets. The technical issues in relation to this are covered in detail by Roy Tennant of the California Digital Library (Tennant, 2002). The abstracting and indexing of chapters of the monographs ensures content is picked up by appropriate indexing agencies. Some of the existing commercial models, such as Oxford Scholarship Online, allow searching across their monograph platforms, and emphasize linkages through abstracts and indices for each individual chapter. This model follows the commercial model of serials from subscription packages to abstracting infrastructure.

As a consequence of the development of such consortial electronic packages, problems might flow for independent scholars who do not belong to an institution. In the past, in most libraries, interested members of the public could enter a physical library and read a book on the shelf, even if they were not affiliated to that institution. However, in the future they will need to be authenticated and, at best, given one-day 'walk-in' privileges. Electronic intellectual ghettos may be created in which the bulk of the population is prevented by passwords from accessing information which was previously available 'free'.

Some ePresses, such as ANU, restrict themselves to the output of their own institution, at least in the first instance. They operate as a 'public good', in the same fashion as the university libraries themselves. Many would agree with the Director of the University of Illinois Press who stated "Universities may find that a more honest way to track the cost of publications would be to fund them up front, publish them electronically and publish them free" (Regier, 2002). The desire to make available the intellectual output, particularly of guild literature from the university is just as valid a resource demand within a university, as the acquisition of research material by the library for the university. The repositioning of the university library in the digital repository movement will mean changes in the role and function of libraries, for example, in the areas of collaborative research, publication and digital archiving. Cervone (2004) has commented that "on the way to changing scholarly communication, libraries may end up changing themselves".

12.   Print On Demand (POD)

Several publishers have found that posting a free copy of a book on the Internet encourages sales of the print copies through their normal press outlet. Jason Epstein, the opening keynote speaker at the 2003 Cairns International Conference on the Book, outlined his vision for the future in commercial POD machines which will be ubiquitous in the delivery of print documents in fashion similar to ATM machines today (Epstein, 2001). The primacy of the printed form will remain as the main access mechanism for research scholars in the social sciences, humanities and discipline area studies. The issues surrounding POD facilities are not new, but the opportunities for printing through institutional network frameworks are now more easily available. Electronic templates can now be filled in at the desktop with either departmental budget codes or personal credit card details. Requests are sent down the line to the university printers to be printed in off-peak times, often within 24 hours. Output can be picked up or delivered from a central university point of sale, for example, the campus bookshop or a Kinko's fast copy type operation.

13. eBooks

Lynch (2001) noted "issues of preservation, continuity of access and the integrity of our cultural and intellectual record are particularly critical in the context of e-book readers and the works designed for them. These have enormous importance both for individual consumers and for society as a whole". Lynch makes a distinction between electronic publishing, which is the incremental evolution of print publishing to the digital world and the new models of digital authorship. There is a requirement to differentiate between the two forms of digital knowledge in an historical and prospective context.

The term eBooks is taken here to refer to text which is created electronically and made available in a variety of forms from POD to eBook readers. Primarily, it does refer to the initial reading or browsing of text on a screen. We are already seeing a variety of eBook offerings. It is clear that many of the models that were adopted for electronic serial sales are now being replicated, rightly or wrongly, (mostly wrongly in this author's opinion) in the eBook arena. It would be wrong if the models for the research monograph, via electronic access, were taken from those publishers who are seeking to make significant profits from the textbook, undergraduate or coursepack market.

The eBook situation is a very confusing one and resembles, at the time of writing, the early days of electronic serial offerings in the myriad of forms, access mechanisms and payments. Publishers are either 'locking up' the text of their offerings, presumably fearful of the distribution of text and thus a loss of revenue, or are making the text available by 24×7 aggregated subscriptions. Apparently, one of the boom areas in the eBook offerings of the British firm Taylor and Francis, is the one-, two- or three-day electronic loans of material by students for relative small prices. Given the total cost of textbooks and the use patterns of the 'Net generation', this perhaps shouldn't come as a surprise.

14. Concluding Comments

It is clear that the digital environment is both a transforming and an uncertain one. The impact of open access initiatives could have a profound impact on scholarly knowledge distribution. The process will be both liberating and disruptive, but in the short term will undoubtedly be a hybrid situation for access to and distribution of knowledge. Liberating in that it could release a large amount of scholarly material in a variety of forms globally, without the financial barriers imposed by multinational publishers. Disruptive in the sense that major changes will be required in scholarly practice to change the paradigms of scholarly communication.

The new business models for ePresses are often predicated on 'public good' foundations rather than a return to the investor in a shareholder context. Prospective viewpoints of the information society are extremely complex and there are no simple answers. Viewpoints vary from the utopian to the share market-driven perspective, to others formed by technological determinism (Hornby & Clarke, 2003). In this process it needs to be recognized that consumers should be the focal point of the knowledge environment, as it is they who will ultimately determine needs and information search patterns.

Libraries are already working in an institutional context to provide coordinated portals within broader content management frameworks. Certainly they need to morph into new roles where they are as much involved with the interactive taxonomy of knowledge as they were initially with the print. Keller, the Librarian of Stanford University has argued that libraries face obsoletion, not simply because they are losing the fight to be the "Internet for eyeballs", but because they are abandoning their role as collection builders and managers (Keller, Reich & Herkovic, 2003).

'Scholar portals' which search across commercial and free databases and customize for the individual at the desktop, will become more widespread both in commercial and non-commercial settings. This is particularly relevant as consumers are time-poor and they are being fast-forwarded in Google-type directions. Research at the Centre for Information Behaviour at City University London has indicated that some users are gradually being divorced from the traditional frameworks of communication and knowledge, and becoming almost "promiscuous " in their information seeking behaviour (Nicholas et al., 2003).

Incentive changes can thus impact on publishing practice. The JISC Open Access survey published in 2004, noted that while almost two-thirds of respondents were aware of open access concepts, only 25% were made aware of this by their institutions. Academics indicated that if publishing work in an open access outlet was a condition of a research grant (and presumably also mandatory university policy) they would comply (Key Perspectives Limited, 2004).

The age of digital information, or rather the age of digital information overload, is certainly with us. Scholarly publishing symbolizes the public/private struggles within the knowledge economy. Willinsky and Wolfson (2003) indicated that the future lies "in convincing scholars, in their capacity as writers, reviewers, editors and professional association leaders, and that it is now time to move away from the commercialization of academic publishing that has taken place over the last four of five decades".

New models will need to be developed which may not fit late twentieth century business models, which may need to change to ones which will utilize and benefit from the public domain infrastructure to support access to scholarly knowledge. As indicated earlier, there are likely to be profound changes in the role and function of many research libraries as user patterns change in terms of accessing information, and libraries become more active partners in the scholarly communication process (Greenstein, 2004). Research and teaching platforms will link appropriate repositories through digital asset management systems, with automated metadata harvesting. Such repositories will be linked to new universal citation processes and open source/open access philosophies.

Access to knowledge in the twenty-first century could be liberated in terms of cost for the vast proportion of material created. As history has shown, the ability to predict knowledge access and transfer patterns is a complicated one. The digital revolution has brought us to another set of information crossroads. While some information highways could lead to scholarly dead ends, hopefully there will be sufficient open access pathways that can be traversed for the benefit of scholars in particular and society in general.

References

ALPSP. Association of Learned and Professional Society Publishers. (2002). *Authors in electronic publishing*. Worthing: ALPSP.

Berners-Lee, T. J. (2003). New Web will enable scientists to share data across disciplines. *Chronicle of Higher Education*, February 7. Retrieved November 15, 2004, from http://chronicle.com/free/v49/i22/22a02502.htm

Cervone, H. F. (2004). The repository adventure. *Library Journal*. Retrieved November 15, 2004, from http://www.libraryjournal.com/article/CA421033

Chartier, R. (2001). Readers and readings in the electronic age. Retrieved November 15, 2004, from http://www.text-e.org/conf/index.cfm?ConfText_ID=5

Cox, B. (2002). The Pergamon phenomenon 1951 to 1991: Robert Maxwell and scientific publishing. *Learned Publishing, 15*, 273–278.

Cronin, B., & La Barre, K. (2004). Mickey Mouse and Milton: Book publishing in the humanities. *Learned Publishing, 17*(2), 85–98.

Daley, E. (2003). Expanding the concept of literacy. *Educause Review*, March/April, 33–39.

Drahos, P., & Braithwaite, J. (2002). Information feudalism: Who owns the knowledge economy? London: Earthscan.

Eisenstein, E. L. (1979). *The printing press as an agent of change*. Cambridge: Cambridge University Press.

Epstein, J. (2001). *Book business publishing: Past, present and future*. New York: Norton.

Esposito, J. J. (2003). The processed book. *First Monday, 8*(3). Retrieved November 15, 2004, from http://www.firstmonday.dk/issues/issue8_3/esposito/index.html

Garca-Berthou, E., & Alcaraz, C. (2004). Quoted in *The Economist*, What is published in scientific journals may not be as true as it should be. Retrieved November 15, 2004, from http://www.library.yale.edu/~llicense/ListArchives/0406/msg00063.html

Greenstein, D. (2004). Library stewardship in a networked age. Retrieved November 15, 2004, from http://www.clir.org/pubs/reports/pub126/green.html

Guedon, J.-C. (2001). *In Oldenburg's long shadow*. Washington: Association of Research Libraries.

Hey, T. (2004). Why engage in e-Science? *Library + Information Update*, (3), 25–27.

Hey, T., & Trefethen, A. (2003). The data deluge. Retrieved November 15, 2004, from http://www.ecs.soton.ac.uk/~ajgh/

Hornby, S., & Clarke, Z. (Ed.). (2003). *Challenge and change in the information society*. London: Facet.

Houghton, J. W., Steele, C., & Henty, M. (2003). *Changing research practices in the digital information and communication environment*. Canberra: Department of Education, Science and Training. Retrieved November 15, 2004, from http://www.cfses.com/documents/Changing_Research_Practices.pdf

James, P., & McQueen-Thompson, D. (2002). Abstracting knowledge formation: A report on academia and publishing. In S. Cooper (Ed). *Scholars and entrepreneurs* (pp. 183–206). Melbourne: Arena.

Jefferson, T. O., Alderson P.; Davidoff F.; & Wager E. (2003). *Editorial peer-review for improving the quality of reports of bio-medical studies*. Oxford: Cochrane Library.

Jeste, D. V. (2003). American Journal of Geriatric Psychiatry. Retrieved November 15, 2004, from http://www.in-cites.com/journals/AmJGerPsy.html

Keller, M. A., Reich V. A., & Herkovic, A. C. (2003). What is a library anymore, anyway? *First Monday, 8*(3). Retrieved November 15, 2004, from http://www.firstmonday.dk/issues/issue8_5/keller/index.html

Key Perspectives Limited. (2004). JISC/OSI journal authors survey report. Retrieved November 15, 2004, from http://www.jisc.ac.uk/uploaded_documents/JISCOAreport1.pdf

Lessig, L. (2003). Open Education interview. Retrieved November 15, 2004, from http://www.elearnspace.org/Articles/lessig.htm

Lessig, L. (2004). Open access and creative common sense. *Open Access Now*, May 10. Retrieved November 15, 2004, from http://www.biomedcentral.com/openaccess/archive/?page=feature&issue=16

Lynch, C. (2001). The battle to define the future of the book in the digital world. *First Monday, 6*(6). Retrieved November 15, 2004, from http://firstmonday.org/issues/issue6_6/lynch/index.html

Lynch, C. (2003). Institutional repositories: Essential infrastructure for scholarship in the digital age. ARL Bimonthly Report. Retrieved November 15, 2004, from http://www.arl.org/newsltr/226/ir.html

Nicholas, D., Dobrowolksi T., Withey R., Russell C., Huntington P., & Williams P. (2003). Digital information consumers, players and purchasers: Information seeking behaviour in the new digital interactive environment. *Aslib Proceedings, 55*(1/2), 23–31.

Oppenheim, C. (2004). Research excellence and academic publications: the parameters for change. Retrieved November 15, 2004, from http://www.humanities.org.au/NSCF/current.htm

Oxford Scholarship Online. Retrieved November 15, 2004, from http://www.oxfordscholarship.com/

Parks, R. P. (2001). The Faustian grip of academic publishing. Retrieved November 15, 2004, from http://econwpa.wustl.edu:8089/eps/mic/papers/0202/0202005.pdf

Regier, W. G. (2002). Quoted in Smallwood, S. The crumbling intellectual foundation. *Chronicle of Higher Education*, September 20, A10.

Rowlands, I. (2003). Knowledge production, consumption and impact: Policy indicators for a changing world. *Aslib Proceedings, 55*(12), 5–12.

Schnoor, J. L. (2003). Making an impact. *Environmental Science and Technology*, March 1, 79A.

SHERPA (Securing a Hybrid Environment for Research Preservation and Access) Retrieved November 15, 2004, from http://www.sherpa.ac.uk/

Steele, C. (2003). Phoenix rising: New models for the research monograph. *Learned Publishing,* *16*(2), 111–122.

Steele, C. (2004a). The wizards of Oz. Retrieved November 15, 2004, from http://agenda. cern.ch/askArchive.php?base=agenda&categ=a035925&id=a035925s13t7/transparencies

Steele, C. (2004b). The sound of one hand clapping: The politics of scholarly communication. Retrieved November 15, 2004, from http://www.lub.lu.se/ncsc2004/

Tennant, R. (Ed.). (2002). *XML in libraries.* New York: Neal.

Willinsky, J., & Wolfson, L. (2001). A tipping point for publishing reform? *Journal of Electronic Publishing* 7(2). Retrieved November 15, 2004, from http://www.press.umich.edu/jep/ 07-02/willinsky.html

Chapter 11

DEVELOPMENT OF, AND TRENDS IN, SCHOLARLY COMMUNICATION IN CHINA

Jinwei Yan and Zheng Liu

1. Chapter Overview

Scholarly communication is a process through which scholars issue and utilize academic information in various subject fields via various channels. With the development of network technology, the traditional paper-based scholarly communication system has been challenged. Library and information science academics in China have been researching scholarly communication in networked environments for some time. There are three aspects to this research: the issue and dissemination of scholarly information, information services, and organizing scholarly information in networked environments.

The information infrastructure in China has made significant progress. Four backbone networks are linked with the Internet, the users of the Internet have rapidly increased, and scholarly information resources on the network have become richer and richer. Several Chinese full-text databases now exist.

In this chapter the results of a survey are reported. The survey concerned both citation analysis and Internet investigation. The survey showed that the environment of scholarly communication and the information behaviour of scholars have changed dramatically in mainland China. The network is now playing a more and more important role in scholarly communication. Although the traditional scholarly communication media such as journals and monographs have not declined and remain as the mainstream media of scholarly communication, the network has brought us a new platform for scholarly communication. Publishers have begun to provide electronic versions of their printed publications, and therefore the spread of academic information is more rapid. Literature databases, with huge amounts of academic information, have broadened the scope of scholarly communication in China. New means of scholarly communication, such as academic forums

H. S. Ching, P. W. T. Poon and C. McNaught (Eds.), eLearning and Digital Publishing, 195–219.

and websites, provide new facilities for interactive scholarly communication. Distinct differences exist between different subject fields, with each subject area developing its own best strategies for scholarly communication.

2. Introduction

Scholarly communication is a process through which scholars spread and receive academic information in various subject fields and via various channels. Generally speaking, researchers issue and gain scholarly information using two main strategies:

1. Informal scholarly communication, including private letters, manuscripts, experimental reports, private periodicals, minutes of meetings, dissertations, introduction of sample products, etc. This can all be called 'gray literature' and is not published.
2. Formal scholarly communication, including textbooks, monographs reference books, journals, newspapers, standards documents, technology reports, audio-visual materials, etc. These are published by formal academic presses or institutes.

Before the Internet, almost all scholarly communication was based on paper media. This so-called traditional scholarly communication system usually is comprised of several elements: scholars, publishers, distributors or service agencies, and libraries. This chain forms the foundation of information services for scientific research and education by which the scholarly information stream is transmitted from one link to another.

With the development of computers, networks and communication technologies, the environment of scholarly communication has undergone a great change. EJournals, databases, eMeetings, mailing lists, and so forth have gradually become more important. The traditional scholarly communication system based on paper media is now under serious challenge. So, it is very important to analyze the change of behaviour when scholars issue and gain scholarly information in networked environments, as this will help us understand trends for the future. This paper is based on the current situation in mainland China, and the statistics and analysis are focused on Chinese academic media.

3. Review of the Research on Scholarly Communication in China

Library and information science academics in China have been researching scholarly communication in networked environments for some time. Through analysis of the articles published, we find that there are three aspects to this research.

3.1.   *Issuing and Disseminating Scholarly Information in Networked Environments*

In paper media environments, the findings of scientific research are published in journals and books. However, in the Internet environment, network technology greatly promotes the development of electronic media, as well as leading to the emergence of digital publications, and this has far-reaching impacts on the issue and dissemination of scientific information. Fang Qing (2000) surmised that publication on the Internet had made the concept of scientific literature more and more obscure, and difficult to distinguish formal and informal forms of literature. Liu Jia (1999) pointed out that one important feature, or advantage, of electronic publishing via the Internet was free issue of information. In addition, Fang Qing (2000–2001) deemed that electronic publishing shortened the delay of issuing scholarly information and greatly satisfied users' demand for timely communication of information.

3.2.   *Information Services in Networked Environments*

Information services are a series of user-oriented actions conducted by institutions to assist patrons to get the scholarly information they need for the process of scholarly communication. Zhang Xiaolin (2000) noted that networked environments greatly change the basic strategies of users in exchanging scholarly information, and also the characteristics and contents of their information needs: all this must change users' information behaviour. Through analyzing these changes, he put forward the concept and pattern of 'knowledge services' in the Internet environment. Fang Qing (2002) pointed out that the reading patterns of users in getting scientific information from a network is changing and a kind of self-aid 'just-in-time' pattern is emerging. This changing pattern of scientific information services has implications for how information is displayed in networked environments.

Regarding information services in academic libraries, Zhang Xiaolin (2000) pointed out that librarians need to sufficiently recognize the impact caused by the re-organization of the scholarly communication system in the society, so as to fully utilize the capacity provided by a virtual system of information services. This could rapidly transform the closed campus information system, based on library buildings and physical collections, into a new open scholarly communication environment which is user-oriented, dependent on networked and digitized communication systems, based on distributed resources and retrieval/delivery systems, and centred on knowledge services to support education and scientific research.

3.3. *Organizing Scholarly Information in Networked Environments*

Organizing information is the premise of information services for scholarly communication. For effective information dissemination, we have to change the methods of organizing scholarly information to adapt to changing situations. In networked environments, there are at least two aspects of change in organizing information. Firstly, the pattern of information structure has changed. Xu Jianhua (2000) noted that the increasing amount of digital information on the Internet is overwhelming for traditional methods of organizing information in libraries. Traditional services involve collecting, classifying, cataloguing, even using MARC (machine-readable cataloguing record) records, and indexing materials; all these are hierarchical strategies. Thus, in order to reveal and organize information resources on the Internet effectively, we must break through the traditional pattern of tree-structures and create network-structures for scholarly information. Further, the object of organizing information has changed. In the Internet environment we must treat the 'knowledge unit' as the object of organizing information instead of a 'document unit', so that we can lay down a series of new standards and regulations for organizing information (He Lingyong, 2000).

Comparing the research in China with that conducted by researchers in western countries, we find that foreigners tend to focus on the impact of electronic publishing and digital libraries on scholarly communication, and there are case studies to learn the changes in scholars' behaviour in searching for the information they need, to evaluate network resources, and so on. In China, people are more interested in exploring the pattern or system of scholarly communication and 'knowledge services' in networked environments theoretically, but there is less research on electronic publishing and scholars' behaviour, and few case studies.

4.   Analysis of the Environment of Scholarly Communication in China

With the development of the network in China, the traditional environment of scholarly communication based on paper media is transforming to a modern environment based on networks.

Table 11-1. Publications statistics in China (from *The Annual of Chinese Publications*)

Year	Books	Journals	Newspapers	Digital publications
2000	143,376	8,725	2,007	2,254
2001	154,526	8,889	2,111	2,369
2002	178,880	9,002	2,137	4,713
2003	190,391	9,074	2,119	4,961

4.1.   The Development of Paper Publications

In non-networked environments, printed monographs and journals are the main media distributing scholarly information. Academic journals, with their ability to establish the priority of findings and deliver information rapidly, play an important role in scholarly communication. Affected by their longer writing and publishing period, academic books may not be a good media to transmit up-to-date scholarly information, but still keep their notable function in scholarly communication because of the diversity of information needs and research styles in different subject fields. Although the Internet has developed by leaps and bounds, the traditional scholarly communication system, with the basis of the two kinds of main paper media, has still developed steadily. Table 11-1 shows that books and journals published in China have kept increasing since 2000.

4.2.   The Development of Digital Publications

The data concerning digital publications in table 11-1 only take account of the number of CD-ROMs published, and there are no more detailed data to separate content types of the CD-ROMs. Digital publications have doubled 2001 to 2003. It is not clear why the statistics of *The Annual of Chinese Publications* does not include full-text databases of journals and books. The possible reason is that almost all of these databases are the digital editions of paper publications.

It is worthwhile considering the nature of several leading full-text databases of journals and monographs in mainland China. There are three Internet-based full-text databases of Chinese journals, namely China Academic Journals, the Full-text Database of Chinese Science & Technology Journals, and the Wanfang Data Digital Periodical Subsystem; these have the widest coverage of contents, the highest utilization ratio, and the heaviest market share in China mainland at present.

China Academic Journals (CAJ) is mainly sponsored by the Tsinghua Tongfang Optical Disc Co., Ltd., the China Academic Journal Electronic

Publishing House, and the China Optical Memory National Engineering Research Centre. Services are provide by local mirror-sites in subscribers' intranets, by authorized remote access to CNKI websites or by CD-ROM. CAJ contains 5,300 journals in full text from 1994 to the present (China National Knowledge Infrastructure website).

The Full-text Database of Chinese Science & Technology Journals has been developed and published by the Chongqing VIP Information Company, and is termed the most complete and comprehensive Chinese periodical database in China. This database has collected 6,000,000 articles from more than 8,400 journals published after 1989; it is divided into seven collections and subdivided into 74 special subjects (VIP information website). The Wanfang Data Digital Periodical Subsystem is one of the series information products of the company. The database holds verbatim contents of more than 2,500 core academic journals in five categories—science, engineering, agriculture, medicine and humanities. The system treats a copy of a journal as the unit, keeps the style of original printed version, and adopts HTML or PDF format (Wanfang Data Digital Periodical Subsystem website).

The eBook market is highly competitive in China. There are four main Chinese eBook systems in the mainland, namely the China Digital Library, the SuperStar Digital Library, the Chinese EBook Network and the Founder Apabi Digital Library. The China Digital Library was created by the National Library of China, and began to provide a remote access service in September 2000. Now it holds 6 billion pages of eBooks and extends its local mirror sites as branches of the digital library. The SuperStar Digital Library was established by the Beijing SuperStar Electronic Co., Ltd. in July 1998 (SuperStar Digital Library website); it has more than 200,000 eBooks now, among which more than 10,000 volumes can be read online freely (Zhang Chunhong & Jiang Gangmiao, 2002). The Chinese E-book Network was established by Shusheng Technology Ltd. in April 2000 by collecting 30,000 new books published after 1999 (Chinese E-book Network website). The Founder Apabi Digital Library was founded by the Beijing Founder Electronic Co., Ltd; it holds 10,000 recently published eBooks (Founder Apabi Digital Library website). All of the four companies claim that they have resolved all copyright problems.

4.3.   The Development of Networked Environments
          for Scholarly Communication

4.3.1.   The Internet in China

According to the *Report on the Development of Internet in China* (online), up to December 31, 2003, the number of computers logged into the network had reached 30,890,000. This was an increase of 48.3% compared with the corresponding period in 2002, and was an increase of 103.3 times compared with the first statistics in October 1997. There were 340,040 domain names registered under CN; this was an increase of 89.4% compared with the same term the previous year. The total capacity of the throughput of the portal going abroad from the China mainland reached 27,216 MB, which was an increase of 190.1% compared with the same term in 2002, and was 1,071.2 times what it was in 1997 when the capacity was 25.408 MB.

With the rapid development of the Internet, the information infrastructure in China has made great progress. The four backbone networks, which are ChinaNET, CSTNet, CERNet and ChinaGBN, are linked with the Internet. Nationwide, ChinaNet covers 31 provinces, CSTNet has connected one hundred institutes of the Chinese Academy of Sciences, CERTNet has linked up more than 800 universities and colleges, and ChinaGBN has its business in 24 cities and provinces. These backbone networks not only supply platforms for scholarly communication, but also promote the construction and utilization of scholarly information resources, especially for the development of academic databases.

4.3.2.   *Users in Networked Environments*

The statistics show that Internet users, who only utilize Internet resources on average at least 1 hour per week, had reached 79 million by January 2004; this was an increase of 34.5% compared with the same term in 2002. The number of network users was 128.2 times as many as the figure in October 1997 which was 620,000. Table 11-2 shows this change.

4.3.3.   *Information Resources in Networked Environments*

In networked environments there are many ways to issue and distribute scholarly information. People can exchange scholarly information through mailing lists, news groups, eBulletins and various websites created by academic organizations, education institutes, enterprises and business, international organizations, and so on. Many academic presses and institutions are creating various databases in their own subject fields besides the eJournals, and eBooks databases mentioned above.

Table 11-2. Statistics of Internet users in China (in millions)

Statistic date	October 1997	July 1998	January 1999	January 2000	January 2001	January 2002	January 2003	January 2004
No. of Internet users	0.62	1.175	2.1	8.9	22.5	33.7	59.1	79.5

So far there are few servers that provide the services of mailing lists or newsgroups in mainland China. Some users discuss the topics they are interested in by subscribing to listserv services available abroad. There are more and more websites created and maintained by various academic organizations or institutes, which have become an essential scholarly information resource for users on the Internet. Some websites function as a virtual community forum, by which the users can get information resources concerning a certain subject field and publish their opinions and ideas. These forums are becoming a popular way for people to exchange scholarly information with others of the same trade or occupation.

The databases are the most important scholarly information resources on the network. There were three nationwide investigations into the databases in mainland China from 1992 to 1998. The first investigation was conducted in 1992 by the Information Department, State Science Committee. The investigation statistics showed that there were only 137 databases at that time in China. The second survey was carried out in 1995, jointly by the State Planning Committee, Information Department of State Science Committee and National Information Centre. The result of the investigation was the book *A complete collection of databases*, which showed that the number of databases then had already reached 1,038, which was nearly eight times the figure of 1992. The third investigation was in 1998, as a research project on the development and utilization of eInformation resources for science and technology in China, headed by the China Science & Technology Information Institute. The final project showed that, up to 1997, there were 171 kinds of Chinese CD-ROM databases, of which 66.7% were on science and technology. Most of the databases provided CD-ROMs and also network services (China Information Almanac website).

Later, according to the statistics on the CNNIC (China Internet Network Information Centre) website, up to April 30, 2001, the number of online databases was up to 45,598. There are altogether ten types of literature resources in the world, namely books, journals, reports on research, proceedings, governmental publications, patents, product samples, technology archives and dissertations. The existing databases in China cover all these types of literature.

5. A Survey of Scholarly Communication in China

To have an overall understanding of the current situation of the development of scholarly communication in China, we conducted a survey to get first-hand data. The survey was divided into two parts: citation analysis and Internet investigation. Through sampling some core journals in different subjects, a citation analysis was made by counting cited literatures in the previous 5 years in order to get an understanding of the changes and regularity of the academic information obtained and utilized by users. The Internet investigation accessed the developmental situation for scholarly resources located in new models of scholarly communication such as academic forums and academic websites.

5.1. Citation Analysis

5.1.1. Research Method

One of the top comprehensive core journals, in Chinese and English, was selected from each of ten subject areas (namely physics, chemistry, biology, medicine, architecture, computer science, law, economics, philosophy, and library & information science). These journals were divided into two groups: Chinese and English.

The Chinese group is *Acta Physica Sinica, Chemical Journal of Chinese Universities, Acta Biochemica et Biophysica Sinica, National Medical Journal of China, Architectural Journal, Chinese Journal of Computers, Chinese Legal Science, Economics Research Journal, Philosophy Research* and *The Journal of the Library Science in China.*

The English group is *Physical Review Letters, Chemical Review, Nature, The Lancet, ACI Structural Journal, IEEE Transactions on Knowledge and Data Engineering, The Yale Law Journal, The American Economic Review, Philosophy of Science* and *Library Trends.*

Statistical analyses were made against the cited references of academic articles published in the above journals from 1998 to 2002 according to the type of their reference sources. The reference sources were divided into seven types: journals, monographs, eSource, conference papers, dissertations, newspapers, and 'others'. The 'conference papers' included proceedings published formally and also unpublished papers; the 'eSource' refers to webpages, websites and some eJournals without printed versions; and the 'others' included laws and regulations, institutional bulletins, projects, standards, handouts, governmental documents, etc.

5.1.2. Results from Citations in Chinese Journals

Figure 11-1 is a column chart according to the sources and types of citation from the ten selected journals published in the previous 5 years. From this it is clear that *journals and monographs are considered as the main source of academic information exchange in China at present in terms of both citation number and disciplinary coverage.* As far as journals and monographs are concerned, the largest citation number is over 6,000; the smallest number is about 150. In the ten investigated subjects, most of the citation numbers are

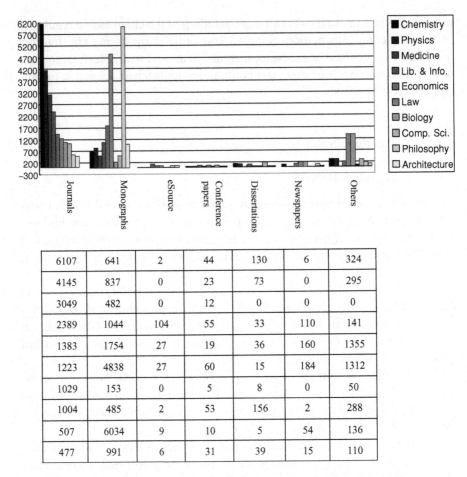

Journals	Monographs	eSource	Conference papers	Dissertations	Newspapers	Others
6107	641	2	44	130	6	324
4145	837	0	23	73	0	295
3049	482	0	12	0	0	0
2389	1044	104	55	33	110	141
1383	1754	27	19	36	160	1355
1223	4838	27	60	15	184	1312
1029	153	0	5	8	0	50
1004	485	2	53	156	2	288
507	6034	9	10	5	54	136
477	991	6	31	39	15	110

Figure 11-1. Sources and types of citation from 1998 to 2002

over 400. In contrast, the quantity of the citations from the other five categories is around 100 except 'others'.

Figure 11-2 is a line chart showing the citation numbers for journals and monographs from the ten mentioned journals in the past 5 years. It illustrates that, in this period, journals and monographs not only have the highest citation number but also present a stable state. The two increasing curves are comparatively smooth, roughly consistent with the tendency and changes in the number of journals and monographs published in recent years in table 11-1.

Only in 2002, there emerged a sharp contrast between the citation numbers from journals and from monographs. It is a little hard to decide whether the sharp contrast occurring in the last 2 years is part of a trend or an isolated occurrence, but we prefer to give the credit to the rapid increase of libraries' subscriptions to the databases of full-text electronic journals, as these have

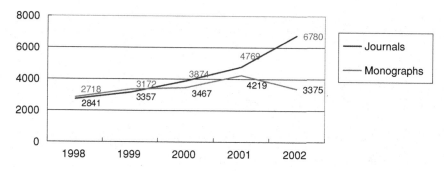

Figure 11-2. Citation numbers for journals and monographs from 1998 to 2002

offered a great convenience for scholars to get scholarly information as they never have been able to before. It is interesting that the databases suppliers would not tell us their market achievement in recent years when we made inquiries of them.

There is a great difference in the number of citations from journals and monographs between different subjects. As figure 11-1 shows, physics, chemistry, and medicine have a heavy reliance on journal citations. In the 5-year period they cited 6,107, 4,145 and 3,049 journal articles respectively. Following these three are library & information science, law, economics, biology and computer science, which have respectively cited 1,000–2,000 articles. In contrast, philosophy and architecture cited fewer articles with number ranging from 400 to 500.

However, when it comes to the number of citations from monographs, philosophy and law rise to the top, with 6,034 and 4,838 respectively, higher than economics and library & information science, which cited 1,754 and 1,044 respectively. Physics, chemistry, biology, computer science and medicine fall behind them, with fewer than 1,000 each.

It is obvious in the contrast above that physics, chemistry and medicine greatly rely on citations from journals, and refer to fewer articles in monographs; however, philosophy and law, which cite a large number of monographs, refer to fewer journal articles. This indicates that in the traditional mainstream system of scholarly communication, the difference among subject fields influences the ways and methods by which scholars exchange academic information. It is not difficult to understand that scholars in physics, chemistry and medicine tend to obtain and utilize the latest academic information via journals which have comparatively short periods for publishing research results because academic information in these scientific and technical fields has, to some extent, a shorter period of effectiveness; while scholars in philosophy, law and some other social sciences tend to use monographs which are relatively stable and contain lasting critical remarks and conclusions; these fields requires less immediacy for academic information.

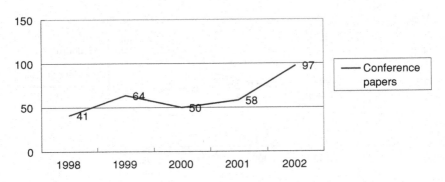

Figure 11-3. Citation numbers for conference papers from 1998 to 2002

Publishing strategies for conference papers greatly influence their impact.
For a long time conference papers belonged to 'gray literature' in the sense
that they were rarely published publicly and their dissemination was usually
confined to a certain subject field or system. Figure 11-3 is a chart showing
the citation numbers of conference papers from articles in the ten Chinese
journals selected.

From figures 11-1 and 11-3, we can conclude that, in the 5-year period,
the citation number of conference papers was not large. However, there are
citations of conference papers in all ten investigated subjects and there is an
upward trend for this. This illustrates that conference papers are still critical
even though they are not the main stream for academic exchange. In addition,
we find in figure 11-3 that before 2001 the citations of conference papers
always ranged from 40 to 60; while in 2002 it reached 97, 2.3 times of that
in 1998, the highest number in the 5 years. This period is also the time when
Chinese information institutes and information suppliers began to pay more
attention to the exploitation and utilization of information resources from
academic conferences. Domestically, there are databases of conference papers
at present as following: the Full-text Database of Academic Conference Papers
published by Wanfang Data, the Chinese Full-text Database of Important
Conference Papers by Tsinghua Tongfang, and the Database of Academic
Conference Papers by CALIS (China Academic Library & Information
System). All of these are databases that spread and exchange conference
papers via the Internet or CD-ROM; they began to offer Internet services
around 2002. This seems a possible explanation for the sharp increase in the
citations of conference papers in 2002.

*The citation of dissertations is influenced by transmission methods and sub-
ject area.* As can be seen from figure 11-1, there are obvious subject differences
in the use of dissertations. Scholars in computer science, chemistry and physics
have a much higher citation number for dissertations, followed by those
in architecture, economics, and library & information science. Scholars of
philosophy, law, biology and other subjects make limited use of dissertations,

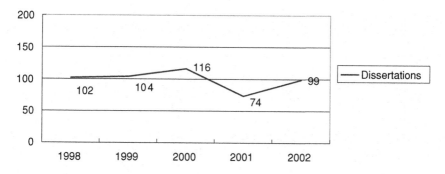

Figure 11-4. Citation numbers for dissertations from 1998 to 2002

and in medicine no dissertations were cited. Figure 11-4 shows the number of citations from dissertations in the ten selected journals from 1998 to 2002.

The exchange and transmission of dissertations have always been plagued with copyright issues. A contrast between figures 11-3 and 11-4 shows that the number of citations from dissertations is higher than that from academic conference papers, but it remains almost constant and even tends to decline in the 5-year period. This is an interesting 'paradox', considering the recognized value and significance of dissertations as academic resources. On one hand, the importance and value of dissertations has been more and more recognized with strategies existing for exchange and transmission. On the other hand, the owners of dissertation collections, including their authors and libraries, tend to add some restrictions to the use of them, which imperceptibly forms a block against the exchange and transmission of dissertations.

In fact, Chinese academic resource providers and information management institutes have recognized the importance of exploitation and utilization of dissertations for a long time. The three aforementioned suppliers of academic information products are also exploring how to exchange and transmit dissertations by the Internet or CD-ROM, and some databases of dissertations have been used, such as the WanFang Dissertation Database, the CDMD (China Doctoral/Master's Dissertations) of CNKI and the Dissertation Database of CALIS. Because they have not resolved the copyright issues appropriately, most of them can just provide abstracts of dissertations and not full-text, so most users have to get full-text dissertations by interlibrary loan or document delivery.

There are some subject differences in academic information transmission by newspapers, codes, standards and other kinds of documents. As can be seen from figure 11-1, although the number of citations from newspapers, codes and standards is not high, they still perform an important function for exchanging and transmitting academic information in some subject fields. For example, newspapers can provide some news, facts and statistics for scholars researching in the fields of law, economics, and library & information science,

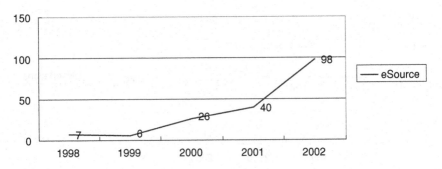

Figure 11-5. Citation numbers for eSource from 1998 to 2002

and thus in these fields there is a certain number of citations from newspapers. Moreover, the number of citation from 'others' of literature in the fields of law and economics is both above 1,300, much higher than in other eight subjects. It is obvious that normative and numerical materials (for example, codes, standards, patents, and advertisements) in 'others' of literature are also an important source for the scholars in these two fields to obtain relevant information.

The function of 'eSource' in scholarly communication is rising rapidly. The eSource category, represented by websites in the citation survey, is a new type of communication media which is increasing rapidly, although it has not been the main source of citation in scientific research. Figure 11-5 shows the number of citations from websites in the ten selected journals from 1998 to 2002.

As figure 11-5 shows, scholars' interest in utilizing eSource material as academic information has increased since 1999. The citation from eSource in 1998 was 7, while it reached 98 in 2002, which is 14 times that in 1998. The combined analysis with figure 11-1 indicates that there is a great difference in the number of citations from eSource among different subjects. Library & information science (104), economics and law have more citations from eSource than others areas. Citations in physics, biology and medicine do not utilize eSource at all. What is the reason for this? We might infer that scholars in library and information science, who are users and researchers of eSource themselves, as well as teaching students and users how to use it, may tend towards paying more attention to new types of media than those of other subject fields. In addition, the majority of Internet-based academic resources are report type at present, but academic information in scientific and technical fields must be accurate and reliable. This might be the reason why scholars utilize more eSources in social sciences than in science and technology.

5.1.3.   Comparative Analysis of Citations in Chinese and English Journals

The discussion above has focused on the habits of Chinese scholars in using references. In order to further analyze the trends in Chinese scholarly

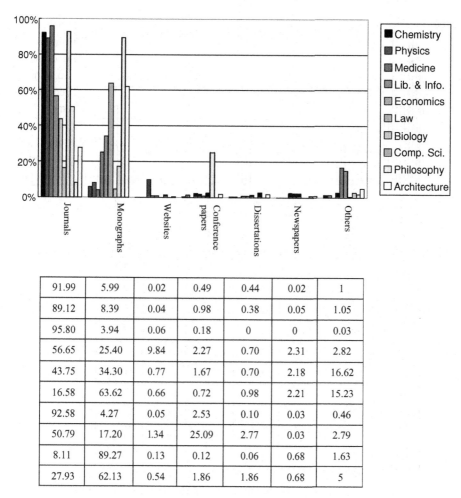

91.99	5.99	0.02	0.49	0.44	0.02	1
89.12	8.39	0.04	0.98	0.38	0.05	1.05
95.80	3.94	0.06	0.18	0	0	0.03
56.65	25.40	9.84	2.27	0.70	2.31	2.82
43.75	34.30	0.77	1.67	0.70	2.18	16.62
16.58	63.62	0.66	0.72	0.98	2.21	15.23
92.58	4.27	0.05	2.53	0.10	0.03	0.46
50.79	17.20	1.34	25.09	2.77	0.03	2.79
8.11	89.27	0.13	0.12	0.06	0.68	1.63
27.93	62.13	0.54	1.86	1.86	0.68	5

Figure 11-6. Percentage of citations from Chinese journals from 1998 to 2002

communication, we compared the citations from these core Chinese and English journals in the ten subjects.

Figure 11-6 illustrates the percentage of citations from Chinese journals in various subjects. The cited materials come from references in both Chinese and non-Chinese languages. Figure 11-7 indicates the citations of English journals in the ten subjects. Comparing the two figures, we find that the strategies for scholarly communication, both in China and other countries, share some similarities and also some differences.

Journals and monographs are still the major sources of scholarly communication. In the types of citations from English journals within the ten subjects, journals and monographs make up a high proportion. The citation of journals and monographs is over 70% in all the subjects except law. This result is similar to the numbers for Chinese citations. The difference is that the

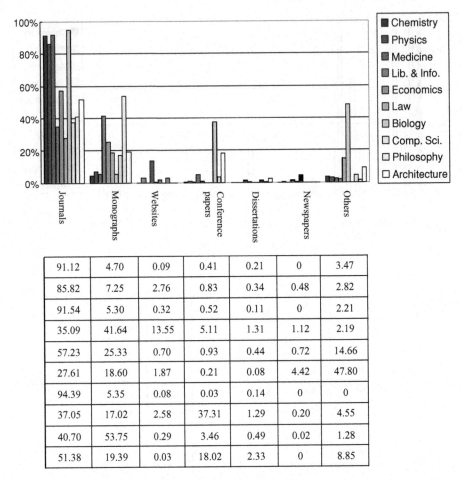

91.12	4.70	0.09	0.41	0.21	0	3.47
85.82	7.25	2.76	0.83	0.34	0.48	2.82
91.54	5.30	0.32	0.52	0.11	0	2.21
35.09	41.64	13.55	5.11	1.31	1.12	2.19
57.23	25.33	0.70	0.93	0.44	0.72	14.66
27.61	18.60	1.87	0.21	0.08	4.42	47.80
94.39	5.35	0.08	0.03	0.14	0	0
37.05	17.02	2.58	37.31	1.29	0.20	4.55
40.70	53.75	0.29	3.46	0.49	0.02	1.28
51.38	19.39	0.03	18.02	2.33	0	8.85

Figure 11-7. Percentage of citations from English journals from 1998 to 2002

Chinese percentage citation numbers are higher than those for English. This might show that, on the one hand, Chinese scholars are more ready to obtain and spread scholarly information by means of books and journals; on the other hand, the scholarly communication in China may still be under transition from the traditional to modern patterns.

The percentage of citation of Internet sources is not high in both Chinese and English scholarly communication. In the citation of English journals, the citation of Internet references for library and information science is 13.6%, and the citations for physics, computer science and law is about 2%. The figures for other subjects are even lower. In the citation of Chinese journals, library and information science also becomes the only subject that makes most use of Internet references with a percentage of 9.8, with computer science taking second place with a percentage of 1.3, similar to that in English journals.

For other subjects the percentage is lower than 1%. However, compared with the citation of Internet references in Chinese journals, the use of Internet references in English journals are wider in both number and percentage for all other subjects except architecture and law.

There are some disciplinary differences in the use of conference papers. From figures 11-6 and 11-7, we know that computer science relies more on conference papers than other subjects. The citation of conference papers makes a large part in computer researches in both Chinese and English journals. The ratios are 25.1% in Chinese journals and 37.3% in English journals. Conference papers are less cited for other subjects, with little change in the 5-year period.

5.2. Quantitative Analysis of Internet-based Scholarly Communication

According to the statistical report issued by CNNIC in January 2003, search engines accounted for 68.3% of the frequently used Internet information services. Among the main instruments through which Internet users could find new websites, search engines ranked top one and accounted for 84.6%. Thus we think search engines are the most frequently used means to access information on the web. We selected several popular comprehensive search engines to make a sampling survey of cyber academic forums and websites in Chinese.

5.2.1. Academic Forums

Using the names of ten subject fields as keywords, we searched the five widely-used search engines (Sina, Yahoo, Sohu, 163 and Google) and limited the matched results with 'forum'. Then from the first 30 results of every subject field, we excluded dead, duplicate and unrelated links. We finally classified and analysed those academic forums left by their creators. The data were collected from March 10 to 12, 2003. From this sampling method, 281 finally matched forums were found, which included 4 library & information science forums, 22 philosophy, 30 law, 29 economics, 9 chemistry, 29 biology, 50 computer science, 33 architecture, and 60 medical science. Figure 11-8 shows the distribution of the academic forums in ten subject fields as a pi-chart.

The number of forums varies by subject. As figure 11-8, the proportion of forums in most subject fields sampled is below 20%. However, we still can classify them into three categories by their distribution levels: first, subjects such as medicine and computer science, each around 20%; second, architecture, biology, economics and law, each around 11%; third, the rest of

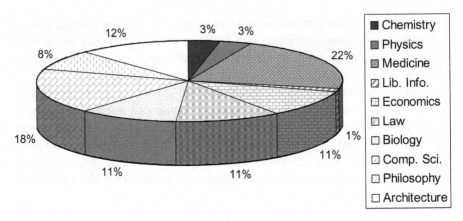

Figure 11-8. Distribution of Chinese academic forums

the subjects falling below 10%—physics, chemistry, library & information science and philosophy.

Forums created by scholars individually are the most common. Figure 11-9 is a column chart based on the type of creators, including institutes and individuals, in selected seven subject fields where the percentage forum number exceeds 8%. Academic forums founded by individuals in each of these subject fields account for more than 40% of the total forums, ranging from 27% in architecture to 69% in biology.

These academic forums provide a platform for people with the same interest to study and discuss topics in a special subject field via the Internet. The quality of the contents and the quantity of participants in the forums are dependent upon the academic level and reputation of the creators. Therefore, academic forums established by individuals can be divided into two categories: the forums founded by web enthusiasts who are skilled at computers and networks, as well as interested in a certain subject, and those by scholars who are the experts of a certain subject field. The quality of the former is uneven due to the limitations of creators' academic skills and personal interests. In any event, since the creators' personal interest may change over time and the maintenance of such forums requires great endeavour and cost, the prospect for this kind of individual forums is not very clear. They are unstable and many have already closed. The latter ones are created by scholars themselves, and provide research materials, academic information and communication platforms for small groups of people working in the same specialties, closely related to the scholars' research fields and reflecting their research topics. This kind of academic forum, small in size but high in quality, appears to be more stable.

The quality of academic forums created by academic institutions or organizations is uneven. This type of academic forum accounts for more

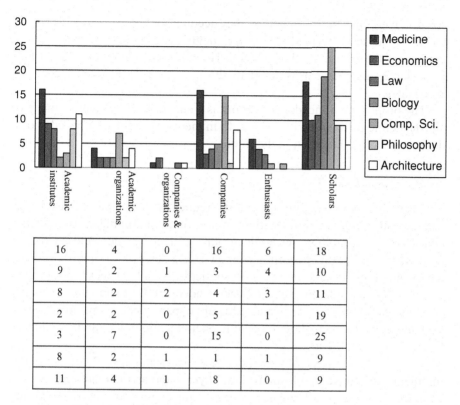

Figure 11-9. Distribution of creators of Chinese academic forums

16	4	0	16	6	18
9	2	1	3	4	10
8	2	2	4	3	11
2	2	0	5	1	19
3	7	0	15	0	25
8	2	1	1	1	9
11	4	1	8	0	9

than 30% of all matched forums, though in biology and computer science the percentage is relatively small. Most of the forums are embedded in the websites of academic institutions or organizations, and the content of the forums closely correlated with the institutions or organizations. To a certain extent, the purpose of establishing the forums was to provide members of the institutions or organizations with a platform for exchanging academic information. The scope of the forums is diverse. Some of them are focused on information related to academic research and education, such as discussion about courses, evaluation of publications and exchange of research ideas. Some have wider content that include plentiful research data and document sources besides the information mentioned above, serving scholars as well as attracting people who are interested in the subject field. Generally speaking, the quality of the forums is uneven, and thus their contributions to academic research are not the same. The state and prospect of these forums relies on the development of academic institutions or organizations themselves.

Forums created by companies themselves, or companies cooperated with academic institutions, obviously vary across subject fields. The proportion of academic forums created by companies alone is small, but in computer science, medicine and architecture, they account for about 30%. This reflects the fact that scholars in these subject fields need more information from companies than those in other subjects. However, the quality of these forums is unstable, and they are related to the aims and business scope of the companies.

The proportion of academic forums as a cooperation between companies and academic institutions is very small; in theory, they fill a real need and so deserve our close attention in the future.

5.2.2.   Academic Websites

Academic websites are the most frequently used way to exchange and spread academic information in a cyber environment. Individuals, educational institutions, academic groups and companies release related academic information by creating their own websites. Some organizations and companies even provide information services and collect fees through their websites. Thus academic websites, independent from the previous scholarly communication systems, have created a public space for academic information exchange; this has constituted a unique phenomenon in the modern Chinese academic environment.

Due to the magnitude of the academic websites and the difficulty of defining them, we selected philosophy, law, physics and architecture respectively from humanities, social science, science and engineering as our research sample. By using the names of the four subjects as keywords, we searched websites through the five wide-used search engines (Sina, Yahoo, Sohu, 163 and Google). From the first 30 results of each subject, we excluded those dead, duplicated and unrelated links and then classified and analysed those matched websites left by their creators. The data were collected from March 12 to 17, 2003. Using this sampling method, we found 157 academic websites, including 45 law websites, 24 philosophy, 61 physics and 27 architecture. Figure 11-10 shows the proportion of academic websites in the four subjects.

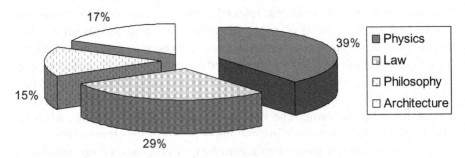

Figure 11-10. Proportion of Chinese websites in four subjects

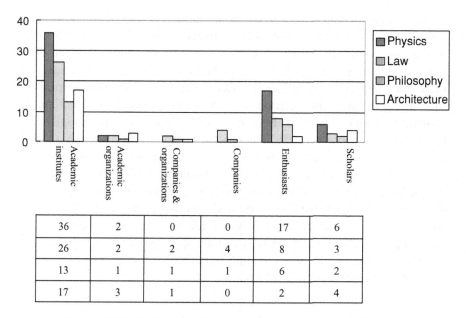

Figure 11-11. Distribution of Chinese website creators in four subjects

Academic websites are distributed reasonably evenly among the subjects. According to figure 11-10, websites of physics account for 39%, followed by law (29%), architecture (17%) and philosophy (15%). The proportions of all four subjects range from 15% to 40%. There is no clear bias among these subjects which indicates that scholars in these subject fields look upon websites as an important way to communicate academic information.

Academic institutions play major roles in establishing academic websites. Figure 11-11 shows that academic institutions have created the majority of academic websites, accounting for more than 50% in each subject. Academic organizations, companies, or collaborations between companies and organizations only created a few academic websites (less than four websites for each category). The proportion of academic websites founded by academic organizations in each subject does not exceed 4%.

However, by browsing the academic websites created by academic institutions, we noted that that the quality of these websites is uneven. Some of them provide comprehensive information, including formally published materials, as well as a great deal of valuable academic information that cannot be normally be found through ordinary channels, for example, teaching notes, conference reports, research reports, internal documents, etc. However, many of them serve only as windows for their own institutions and seldom offer research information to other scholars.

Websites established by individuals are notable. Figure 11-11 also shows that web enthusiasts and scholars are actively involved in the establishment of academic websites. Although web enthusiasts created more websites than scholars in three subjects, the difference of the websites in terms of academic value and stability are just like the above analysis of academic forums. In addition, in terms of the distribution of websites created by web enthusiasts in different subjects, physics accounts for 28%, followed by philosophy 25%, law 18%, and architecture 7%. The ratio of websites established by scholars is 15% in architecture, 10% in physics, 8% in philosophy, and 7% in law. This result shows that web enthusiasts and scholars have different interest in establishing academic websites. In the field of physics, there are a number of academic websites created by individuals. However, since most of them are established by web enthusiasts, the academic value and stability are not satisfying. Though the number of architecture websites is not high, most of them are established by scholars, and thus there is a higher expectation of obtaining valuable academic information.

5.2.3.   Comparison between Chinese and American Websites

In order to have a further understanding of the development of Chinese scholarly websites, we also made an investigation of academic websites in the US. Just as the investigation on Chinese websites, we used philosophy, law, physics and architecture respectively from humanities, social science, science and engineering as our research sample. Taking 'philosophy', 'law', 'physics' and 'architecture' as keywords, we searched websites through four widely-used search engines, Yahoo, Google, Lycos and Hotbot. From the first 30 matched records of each subject, we ruled out those dead, duplicated and unrelated links, and then classified and analysed the academic websites according to the creators. The data were collected from July 2 to 5, 2004. Altogether we obtained 93 academic websites among which 30 are about law, 21 about philosophy, 23 about physics and 19 about architecture. Figure 11-12 is a distribution of the creators of the academic websites for the four subjects. Comparing figure 11-12 with figure 11-11, we note the following findings.

Academic institutions and organizations are the major force in construct-ing academic websites. The academic websites in both mainland China and America are mainly created by academic institutions and organizations. Such websites constitute about 50% of academic websites.

Academic websites established by web enthusiasts are a notable feature of Chinese scholarly communication. From figure 11-11 we find that web enthusiasts establish several Chinese academic websites in the four subjects. This phenomenon is not obvious in American academic websites. From the introduction of the websites we know although there are some academic websites established by individuals in America, these individuals themselves

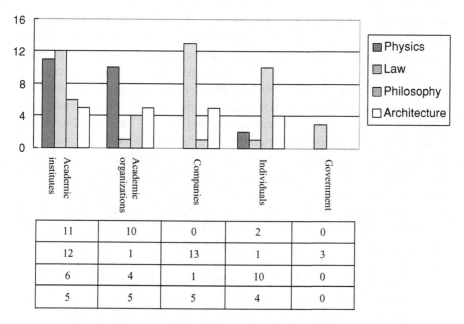

11	10	0	2	0
12	1	13	1	3
6	4	1	10	0
5	5	5	4	0

Figure 11-12. Distribution of American website creators in four subjects

are mostly researchers or educators in these fields. They are not web enthusiasts who establish websites just for individual interest.

Some academic websites in applied sciences are established and managed by companies in America and provide free or charged information services. However, there are few such websites in China. Websites established by companies in China are mainly taken as advertising windows. They do not work as academic websites, nor do they provide information services. A case in point is an architecture website 'Architectureweek', which is not only an online magazine, but also functions as a news group, searching professional information and recommending good books (Architectureweek website).

6.   Conclusion

As a result of the development of information and network technologies, the present environment of scholarly communication and the behaviour of scholars issuing and gaining academic information have changed dramatically in mainland China. Networks are playing an increasingly important role in scholarly communication. Although people embrace the Internet ardently, the traditional scholarly communication media such as journals, monographs and newspapers are not declining in the face of the challenge of networks; they remain as the mainstream media of scholarly communication. The publication and distribution of printed literature are steadily growing, and printed materials are still the major citation sources for scholars to utilize academic information.

Nevertheless, the Internet has brought us a new promising platform for scholarly communication. Network-based scholarly communication is flourishing. On one hand, publishers begin to provide electronic versions of their printed publications, and therefore enable academic information to spread more quickly and conveniently through digital media and networks. Conference papers and dissertations, which are difficult to disseminate through traditional media, can be delivered and utilized in a new way after being digitized. Literature databases, integrating a huge amount of academic information, provide unprecedented academic resources to scholars, and broaden the scope of scholarly communication. The digitized academic resources are growing rapidly in mainland China, and the means utilizing the resources have been gradually accepted by scholars. In addition, new instruments of scholarly communication, such as academic forums and websites, provide a new type of platforms for scholarly communication interactively. Although these new methods of scholarly communication are not widespread in mainland China yet, they are increasingly influencing scholars' habits for releasing and acquiring academic information, transforming people's behaviour to exchange information.

Not all subjects fall into the scholarly communication system built up by the pervasive Internet. At least under the current circumstances, distinct differences exist in different subject fields. Due to the differences of communication systems and the scholars' attitude to accept different methods, each subject has its own best ways for scholarly communication. Even within the same subject field, different communication instruments and channels are selected according to different contents and purposes of the communication.

Our study is based on the investigation into citations of journal articles, academic forums and websites. The samples to some extent could represent the current situation of scholarly communication in mainland China, but there still are some limitations in the study in that the situation is rapidly evolving. Network-based scholarly communication has provided new opportunities of development for teaching, publishing, library services and so on. Some higher educational institutions are developing courseware to perform teaching through the network. The State General Bureau of News and Publication of China has made relevant rules for management of publication, production, duplication, issuance and sales of digital publications. Libraries have brought various network information resources into their collections and tried to combine them with the traditional collection resources. They also provide various new kinds of information services, such as network navigation and virtual reference services, with the help of network technology. However, as a developing country, China is still at the beginning of network-based scholarly communication and there is much room for improvement.

References

Architecture Week. Retrieved January 21, 2005, from http://www.architectureweek.com

China Information Almanac. Retrieved January 21, 2005, from http://www.jcinfo.gov.cn/infomation/cyfz_6.htm

China Internet Network Information Centre (CNNIC). Retrieved January 21, 2005, from http://www.cnnic.net.cn/

China National Knowledge Infrastructure (CNKI). Retrieved January 21, 2005, from http://www.cnki.net

Chinese E-Book Network. Retrieved January 21, 2005, from http://www.21dmedia.com

Fang Qing. (2002). Discussion on science information service based on network carrier. *Information Science, 2,* 209–221.

Fang Qing. (2000–2001). Research on the science information communication in network environment. *Annual Review of Information Science Progress*, p. 125. Beijing: National Defense Industry Press.

Fang Qing. (2000). The influence of network publishing on communication of science information. In *Research on the development of publishing in the trans-century period* (p. 178–181). Wuhan: Wuhan University Press.

Founder Apabi Digital Library. Retrieved January 21, 2005, from http://www.apabi.com

He Lingyong, & Xiao Zili. (2000). From development of literature resources to access of knowledge information. *Information and Documentation Work, 4,* 8–11.

Liu Jia. (1999). Academic resources in network environment. *Journal of the Library Science in China, 11,* 53–59.

SuperStar Digital Library. Retrieved January 21, 2005, from http://www.ssreader.com

The report on the development of Internet in China. Retrieved January 21, 2005, from http://www.cnnic.net.cn/index/0E/00/11/index.htm

VIP Information. Retrieved January 21, 2005, from http://www.tydata.com

Wanfang Data Digital Periodical Subsystem. Retrieved January 21, 2005, from http://www.periodicals.com.cn

Xu Jianhua. (2000). Studies on organization and revelation of network information resources. *Information Science, 6,* 497–501.

Zhang chunhong & Jiang gangmiao. (2002). A comparative study on several Chinese E-Book systems. *Journal of Academic Libraries, 1,* 35–41.

Zhang Xiaolin. (2000). Reconstruction of academic information exchanging structure and rebuilding of the information service model in universities. *Journal of Academic Libraries, 1,* 16–21.

Zhang Xiaolin. (2000). Towards knowledge services: Seeking development opportunities of library and information services in the 21st century. *Journal of the Library Science in China, 5,* 32–37.

Chapter 12

GLOBAL CHANGES IN SCHOLARLY COMMUNICATION

Suzanne E. Thorin

1.   Chapter Overview

For more than a decade, the cost of print and electronic journals, particularly in the sciences, has increased rapidly at the same time as the amount of research being reported via published articles has grown exponentially. The publicity surrounding the cost of finished publications has come about because librarians, in a growing number of cases, simply can no longer afford to purchase some journals. At first blush, the traditional scholarly communication system, apart from the pricing structure, still seems to work. However, under what is still on the surface a relatively stable environment for teaching, learning and scholarship, potentially seismic changes are occurring that are affecting each stage of the scholarly communication process. These challenges include lack of communication between disciplines and a lack of understanding of the social and cultural practices of various disciplines.

When looking closely at the term scholarly communication, it has a somewhat broader meaning than publication, as it also includes the processes by which scholars communicate with one another as they create new knowledge and by which they measure its worth with colleagues prior to making a formal article available to the broader community, which is then purchased and preserved or licensed by academic libraries world-wide.

This chapter divides the scholarly communication process into three distinct aspects: (1) the process of conducting research, developing ideas and communicating informally with other scholars and scientists; (2) the process of preparing, shaping and communicating to a group of colleagues what will become formal research results; and (3) the ultimate formal product that is distributed to libraries and others in print or electronically. The chapter describes some of the strategic issues within the traditional system of scholarly

H. S. Ching, P. W. T. Poon and C. McNaught (Eds.), eLearning and Digital Publishing, 221–240.
© 2006 *H. S. Ching, P. W. T. Poon and C. McNaught.*

communication. It also investigates some of the changes in informal and formal communication between scholars and scientists that are destabilizing longstanding traditions and looks at emerging spaces that scholars are using to conduct and to disseminate the results of their research.

2.   Introduction

For more than a decade, the cost of print and electronic journals, particularly in the sciences, has increased rapidly. At the same time, the amount of research being reported via published articles has grown exponentially. With academic libraries less and less able to purchase the journals needed by their communities, the use of the term *scholarly communication* has evolved to illustrate the breakdown of the process of traditional scholarly publication which, as a means of disseminating research results, no longer meets the needs of the scholarly community at large.

When looking closely at the term scholarly communication, it has a somewhat broader meaning than publication. It also includes the processes by which scholars communicate with one another as they create new knowledge and by which they measure its worth with colleagues prior to making a formal article available to the broader community. For the purposes of this chapter we are dividing the scholarly communication process into three distinct aspects: (1) the process of conducting research, developing ideas and communicating informally with other scholars and scientists; (2) the process of preparing, shaping and communicating to a group of colleagues what will become formal research results; and (3) the ultimate formal product that is distributed to libraries and others in print or electronic format. In addition to describing each of these aspects, we will illustrate some of the changes that are destabilizing longstanding traditions.

The publicity surrounding the cost of the final product has come about because librarians in effect stand at the end of an assembly line holding an item that, in a growing number of cases, we simply cannot afford to buy. At first blush, the assembly line where the product itself is created appears to function in a business-as-usual mode: humanities scholars mostly remain solitary researchers as they accomplish their work and physical scientists work together as they have for decades while conducting research; traditional peer review continues as per the traditions of each disciplinary group; and applications for tenure and promotion are reviewed by academic committees using standards that can be more than a century old.

For some time, much of the academic world has been perplexed as to why librarians are creating such a fuss about the price of journals. Many academics are only vaguely aware that library budgets have shrunk in buying power, and some express frustration with the amount of funding given to building complex information technology environments at their campuses instead of allocating it to meet their direct needs, including books and journals in their fields. Under what is still on the surface a relatively stable environment for teaching, learning and scholarship, seismic changes are actually occurring that are affecting each stage of the scholarly communication process. Springing up wildly and seemingly from nowhere are 'sudden' changes that are ensuing from the increasing use of sophisticated digital technology by scholars and scientists. Massive and profound changes are occurring that are not only affecting teaching, learning, research and administrative processes but which are reshaping the academy itself (Hawkins & Battin, 1998; see also Duderstadt, Atkins & Van Houweling, 2002).

This chapter addresses some of the strategic issues that relate to the traditional system of scholarly communication by looking at changes in informal and formal communication between scholars and scientists, and at emerging spaces that scholars are using to conduct and to disseminate the results of their research.

3. Beginning at the End: The Product

The extreme price hikes that have occurred over the past decade for journals, especially those in science, technology and medicine (STM), are often described as a 'serials crisis'. This worrisome situation has had the effect of limiting the number of monographs that libraries can purchase as we divert a growing percentage of our acquisition budgets to science serials and away from books. The price increases have been well-documented by the Association of Research Libraries (ARL)[1]: the unit cost paid by research libraries for serials increased by 226% between 1986 and 2000, while the consumer price index increased by only 57%. Coupled with decreasing annual increments and one-time infusions to library budgets as universities have had to make other large financial commitments, including the allocation of substantial funds for building information technology infrastructures, university libraries have lost significant purchasing power. Mary Case (2002), Director of the Office for Scholarly Programs at ARL, describes the effect on libraries:

> Even though the typical research library spent almost three times more on serials in 2000 than in 1986, the number of serial titles purchased declined by 7%. Even more dramatically, as libraries diverted resources to support journal subscriptions, book purchases declined by 17%. Based on 1986 acquisition levels, this figure represents over 6,000 monograph volumes a year not purchased by the typical research library. With such a drastic erosion in the market for books, publishers had no choice but to raise prices. By 2000, the unit cost of books had increased 66% over 1986 costs.

Within these two interlocked pricing spirals, the most dramatic increases have occurred in STM journals that are produced by commercial firms. As Case (2002) states, "Data consistently show that the cost-per-unit of content, the cost-per-citation, and the cost-per-use of commercially produced journals are higher than those of journals produced by society and not-for-profit organizations".

Librarians have been placed in a position of defending the purchase or licensing of expensive journals for science academics over books and journals for humanities academics, even though science academics also continue to receive a much greater share of governmental grant support than do their humanities colleagues. This situation, which initially appeared to some to be a library's poor management of existing funds or its ineffective lobbying for additional library funding from the university, was actually a logical and perhaps predictable next step within a much more complex environment that has evolved in the field of scientific research publication for more than a decade. Librarians, who have been described more than once as whiners, actually have a relatively minor role in a complex drama being played for power and profit by international commercial firms, with sometimes unknowing support from academics seeking promotion, tenure and the confirmation of status in their fields. And, this academic role has not been undertaken with malice toward libraries; rather, academics are participants in the complex social and intellectual process that has worked for more than a century to make scientific research available to the community. To understand the process, we need to understand the history and the ingredients that led first to success and now to a growing and urgent need for disruption and change.

Jean-Claude Guédon (2002), historian of science and professor of comparative literature at the Université de Montreal, has written a definitive and elegant explanation of 'how we got to where we are today'. It all began, Guédon writes, with Henry Oldenburg, who created a journal called *Philosophical Transactions of the Royal Society of London* (*Phil Trans* for short) in 1665. Oldenburg's aim was to document and distribute original contributions to knowledge. As Guédon (2002) notes, "In particular, it [*Phil Trans*] introduced clarity and transparency in the process of establishing innovative claims in natural philosophy, and as a result, it began to play a role not unlike that of a patent office for scientific ideas". In other words, publication in this journal not only dispersed scientific ideas to the world at large, but it also provided, in effect, a record of who introduced what new knowledge and when. Critical to Oldenburg's strategy was being able to attract the best authors from England and Europe. There were many reasons that Oldenburg did not achieve his goal of placing all knowledge of the natural sciences in his journal for distribution to the community at large. Guédon notes that the roles of writers, printers and bookstore owners were still being explored in the 17th century, much as the relationship between Internet service providers, networks, authors and users are still evolving today.

The purpose of a scholarly journal is not only to disseminate information to the community but, in its present configuration, it also provides quality control, a trusted archive and author recognition (Rowland, 1997). However, throughout the history of scientific publication, profit has also been an ingredient. And, as Guédon describes, the scientist/scholar can take either of two roles. The first role, as a scholar/ member of an academic faculty seeking published research of others or her/his own published research, allows the academic to complain loudly about how inequitably the library's acquisitions budget has been spent and particularly about any serials cancellations in his/her field. The second role, which is considerably nobler, is one that s/he assumes as author. Ignoring any economic considerations, s/he cares about the visibility of the journal, its authority, prestige and its so-called impact factor. That the journal where the article appears is enormously expensive is possibly a factor that even increases its prestige.

In the traditional process of publication a completed article, as opposed to a preprint, is necessary because the article needs to be validated through peer review and its ownership recognized. As an author is footnoted by others, the quality of the journal cited helps to build the reputation of the author. But the location of the article in a distinguished journal is paramount because it helps to 'brand' the author by linking her/his name and work to that journal. Guédon compares being published in the most prestigious journals to being on prime time television as opposed to the local news. The author is placed in an exclusive 'club' of the very best researchers and his/her ability to get grants, tenure and promotion is enhanced.

Another player in journal publishing is the editor, whose role is gatekeeper, according to Guédon (2002). "Silently, the journal's editor... has come to occupy the role of guardian of truth and reality or, in other words, the role of a high priest." The editor also gains prestige when the journal that s/he edits is referenced repeatedly and as the journal gains a reputation for being a major contributor to the record of science. When one understands the Janus-like role of scientists and scholars in the publishing process, the librarian, who plays a walk-on part and who sits well below the academics in the university hierarchy, is relegated to a reactionary role.

There are ingredients that are causing this stable, albeit imperfect, system to begin to come apart. Several components that keep the process together have begun to fragment. The first weakening began with the explosion in the amount of research that came about after the Second World War. Until World War II, most scholarly publishing was supported by not-for-profit scholarly societies. The rapid growth of research in universities after the war resulted in more articles than could be handled by the existing societies. Impatient authors, who wanted to see the results of their research published more quickly, turned to commercial journals which previously had no or little interest in articles which they believed held no hope of profit.

Guédon argues that there are two other issues: (1) the concept of *core journals* evolved, and (2) the *Science Citation Index (SCI)* began to be published in 1961. With limited budgets, we librarians have always wanted to find a way to buy only what is needed by our constituencies. We proceeded to identify and codify the critical serials for each discipline, believing we could satisfy most needs of our local research scientists through what were subsequently called core collections. In the print world this was a fairly reasonable approach because each library needed to collect virtually the same volumes. When the Institute of Scientific Information (ISI) published the SCI, it enabled one to trace citations for articles across all science journals. From this feature came the 'impact factor', that is, the number of times an article is cited directly relates to its importance in the field. As we have already noted, it is the journal itself, not the individual articles, that gain status from being cited because it is the journal's impact that brands the scientist. By making the journal the most important element in publication, Guédon argues, researchers seek the "visibility, prestige, and authority (and improved institutional ranking) in these publications". And further, by limiting the citation analysis to a core of journals, the SCI made these journals élite. This argument is important because it sets the stage for why the ensuing price increases could occur.

It is likely that the entry of commercial firms into scientific journal publishing probably produced some healthy competition between the groups at first. But once the core journals had been defined by libraries and the SCI data became integral to the prestige of these journals, librarians had no choice but to purchase the core journals, and we did. The stage was now set for dramatic price increases within a closed market and for the ensuing mergers where publishers have attempted to increase their profits by buying other companies that shared the market.

In its attempt to capture the lucrative science market, the commercial publishing world buys and sells firms regularly. It is well known that Reed-Elsevier now publishes about 20% of the core science publications available commercially. In May 2003, the German conglomerate Bertelsmann announced that, subject to regulatory approval, it was selling its Bertelsmann Springer science-publishing operations to the British private equity firms Cinven and Candover for just over 1 billion euros. (See http://www.bertelsmann.com/documents/en/BSpringer_e.pdf. Bertelsmann is selling Springer to reduce its debt load.) This acquisition places Cinven and Candover, which acquired Kluwer Academic Publishers in 2002 for over 600 million euros, second only to Reed Elsevier in market share. Cinven and Candover publish nearly 1,500 journals and about 5,000 books annually.

With the introduction of electronic versions of articles, journal publication has become even more complicated. Instead of placing the electronic article within the framework of copyright law, the first experiment (Elsevier's TULIP[2]) made the articles available as materials licensed, rather than purchased by the libraries, and this model is now the norm. An exciting project from the view point of what digital technology could deliver, TULIP also set up a new role for the library, one of an access point, rather than an owner of intellectual products. As the number of electronic journals grew, librarians became deeply immersed in a new and highly complex world where we seek to cut the best licensing contracts for our constituencies.

And, while we librarians still seek to bring our own academics and students what they need when negotiating licensing contracts, we have found most of the time that larger contracts and bigger constituencies bring better deals. A state-wide consortia, such as OhioLINK in the US with 450,000 full-time equivalent users, is able to negotiate the price of products more effectively. The Canadian National Site Licensing Project has also achieved some success, and licensing contracts for entire countries are common in Europe and the Far East.

As users come to rely on a certain scale of electronic resources negotiated for substantial savings in the first round of negotiations, librarians fear that it will become more difficult to negotiate effectively the second and third time around because our users will have come to rely on the products. In addition, there are other elements when one commits to what is now called the Big Deal as described by Ken Frazier (2001), Guédon and others. With a high percentage of a library's or consortium's budget being spent to fund resources from one publisher, there is a danger that subscriptions from other publishers will be cancelled to the detriment of what competition there is left standing.

In addition, the Big Deal publisher (Elsevier at this point) ends up dominating the users' space. With the ease of finding so many articles online, users rely on what is available. If Elsevier dominates, more Elsevier articles will be read and cited. Guédon notes that Elsevier, with about a 20% share of the entire scientific market, accounts for 68.4% of the articles downloaded in OhioLINK. Recalling the impact factor, Elsevier journals cited then get added to the impact and the reputation of the journal goes up.

So, has the genteel world that we used to imagine ended? Yes! Moreover, there is near consensus by university librarians and administrators that the current system of scholarly communication in the sense of publication is not sustainable. Fortunately, the very growth of digital technology that has helped to produce the problematic situation that we have just described is also helping scholars and librarians to explore new directions. The sophistication and accessibility of digital tools is enabling all sorts of creative efforts to flower that may eventually lead to a new system of scholarly communication.

4.   **Midway: The Process of Shaping Research**
            into a Finished Product

In July 1998, Myles Brand, then president of Indiana University (US), convened a university committee on scholarly communication and charged it to look at the national efforts afoot that were seeking to change the environment and to plan a course of action that would be undertaken at Indiana University. It was no surprise that one of the committee's charges was to analyze the impact of high prices on library acquisitions and to develop policy changes to maximize access by academics to the materials they need.

The committee was co-chaired by this author (dean of the libraries) and the chair of the Chemistry Department. It included two other librarians who were collections and reference experts, as well as representatives from philosophy, history, law, business, library and information science, psychology, geology, physiology and biophysics, and mathematics. The director of the university press and a copyright lawyer also participated.

After considerable discussion about the process by which articles are published, the committee decided it would review the communication processes that are involved when an author initially begins to create what will become a publication and to move through the peer review process. Because the committee did not have enough time to look intensely at all the disciplines, the group agreed to use its own expertise to present and discuss communications practices in two areas in the sciences (chemistry and mathematics), two in the humanities (history and philosophy), and in two professions, law and business.

Before the academics began their presentations, it was clear that most committee members believed they would be listening to a redundant one-size fits all description of peer review and other informal communication. This assumption fell apart immediately as it became clear that none of the academics knew anything about disciplines other than their own. Each had assumed wrongly that other disciplines functioned as theirs did.

Overall, each committee member knew at the outset that academics in the humanities published books and science academics produced articles. They also knew that monographs were critical for obtaining tenure and promotion in many areas of the humanities and that books were increasing in price at a slower rate than were journals. A few realized that because of the need to fund expensive journals, particularly in the sciences, fewer monographs were being purchased by the libraries for humanities academics. They learned, however, that in some areas of the humanities, such as philosophy, monographs play a much smaller role than do journals.

In business, journal articles are the main outlet for research results. Monographs and conference proceedings are of secondary importance. Both association and commercial journals are important. Association journals are significantly cheaper than commercial journals and electronic versions of journals and working papers are becoming more common.

The field of law is radically different from both the humanities and the sciences. Articles are generally not peer-reviewed, but are most often reviewed by students who edit the law journals. The journals are inexpensive and largely subsidized by the universities that publish them; commercial journals are not the most prestigious, but institution-sponsored law journals are, and their importance generally comes from the ranking of the law school that sponsors them.

When a committee member described the kinds of publications that are important in his/her field, the others were surprised. Most of the literature and rhetoric that describes the so-called crisis in scholarly communication in no way captures the distinct and fine differences in the way scholars in different disciplines work. The professor describing processes in history brought with him an example of a book in case his scientist colleagues had forgotten what one looked like!

Even more fascinating were the reactions to how academics in different disciplines communicate with one another as they began to draft ideas. In some cases, history being one, other colleagues do not regularly read and criticize another colleague's ideas. The exception is a trusted 'invisible college'; this is a trusted community of scholars, who share an interest in a common subject or discipline and who communicate informally and often privately. Even the sciences vary in how much they communicate and how widely. High-energy physicists, with their need for expensive equipment, have traditionally communicated through preprints and multi-layered conversations, even before electronic preprint servers and email. Chemistry, perhaps because of its close association with business and the need to patent results, does not communicate broadly within the profession.

Even peer review, a fairly homogeneous process, except for law as noted above, had disciplinary variations. In some disciplines, authors know who their reviewers are and, in others, the reviewers remain unknown (blind review). Committee members were actually shocked at the different practices that had evolved over the years. While the variations in practices may have been known to a few on the committee, possibly the copyright lawyer and the librarians, most members of the committee were surprised by how widely the norms of scholarly communication and the markets for scholarly materials differ among the disciplines. As a result of the wide divergence, the committee ended up believing that it was unlikely that any single solution would emerge to address the wide range of issues connected with scholarly communication. Put bluntly, they found no 'magic bullet' that would correct the present system of price increases for scholarly publications.

Tony Becher (1989) has called the various disciplines 'tribes'. The *Oxford Encyclopedic English Dictionary* defines a tribe as a group of families or communities, linked by social, economic, religious, or blood ties, and usually having a common culture and dialect and a recognized leader (Pearsall & Trumble, 1995). Implicit in Becher's use of the word tribes to describe the different disciplines is the notion that even though each group is similar, that is, all are scholars or scientists, the traditions and rules that govern a tribe's work processes have evolved over a period of time and are different from other tribes. These processes were stable before electronic publication began to emerge and are still, with some exceptions, stable today.

Furthermore, there would be no reason for tribes to explore practices of other tribes because each tribe is fairly independent. An American university's promotion and tenure process begins in a discipline-centred department that, as one tribe, makes its processes and values a part of the collegial environment. Other considerations come up as the tenure and promotion folders are forwarded to the university's promotion and tenure committee and the provost. But even when particular tribal customs and values are questioned by the university committee or provost, as far as we can tell, the procedures and values do not need to be defended, but simply explained by tribal representatives.

As for the President's Committee on Scholarly Communication, its six long sessions were incredibly illuminating to the diverse group (and especially to the librarians), but plans to educate colleagues through a series of seminars were never realized, we believe, because each academic wanted to get back to the focused work of the discipline with its many pressing issues and duties. The overview the committee members gained was impressive, but their interest in the overview was far superceded by a consuming interest in their own areas. It was also clear that the underlying differences in how each discipline works are complex and so are academics' relationships with publishers of their work. With no clear path toward victory, the committee never made a final report.

At the point the committee discussed the sciences, we invited Rob Kling (2000; Kling and McKim, 1999), an Indiana University academic, to discuss his extensive research in disciplinary differences[3]. Kling (2000) concluded that "communicative plurality and communicative heterogeneity are durable features of the scholarly landscape, and that we are likely to see field differences in the use of and meaning ascribed to communications forums persist, even as overall use of electronic communications technologies both in science and in society as a whole increases". In his work, he describes the differences in how three scientific fields—high-energy physics, molecular biology and information systems—are using and shaping 'electronic media'.

The first field, high-energy physics, works on a small number of projects that last for 2 to 3 years or longer. The scientists, whose very expensive projects are supported by grants of hundreds of millions of dollars, use expensive equipment. Multi-institutional collaborations that can involve hundreds of scientists and more than two dozen institutions have long been common because of the nature and expense of this research. A new $1 billion project, the ATLAS experiment, will begin in 2007 and will include nearly 2,000 physicists from more than 150 universities and laboratories in 34 countries. The project's locus is the CERN laboratory, the European Organization for Nuclear Research, in Switzerland, and it is funded by the National Science Foundation (US) and the Department of Energy (US).

It is not surprising that physicists have led the sciences in the use of electronic media because they have a strong need to communicate and have done so through various means, including preprints, before they used electronic communication. The working paper has long been a main source of communication between scientists and, since the 1970s, physicists have submitted their papers to clearinghouses that then redistributed them to researchers. Kling notes that even though the Los Alamos ePrint server (now called arXiv and located at Cornell University; http://arxiv.org/) has become the most famous there are approximately 11 others, including the CERN preprint server (http://cds.cern.ch/), DESY preprints (ftp://ftp.desy.de/pub/preprints/), and one from the American Physical Society (http://publish.aps.org/eprint/). For purposes of archiving and for "prestige and reward allocation" the electronic preprints are also formally published, but the article is usually also available electronically on a preprint server.

Molecular biology is the second area Kling describes. Here the biologists also circulate preprints, but only within small so-called 'invisible colleges'. Preprint servers do not play as significant a role in communication as they do in high-energy physics. But, Kling points out that the field of biology does use shared databases and data sets in its research. The Protein Data Bank, a repository of experimentally determined three-dimensional structures of biological macromolecules; Flybase, a database that maps the genetics of Drosophila (the fruit fly) and into which biologists submit genomic data; and AceDB (A C. Elegans Data Base) which studies Nematode worms are three examples. Moreover, adding data to these shared knowledge databanks is sometimes required before the researcher publishes an article. "The 'accession number,' a unique number identifying a dataset submitted to one of these databases, is then published along with an article in a paper journal, allowing readers to obtain research data almost instantly, if desired" (Kling, 2000). These digital corpora, Kling notes, are critical to the communications system in molecular biology, but they operate synergistically with print journals.

Information systems is the third discipline Kling describes. A new field, it seeks to decide which activities in an organization need to be computerized, how they should be computerized and evaluated, and how people use systems.

Within these three disciplines, high-energy physics alone uses ePrint servers; information systems alone communicates through 'pure' electronic journals; molecular biology and information systems build digital disciplinary corpora, but high-energy physics does not; information systems alone produces shared digital libraries; and all three publish additional data or enhancements in paper-electronic journals, high-energy physics and molecular biology in *Science Online* and information systems in the *MIS Quarterly*.

The complexities and traditions in each discipline even in the sciences, Kling argues, are driving their use of information technology differently in all aspects of research, communication and publication. He disagrees heartily with the notion that all disciplines will use technology and communication practices common in high-energy physics. Stevan Harnad, Andrew Odlyzko and Paul Ginsparg[4] are probably the best known promoters of what Kling calls the electronic publishing reform movement. All believe that electronic scholarly communication is better than communication via print. They describe it as being less expensive and faster and having easier access. They claim that the push toward total electronic communication is inevitable. Though this may be true, by advocating a single model as appropriate for all scholarly communities and by dominating the press about scholarly communication, the heterogeneity of the disciplines that actually is driving different solutions suitable to longstanding disciplinary practices is lost in discourse on this topic, particularly by libraries and university administrations (Valauskas, 1997).

By ignoring the complexities embedded in the disciplines, there is a danger that librarians and university administrators might use limited funding toward solutions that may appear obvious at first but actually are unworkable and engage in frustrating dialogues with publishers because they believe that the scholarly world is moving in one direction lock step. For example, several years ago there was a growing public dialogue among university presidents to 'take back' the scholarly articles that they said American university professors had written while being supported by university funds and in many cases by government grants. Implicit in this argument was their belief that most articles were written by American professors. Representatives from six scientific publishers who spoke with university librarians from 12 major Midwest universities in the US (The Committee on Institutional Cooperation), however, told the group that more than 60% of their authors were not academics at US universities but were located throughout the rest of the world. We mention this because librarians and others have the responsibility to help presidents shape their strategies. And, unless we understand these complex issues ourselves, we cannot harness the power of our administrators to help us.

5.   Starting at the Beginning: Conducting Research

Massive and complex changes are occurring in how scholars conduct their research, mostly in the sciences, but also in the humanities, due to a small number of intrepid humanists who are pursuing the use of technology far beyond the publication of research in electronic format instead of, or along with, the print publication. Perhaps the best place to begin is the report of the National Science Foundation (NSF) Blue-Ribbon Advisory Panel on Cyberinfrastructure which itself links to similar efforts in Great Britain and the European Union (Atkins *et al.*, 2003). These changes will eventually transform the research community, scholarly communication and the role of the research library.

The NSF Blue-Ribbon Advisory Panel, which was chaired by Dan Atkins (Atkins *et al.*, 2003), an engineer and founding dean of the School of Information at the University of Michigan in Ann Arbor (US), was charged "to inventory and explore current trends and to make strategic recommendations on the nature and form of programs that the NSF should take in response to them". The report uses the term 'infrastructure' in the broadest sense—the structural foundations of a society or its economic foundations, including roads, bridges, sewers, telephone lines, power grids, etc. and adds the prefix 'cyber' to refer to the growing distributed computer, information and communication technology. "If infrastructure is required for an industrial economy, then we could say that cyberinfrastructure is required for a knowledge economy" (Atkins *et al.*, 2003).

The technologies supporting a cyberinfrastructure are the "integrated electro-optical components of computation, storage, and communication that continue to advance in raw capacity at exponential rates" (Atkins *et al.*, 2003). They also include enabling hardware, software, instruments, algorithms, data, information, services, social practices, disciplines, and communities of practices, communications, institutions, and personnel. Put another way, there are two overall ingredients: the layers of enabling technology and the complex social practices of the people who use the technology. Atkins' team was concerned about building the required technology infrastructure, but also about redundant activities resulting from lack of communication between disciplines and a lack of understanding of the social and cultural practices of various disciplines, both of which could prevent full use of technology that he contends will help humankind and the planet Earth to survive and prosper.

The report emphasizes the need for comprehensive libraries of digital objects and for curators who will organize and preserve them. It also emphasizes that efforts should transcend individual agencies and institutions and be international in scope. Because of the growth of the cyberinfrastructure, scientists have been able virtually to revolutionize their research through the use of digital data and networks. Simulation and modelling have been added to the more classic theoretical/analytical and experimental/observational approach in such fields as scientific and engineering research, including the biological, chemical, social and environmental sciences, medicine, and nanotechnology. In all these fields, data has been collected and is available online. Modern genome research is probably the most well-known example, but astronomical research is also being redefined. The report notes that scientific publication is now almost totally online, that publications are beginning to incorporate rich media (hypertext, video and photographic images), and complex data sets are being visualized in new ways that will lead to a better understanding of their meaning. The report also states that researchers could not do without email and the web.

Within this growing environment, the report lists some serious concerns:

- Researchers in different fields may adopt different formats and representation of key information that will be impossible to combine or reconcile.
- The lack of systematic archiving and curation of data, gathered at great expense, is endangering its long-term existence.
- Incompatible tools among the disciplines will serve to continue to isolate scientific communities.
- Groups who are building their own software are unaware of comparable needs elsewhere.
- Forthcoming changes in computing and applications could render some projects obsolete before they are completed.
- If the sociological and cultural barriers to technology adoption are not addressed, large investments in technology may be wasted.

The issues above address an overall need to coordinate change and to educate and influence the various communities to adopt new ways of working. In this sense, the research process, the first step in scholarly communication, as we have defined it, is the appropriate place to begin and to influence other informal communication and eventual publication in whatever format. As we have seen, however, the traditions within each discipline have worked for many years; modifying these processes will take time for the disciplines to adopt new technology and to make use of it in concert with their own practices. The prospect of fully employing technology and conducting research in comprehensive digital environments that are interactive and that have high levels of computational, storage and data transfer may push changes that could not have happened before.

This report also emphasizes the need for the research community to find "trusted and enduring organizations" to preserve and make available scientific data. As research libraries experience the move of many serials and some monographs to digital only—or digital and electronic—we need a dialogue that expands from preserving ePublications to our potential responsibility for preserving other scholarly and research output both in the sciences and the humanities.

An interdisciplinary conference, 'Transforming disciplines: Computer Science and the Humanities', held in Washington, DC in January 2003, helped to illuminate some of the current groundbreaking computer projects in the humanities (Davidson & Thorin, informal notes, January 17–18, 2003). Its goal was for computer scientists and humanities computing practitioners to review current needs and policy issues and to identify areas of research that would benefit from cross-disciplinary applications conducive to new discovery and long-term collaboration between the humanities and engineering sciences.

Linking engineering to the humanities, keynote speaker William Wulf (National Academy of Engineering) stated that he believed that the computer can do the same thing for the humanities that it has done for the sciences. He described the profound changes occurring in the scientific method from the practice of simulation. Instead of waiting for two galaxies to collide and observing the results, the results can be observed through computational simulation.

Other humanities scholars who spoke illustrated how they are building data and using it to draw conclusions. They included:

- Gregory Crane, a professor at Tufts University (US) who is dissecting languages to find patterns/data that will lead to discovery and conclusions. See http://www.perseus.tufts.edu and http://www.darpa. mil/ipto/programs/tides/index.htm;
- Douglas Greenberg, who directs the project, 'Indexing Memory: The Shoah Foundation Archive of Holocaust Testimony'. The Shoah Visual History Foundation has collected on digital tape 52,000 testimonies, the average being 2–3 hours in length. See http://www.vhf.org/;
- Steven Murray, professor at Columbia University (US), who spoke on generating humanistic knowledge through the media and who illustrated through a video based on computer modelling, which was in turn derived from other manual measurements and analysis, that illustrates how a cathedral at Amiens, France was constructed. See http://www. mcah.columbia.edu; and
- Will Thomas, professor at the University of Virginia (US), who spoke on the differences slavery made in two communities located in the southern United States. See http://valley.vcdh.virginia.edu/.
- Three other interesting examples are: (1) The Physics of Scale Project in the History of Recent Science and Technology (http://hrst.mit.edu) at the Dibner Institute (http://dibinst.mit.edu/); (2) the work of the Center for History and New Media, George Mason University (http://chnm. gmu.edu); and (3) the William Blake Archive, Monuments and Dust, and the Complete Writings and Pictures of Dante Gabriel Rossetti: A Hypermedia Research Archive, projects of The Institute for Advanced Technology in the Humanities, University of Virginia, U.S. (www.iath.virginia.edu) (Smith, 2003).

Note: All URLs accessed on January 22, 2005.

In the discussions that followed, it was clear that the vast majority of humanities scholars at universities are not yet working in new media. Those who do, usually work in centres or institutes, and their work is often misunderstood by colleagues. The use of data by humanists brings up the question of sharing data, a practice common in most of the sciences but not in the humanities. The humanities are now using technology in a way that incorporates long-held practices, but as the potential of better research through the effective use of digital technology is realized, traditional practices may change. At this point, progress is not exponential.

6.   Conclusion

Because the overall shape of the traditional system of scholarly communication is similar among all the disciplines, some have assumed that the entire process of research and communication is uniform throughout. The dominating rhetoric among some scientists is evangelical in its desire to transform scholarly communication through a single electronic approach. Taking that very interesting and compelling viewpoint and broadening it to include all the scientific, social sciences and humanities disciplines has resulted in a picture being drawn that is too simple, given the heterogeneity of the various disciplines. The library profession is only now growing in its knowledge of scholarly communication processes and beginning to be able to understand the similarities and differences. This understanding is vitally important for at least two reasons:

First, academic librarians and particularly library directors, whose knowledge should span the disciplines, can only be effective communicators with our administrations if our knowledge of the disciplines is deeply rooted. We have already seen that academics are profoundly (and narrowly in the best sense of the word) involved in a particular discipline or a sub-discipline. Even those who are interdisciplinary in scope, focus intensely on the particular subject areas and their relationships. In any case, a scholar's job normally is not to understand practices in other disciplines, but to relate subjects, develop ideas and publish them. Up to this point, the academic library profession has not deeply explored the dimensions of changes in scholarly communication beyond rapidly escalating prices for journals and the effects of mergers of the conglomerates that publish significant academic output. Both of these troubling practices are important, however, and we have already described how the pricing situation evolved.

But to take only the pricing issues into account and not to understand that each discipline is different in its practices, we have perhaps proposed simplistic solutions to our university presidents and provosts and may have placed them in the position of advocating unworkable solutions. A good comparison exists in the world of digital libraries. When libraries first began to develop digital libraries, staff looked for what is called in digital parlance, the 'killer application' (killer app)—the overall solution that would obviate the need for slow and painful progress. As digital librarians grew more sophisticated, both in experience and expertise, the 'killer app' idea was left behind (Greenstein & Thorin, 2002). The same is true in the changes that are occurring in scholarly communication. While there are some dramatic changes occurring, those changes are not transforming scholarly communication in the same way or at the same pace.

Second, in reshaping the role of the library to accommodate and support change, it is equally important to understand how each facet of the scholarly community works. We have seen that some communities are comfortable with preprints and others are not. Some scholars work alone and others in groups. Some are constructing data sets together to analyze as a community. There is even some use of, and interest in, data sets in the humanities. But each group is using technology a little differently and at a different pace. Most important, each group is working with technology within the framework of its own traditions.

As we look at how our libraries are organized to support the changes that are occurring, our understanding of what the changes are is vitally important. While our old print library system was not a simple one, we knew who we were and what our job was. Scholars and scientists came to us to find and to use books and journals they needed. Our responsibility was to acquire, catalogue and preserve those materials and to make them accessible to our communities. The physical arrangements in our libraries reflected these purposes. Now, we find that scientists are creating complex online communities where they share research, conversation and ideas, build datasets and publish. Humanities scholars come to the library less often because they now have online journals and in some cases publishing processes which are close to being completely online.

If we can understand and grapple effectively with the changes occurring now and in the next few years, we have the opportunity to move our relationship with academics from one of facilitator to one of partnership, and this is unprecedented. Interestingly, one of our traditional roles, that of archivist, is being explored in the digital environment. For example, LOCKSS (Lots Of Copies Keep Stuff Safe) is a prototype of a system to preserve access to scientific journals published on the web (see http://lockss.stanford.edu/). But not only do we have the potential to have a major role in digitally preserving electronic journals, we also have the opportunity to be a part of archival solutions for more informal scholarly communication through institutional repositories. To build an effective repository, however, we must build new relationships with the academic staff.

In addition, many of us are digitizing important historical collections. Not only are we digitizing text, but a growing body of photographs, film and audio. With the growth of the Internet, we are beginning to understand that we must create for our users a more coherent digital environment that includes the materials our own libraries digitize, our online catalogues, as well as materials available globally through the web. Many of us are exploring the technical and cultural challenges of being able to search across numbers of digital resources and pulling out those materials needed in a particular field. Some of us are also finding that scholars are suddenly locating materials online that they had not explored before because those materials had been 'classified' in another discipline. With so much available to them, scholars are now beginning to expect that they will be able to move these digital materials into their own digital surroundings and modify them for use in their research and teaching. As we work with scholars and scientists, if becomes imperative that we know how they work in order to shape our access tools into effective mechanisms for delivery.

The number of simultaneous developments occurring presently in the way scholars and scientists work and communicate will eventually result in a greatly modified or even new system of scholarly communication, one that will sustain itself in a digital environment. At this point it is difficult to understand completely what the role of an academic library will be, that is, how libraries (and librarians) will be involved in the new system. We do know, however, that the days of an academic library standing alone are gone; those of us responsible for managing staff and those librarians who understand these changes, need to work effectively together to build a completely new environment, one that is fraught with challenges, but one that will transform libraries in synchronization with the evolution of scholarly communication.

References

Atkins, D. E., Droegemeier, K. K., Feldman, S. I., Garcia-Molina, H., Klein, M. L., Messina, P., et al. (2003). Revolutionizing science and engineering through cyberinfrastructure: Report of the National Science Foundation Blue-Ribbon Advisory Panel on Cyberinfrastructure. Retrieved January 22, 2005, from http://www.communitytechnology.org/nsf_ci_report/report.pdf

Becher, T. (1989). *Academic tribes and territories: Intellectual enquiry and the cultures of discipline*. Buckingham, Philadelphia: Society for Research into Higher Education and Open University Press.

Case, M. M. (2002). Igniting change in scholarly communication: SPARC, it's past, present, and future. *Advances in Librarianship*, 26, 1–26. Retrieved January 22, 2005, from http://www.arl.org/sparc/pubs/docs/SPARC_advances.pdf

Davidson, M. W., & Thorin, S. E. (2003). Informal notes from the Interdisciplinary Conference Transforming Disciplines: Computer Science and the Humanities. Sponsored by the National Initiative for Networked Cultural Heritage, January 17–18, 2003.

Duderstadt, J. J., Atkins, D. E., & Van Houweling, D. (2002). *Higher education in the digital age: Technology issues and strategies for American colleges and universities.* Westport, Connecticut: Praeger: American Council on Education.

Frazier, K. (2001). The librarians' dilemma: Contemplating the costs of the 'big deal.' *D-Lib Magazine, 7*(3), 1–8. Retrieved January 22, 2005, from http://www.dlib.org/dlib/march01/frazier/03frazier.html

Greenstein, D., & Thorin, S. E. (2002). *The digital library: A biography.* Washington, DC: Digital Library Federation and Council on Library and Information Resources. Retrieved January 22, 2005, from http://www.clir.org/pubs/reports/pub109/pub109.pdf

Guédon, J.-C. (2002). In Oldenburg's long shadow: Librarians, research scientists, publishers, and the control of scientific publishing. Washington, DC: The Association of Research Libraries. Retrieved January 22, 2005, from http://www.arl.org/arl/proceedings/138/guedon.html

Hawkins, B. L., & Battin, P. (1998). *The mirage of continuity: Reconfiguring academic information resources for the 21st century.* Washington, DC: Council on Library Information Resources.

Kling, R. (2000). Not just a matter of time: Field differences and the shaping of electronic media in supporting scientific communication. *Journal of the American Society for Information Science, 51*(14), 1306–1320. Retrieved January 22, 2005, from http://www.slis.indiana.edu/CSI/WP/wp99_02B.html

Kling, R., & McKim, G. (1999). Scholarly communication and the continuum of electronic publishing. Retrieved January 22, 2005, from http://xxx.lanl.gov/ftp/cs/papers/9903/9903015.pdf

Pearsall, J., & Trumble, B. (Eds.). (1995). *The Oxford Encyclopedic English Dictionary.* New York: Oxford University Press.

Rowland, F. (1997). Print journals: Fit for the future?. *Ariadne: The Web Version, 7,* 1–5. Retrieved January 22, 2005, from http://www.ariadne.ac.uk/issue7/fytton/

Smith, A. (2003). *New-model scholarship: How will it survive?.* Washington, DC: Council on Library and Information Resources. Retrieved January 22, 2005, from http://www.clir.org/pubs/reports/pub114/contents.html

Valauskas, E. J. (1997). Waiting for Thomas Kuhn: First Monday and the evolution of electronic journals. *First Monday, 2*(12). Retrieved January 22, 2005, from http://www.firstmonday.dk/issues/issue2_12/valauskas/

7. Endnotes (all URLs accessed January 22, 2005)

1. The Association for Research Libraries is a membership organization of 114 large research libraries in the United States and Canada. For more information, see http://www.arl.org/stats/index.html and http://fisher.lib.virginia.edu/arl/index.html
2. TULIP (The University LIcensing Program) was a collaborative project (1991–1995) of Elsevier Science and nine American universities to test systems for networked delivery to and use of journals at the user's desktop. For more information, see http://www.elsevier.nl/homepage/about/resproj/trmenu.htm
3. Before his untimely death in May 2003, Rob Kling was a professor in the Indiana University School of Library and Information Science and the director of the Center for Social Informatics. The following pages rely on two of Kling's publications.
4. Stevan Harnad is a Professor of Cognitive Science at Southampton University and the founder of the CogPrints Electronic Preprint Archive in the Cognitive Sciences, http://www.

ecs.soton.ac.uk/~harnad/; Andrew Odlyzko is Director of the interdisciplinary Digital Technology Center and is an Assistant Vice President for Research at the University of Minnesota, http://www.dtc.umn.edu/~odlyzko/; Paul Ginsparg is a Professor of Physics and Computing and Information Science at Cornell University. He developed the Los Alamos National Labs Physics e-Print Server, now located at Cornell University, http://xxx.arXiv.cornell.edu

Glossary of Acronyms

AASL	American Association for School Librarians
ACM	Association for Computing Machinery
AECT	Association for Educational Communications and Technology
ALA	American Library Association
ALPSP	Association of Learned and Professional Society Publishers
ANU	Australian National University
ARL	Association of Research Libraries
CAJ	China Academic Journals
CALIS	China Academic Library & Information System
CD-I	Compact Disk—Interactive
CDMD	China Doctoral/ Master's Dissertations
CD-ROM	Compact Disk—Read-Only Memory
CERN	European Organization for Nuclear Research
CMC	Computer-Mediated Communication
CNKI	China National Knowledge Infrastructure
CNNIC	China Internet Network Information Centre
DistEdNet	Global Distance EducationNet
DLESE	Digital Library for Earth System Education
DLT	Deakin Learning Toolkit
DSO	Deakin Studies Online
DVD	Digital Video Disk
EP	Electronic publishing
FTE	Full-Time Equivalent
HKCAA	Hong Kong Council for Academic Accreditation
HTML	HyperText Markup Language
ICT	Information and Communication Technology

ISI	Institute of Scientific Information
IT	Information Technology
JISC	Joint Information Systems Committee (UK)
LiPACE	Li Ka Shing Institute of Professional and Continuing Education (OUHK)
LOCKSS	Lots Of Copies Keep Stuff Safe
MARC record	MAchine-Readable Cataloguing record.
MIT	Massachusetts Institute of Technology (US)
MOO	Multi-user Object Oriented
NELINET	New England Library and Information Network (US)
NSF	National Science Foundation (US)
OEB	Open eBook (refers to standards)
OLMS	Office of Leadership and Management Services (of ARL)
OUHK	The Open University of Hong Kong
PDA	Personal Digital Assistant
PDF	Portable Document Format
POD	Print-On-Demand
RoMEO	Rights MEtadata for Open archiving
SCI	Science Citation Index
SHERPA	Securing a Hybrid Environment for Research Preservation and Access (UK)
SIUC	Southern Illinois University Carbondale (US)
STM	Science, Technology and Medicine
SU	Simultaneous User
TLSU	Teaching and Learning Support Unit (Deakin University, Australia)
TULIP	The University LIcensing Program (US)
UC	University of California (US)
UK	United Kingdom
URL	Uniform Resource Locator
US	United States
XML	eXtensible Markup Language

Subject Index